D0407879

Violence in the Lives of Adolescents

Martha B. Straus, Ph.D.

W.W. NORTON & COMPANY New York London

A NORTON PROFESSIONAL BOOK

Edited by Martha B. Straus

Abuse and Victimization Across the Life Span

Composition by Bytheway Typesetting Services, Inc.
Manufacturing by Haddon Craftsmen, Inc.

Library of Congress Cataloging-in-Publication Data

Straus, Martha B., 1956–
  Violence in the lives of adolescents / Martha B. Straus.
    p. cm.
  "A Norton professional book."
  Includes bibliographical references and index.
  ISBN 0-393-70186-7
  1. Violence in children—United States—Case studies. 2. Juvenile
delinquency—United States—Case studies. 3. Teenagers—Mental
health. 4. Family violence—United States. I. Title.
RJ506.V56S77   1994
616.89′022—dc20   94-27718   CIP

W. W. Norton & Company, Inc., 500 Fifth Avenue, New York, NY 10110
W. W. Norton & Company, Ltd., 10 Coptic Street, London WC1A 1PU

1 2 3 4 5 6 7 8 9 0

To my HB

Many men go fishing all of their lives without knowing that it is not fish they are after.

—Thoreau

Contents

v

Acknowledgments

I am grateful to many people who made it possible for me to write this book. Foremost, I want to thank my own family, who have demonstrated to me beyond a doubt that we all need people we can call our own: my parents Betty and Nathan, my siblings, Andi and Joe, his wife, Sally, my husband Harry, and our girls, Lizzie and Molly. They keep me hopeful when the world seems more violent than kind.

Thanks to Susan Munro, a patient editor indeed, who hung in with me long past the deadline, accepting the birth of a child as a perfectly good reason for an extension, and then editing with kindness and wisdom.

Thanks to my friends and relatives who helped with early drafts of the manuscript: Becky Coffey, Margaret Wimberger, Cleary Donovan, Joe Straus, Harry Bauld, John Kronenberger, and Chard DeNiord.

And, thanks to the adolescents and families who continue to teach me and allow me to become part of their lives for a time.

Preface

In my practice as a clinical psychologist over the past ten years, working in the city, the suburbs, and the country, I have seen an increasing number of adolescents who were either victims or perpetrators of violence. One day, several months ago, I sat in my office reviewing summaries of completed therapy cases. These included Susan,* age 15, who had made a serious suicide attempt with an overdose of different kinds of pills taken impulsively and randomly from the medicine cabinet; Michelle, age 14, who had run away from home many times and lived on the streets to avoid sex with her stepfather; Richie, age 16, who had knocked over an elderly man coming out of church in order to rob him; Paul, age 15, who had sexually abused small children after finding a neighbor's pornography collection in his garage; and Dawn, age 16, who had been frequently attacked physically by her drunken father. As I went back through my notes, I considered the degree to which violence, in a staggering array of guises, dominated the lives of my adolescent patients. Unlike the children and adults I was treating, these adolescents had to face life's margins as a matter of course.

What I encounter in my clinical practice is consistent with many recent accounts of the increasing frequency and severity of adolescent delinquency, running away, truancy, drug and alcohol use, prostitution, sexual and physical abuse, teen pregnancy, and juve-

*All names and some identifying information have been changed.

vii

nile homicide, parricide, and suicide. Statistics on incidence and prevalence that are provided by national surveys and clinical samples clearly demonstrate that violence in the lives of adolescents is not just an aberration requiring psychotherapy or detention, or something that happens only on the fringes of society to the marginal, the underclasses, and the insane. Violence can, and does, happen in any family with adolescents. The families I have treated in private practice, hospitals, and outpatient clinics come from *all* social, economic, and racial groups.

Each day, contemporary adolescents must make choices about the extent to which acts of violence will shape their lives. The decisions they make ultimately affect specialists in education, law, health, and mental health—and virtually everyone else. Unlike pancreatic disorders or anxiety, the problems of adolescents are no longer restricted to the purview of trained professionals. Violence in adolescence touches us all. How did this happen? What can we do to shape safer lives for the adolescents we know? *Violence in the Lives of Adolescents* is written to ponder these questions, using case material as the foundation for a broader exploration of the issues.

All therapists operate within a philosophical framework; I have tried to reveal mine in this book to the extent that I am conscious of it. With adolescents in particular, we have to be aware of our belief system or we will be working at a great disadvantage when, as invariably happens, we are challenged.

I believe, for example, that families and communities become more powerful when they have education, support, and resources. When I work with parents, I provide them with information about their changing parental jobs and about what they can reasonably expect from their adolescents. I listen to them, but I also help establish them in their neighborhoods by providing links to individuals and agencies that offer concrete solutions and services.

I also believe that individual therapy alone is insufficient for stopping violence in adolescence. *Violence in the Lives of Adolescents* is written from an ecological perspective. From this vantage point, I work on four concurrent levels. At the most basic is the very private, personal connection with a troubled teenager. The second level is family therapy and education, helping other family members to change and grow with their adolescent. Modifications in family structure and functioning may enable family members to stay together until the adolescent is prepared to engage in the ritual of leaving home. Since adolescents of violence can come into contact with so many institutions and individuals outside of the family, I also engage routinely with aspects of the third level—the community. Links to resources in the neighborhood are often critical when a family is overwhelmed by problems associated with violence. Finally, I also consider how social policy cradles and shapes the community, the family, and the adolescent. As a therapist, I serve on committees and advisory boards, I lobby for policy reforms, and I vote. All four intervention levels affect the extent to which violence will define the lives of adolescents. Although we may prefer to work with individuals or with families, I don't think we should delude ourselves into believing in any single type of intervention; alas, there are no ruby slippers here to get an adolescent home safely.

Another belief I have is that men are responsible for a disproportionate amount of the violence against and by adolescents. When colleagues read early drafts of this manuscript, they often observed that "guys don't come out looking too good," and they were correct. While I have had cases in which women were violent perpetrators of physical abuse, and have treated girls with memberships in tough gangs, these are still the exceptions in what I've seen of the violent experiences of adolescence. Violence of all kinds is first and foremost the abuse of power. And I believe that the limbo-land of adolescence in our culture makes teenagers particularly vulnerable to the patriarchal structure that denies employment, status, and resources to adolescents (and, not coincidentally, to the women who care for them). I'm forced to conclude that violence is caused, in no small part, by male domination, and by the economic, social, and political inequality that stems from it. Ending violence in adolescence ultimately means doing something about the balance of power, so that all adolescents will be entitled to a safe and productive future.

Realistically, we must adapt to an evolving world and live in it as it comes to us. But today's victims are not inevitably tomorrow's victims and offenders. In the vast majority of cases, the family, whatever its membership, is exactly the environment contemporary adolescents need. Families *can* break the cycle of violence. In a violent world, adolescents can be buffered immeasurably by someone who will love them irrationally. It has been my experience that there is usually someone in every family who can do this. Since one of the major developmental tasks of adolescence is leaving home, both metaphorically and pragmatically, it is crucial that the adolescent have a home to leave.

Despite popular convention, parents and children need not struggle and suffer en route to a twenty-first birthday. In a family, everyone is changing and growing—not just the adolescent; our identity develops throughout our lives. Adolescence is just one of the developmental periods over the life span, though with some uniquely important tasks. While the problems associated with violence are indeed numerous, the adolescent has a remarkable capacity for change and growth. So much of what I have seen and experienced in therapy tells me that adolescents are quite capable of seizing the chance to break the cycle of violence. Despite the difficulties living with, working with, and being an adolescent, this developmental period offers wonderful opportunities. So, despite the distressing content of this book, I am still filled with enormous hope. I believe, most of all, that people can change and that violence can be stopped.

This book is organized around five cases from my practice of psychotherapy. The introductory chapter offers a brief history of adolescence in America and a more comprehensive discussion of the four-level ecological model used for the subsequent chapters. Chapter 1 looks at the effects of violence on normal adolescent development. In the five case chapters I explore individual- and family-therapy approaches to particular areas of violence. In Chapter 7, I then address the ways in which communities are working to solve the problem of violence. Finally, in Chapter 8, I describe how social policy defines the issues for individuals, families, and communities. Those of us treating adolescents are not merely therapists; we are also parents, neighbors, friends, and citizens. We need to view violence through personal, professional, and political lenses. With this broader understanding put into action, we may truly be able to stem the rising tide of violence.

Introduction

Most of the violence associated with contemporary adolescence did not exist a century ago and is not inevitable now. In fact, adolescence as a special stage in human development is a very recent concept in family history. Adolescence is, in many ways, the story of an invention which then required an increasingly complex support apparatus to sustain it. Programs and institutions designed expressly to help adolescents have increased and grown exponentially in recent decades. The significance of adolescence as a distinct period in the life span has been further fueled by changing demographics and enduring myths about being American.

Adolescence as we regard it today appears to have emerged in America in the late nineteenth century, as Americans made the transition from an agrarian, small-town social order to one characterized by large-scale industrialization and urbanization. By the turn of the twentieth century, the transition from childhood to adulthood became ambiguous and prolonged, and adolescence was invented. In a short period of time, three major social policy changes occurred: the juvenile justice system was separated from adult procedures, compulsory high-school attendance was established, and legislation preventing child labor was passed. As industrialism narrowed the labor market, childhood was extended to exclude adolescents from competing with adults for jobs. These changes reverberate today in the overcrowding of juvenile courts, rehabilitation and detention facilities, the high school drop-out and illiteracy rates, and lack of jobs for adolescents ready and needing to work. These issues continue to concern government at all levels and receive much attention in the popular press. The time of adolescence cannot be *un*invented, but our expectations for violence in the teen years do need to be reexamined.

Contemporary Adolescents

The increase of violence in adolescence has been tied to some key demographic changes in the racial and ethnic composition of American families, marital instability, and fluctuations in parental employment and income over the latter course of this century. These changes have all had dramatic and often deleterious effects on the nurturing capacity of the family and on the ability of adolescents to make the long leap into adult life and responsibility.

Currently, there are about 28 million 10- to 17-year-olds in the United States, with half a million more boys than girls. The number of young people will increase over the next decade by about 10 percent because the number of births has increased every year since 1978, when the current 15-year-olds were born. The vast majority (81 percent) of young people, ages 10 to 17, in the United States are white, with 15 percent black and 4 percent other races. According to census reports, 10 percent are of "Spanish origin" and are described as either white or black. The minority population is growing both from higher birth rates among nonwhites and from immigration. The Census Bureau predicts that by the year 2000, 20 percent of the youth population will be black and 18 percent Hispanic, and that, a decade later, the Hispanic portion of the youth population will have increased to 23 percent, while blacks will make up 21 percent (Dryfoos, 1990). These trends point to the potential for an ever-expanding underclass that will have to struggle to survive in mainstream America.

One in four adolescents lives with only one parent, most typically a mother. Because of separation and divorce, nearly half of all adolescents can expect to live with a single parent at some time. Fewer than half of all black adolescents have a father with whom they live. Seventy percent of women with children between 14 and 17 years of age are currently in the labor force. Contemporary adolescents may have less attention and monitoring, and be more vulnerable to all forms of violence, because of these significant alterations in family structure and functioning.

Another factor related to adolescents' adjustment problems is mobility. Contemporary Americans move a lot. During the past five years, two out of every five 10- to 14-year-olds moved, almost half of them to a different county. This increased relocation stands in stark contrast to early generations of Americans staying on the family farm, and indicates the extent to which young adolescents must endure shifting environments, with frequent changes in schools, family structures, and communities. Homelessness also involves growing numbers of adolescents, whose numbers are included in the estimate of 2.5 million homeless children in America.

The relationship among poverty, decreased access to resources, and adolescent violence has been amply documented in both the professional press and through media coverage. Currently, 21 percent of young people aged 10 to 14 are in families with incomes below the poverty level, as are 17 percent of 15- to 17-year-olds. (In 1987, when the median income for a family of four was over $30,000, the poverty rate was set at an unliveable $11,611.) The younger the children in the home, the greater the chances that a family will be poor. In 1986, about 5.5 million 10- to 17-year-olds lived in such impoverished situations. Black and Hispanic children were much more likely to be poor than white children: 45 percent (1.8 million) of black and 41 percent (1.2 million) of Hispanic youngsters were in poor families compared with 13 percent (3.5 million) of white young people. While the problems of poverty and racism are clearly linked, most poor families (64 percent) are white.

Living in a female-headed household increases the probability of poverty. While 11 percent of all families live in poverty, 46 percent of the female-headed households that include children are poor. The median income for a mother raising children on her own is around $9,000 (compared with dual-income and father-headed households that have a median of more than three times that figure). And the more children, the greater the chances of being poor. Many of these families rely on public assistance for support. The 3.7 million families currently receiving Aid to Families with Dependent Children (AFDC) include approximately 3 million children aged 10 to 17. Thus, roughly two thirds of the nation's youth who live in poor families are currently welfare recipients (Children's Defense Fund, 1989).

Race and poverty dictate the amount of exposure to violence that an adolescent will endure. The deadly combination of guns, gangs, drugs, poverty, and frightened, hopeless youths has killed nearly 50,000 young people since 1979—a number equivalent to the total battle casualties in the Vietnam war (Children's Defense Fund, 1994a). Gun violence is probably the greatest adversity of all that increasingly plague American youth in the inner city. Abuse and neglect, dense living conditions, and grossly inadequate schools have also contributed to a generation of anxious, terrified children. In a recent national *Newsweek*/CDF poll (Children's Defense Fund, 1994b), children between 10 and 17 years of age, as well as their parents, stated that their greatest worry—more than economic or health concerns—was the threat of violent crime. Although poor children and parents and those in inner cities felt the most threatened by violent crime, small-town and suburban families echoed this deep anxiety. Between 50 and 60 percent of the youngsters questioned, regardless of their family income or the size of their community, knew someone who was severely beaten up or threatened with a knife or gun. However, in many reports, the presence of violence in the lives of urban youth is even greater. For example, in a study of 8th graders in Chicago, 73 percent reported seeing someone shot, stabbed, robbed, or killed (American Psychological Association, 1993). While exposure to violence is a real threat for all adolescents, urban, poor, and minority youth are at the greatest risk of being perpetrators, witnesses, or victims of crime.

Recent research (Dryfoos, 1990) has identified that one in four adolescents (7 million youngsters) are at risk for problems so severe that they have little chance of becoming responsible adults. They are not learning the skills necessary to participate in the educational system or to make the transition into the labor force. They cannot become responsible parents because they have limited experience in family life and lack the resources to raise their own children.

Summarizing her research, Dryfoos states that "a new class of 'untouchables' is emerging in our inner cities, on the social fringes of suburbia, and in some rural areas: young people who are functionally illiterate, disconnected from school, depressed, prone to drug abuse and early criminal activity, and eventually, parents of unplanned and unwanted babies" (p. 3).

For a time, just a century ago, all adolescents were essential assets to the economic and social stability of the family (Elder, 1987). Now, a quarter of youth find no place for themselves in the adult world. As society has become more complex, and adolescents have gradually spent less and less time with their families, the (unrealistic) expectation that school alone should ready them for work and life has increased correspondingly.

However, as adolescents have been removed from responsibility for the welfare of the family, and cut off from the world of work, the role of school has become increasingly meaningless for many of them—even those who are able to do well there. Despite these remarkable demographic and social changes, the nuclear family is ultimately blamed for its problems and weaknesses, and rendered incapable of solving them.

The Family in Context

Americans have always assigned a primary causal role to family life: Good homes will create a good society (or, from the standpoint of reform, change the family and you will change everything else). To be sure, there is a certain logical plausability here; it also feels good to believe that we have control over our lives in this way. But, in practice, it is much easier to trace those processes that move the other way—that is, *from* the society at large *to* the family in particular. In the history of social institutions, the family seems to display a markedly reactive character. Time and again, it receives influences from the outside, rebuffs and modifies them, and eventually adapts to them. There are dynamic and reciprocal aspects in all of this, but, even so, the power of influence is largely unidirectional; the effect of a family on a community is generally much less (Keniston, 1977).

The family, considered as a species, is molded by history and thus lies beyond our power to control. Not so those *particular* families to which we personally belong. The past lives in us always, but we may have control over what we make of it individually. Violence in adolescence persists and increases in no small part because this distinction is one that Americans have difficulty embracing.

Four myths have endured to reinforce the illusion that adolescents and their families are responsible for their own misery. The first myth is that problems of individuals can be solved by changing the individuals who have the problems. This myth also implies that

families are free-standing, independent, and autonomous units relatively free from social pressures. If family members ask for help,
then they are by definition not an "adequate" family. Adequate families, the assumption runs, are self-sufficient and not influenced from
outside. For families with adolescents, this myth serves to isolate
members from community supports, even as it denies social pressure.

This myth is, in turn, closely connected to another myth about
the work ethic. For children and adolescents in particular, "industry" has always been a moral quality as well as a useful one: It shows
"good character." The emerging capitalism of the early nineteenth
century provided enough examples of success apparently achieved
through industriousness to make this myth believable (but there are,
and have always been, many powerful exceptions). Such stories add
fuel to the myth that unemployed adolescents are to be feared and
derided. Within the logic of this myth, it is unimportant that schools
may not be preparing adolescents for adequate employment, or that
jobs may not be available for adolescents wanting meaningful work.

A third myth involves the role of the American family as a sanctuary from the world's problems. As the nineteenth century passed,
Americans came to define the ideal family as one that was not only
independent and self-sustaining, but almost barricaded—as if the
only way to guard against incursions from the outside was to reduce
all contact with the rest of the world to a minimum. Laws protecting
family privacy reinforce this myth of family as haven. In reality,
though, millions of homes are more dangerous to adolescents than
the streets are.

A fourth and more recent myth has developed alongside the
family-as-sanctuary myth. In this myth, changes in the American
family, especially divorce and remarriage, are viewed as good for
children and adolescents. The expectation is that every historical
period gets the family form it needs and deserves. Thus, the obvious
outcome of a more technological and complicated world is a more
diverse and stratified family form. Recent research has demonstrated amply that this myth has developed because it is difficult for
us to tolerate the notion that the interests of children and of adults
may be diametrically opposed. But children and adolescents are
truly conservative by nature. The more stable and predictable their
world, the happier they are. Changes in family structure are seldom
as beneficial to the involved children as adults would like them to

be, and are often associated closely with emotional problems and violence of all kinds.

Despite ample evidence to the contrary, these myths—of the self-sufficient individual and of the self-sufficient, protected, and protective family—have prevailed. Even those who cannot make such myths real in their own lives often subscribe to them and feel guilty or angry about not meeting their standards. The myths determine who is virtuous and who is wanting; they have always provided the rationale for defining familial adequacy and morality. This moralizing quality is one of their most significant features, for these myths tell us that those who need help are ultimately inadequate—that for a family to need help, or at least to admit it publicly, is to confess failure. In cases of violence, these myths can be deadly. Moreover, to give help, however generously, is to acknowledge the inadequacy of the recipients and indirectly to condemn them, to stigmatize them, and even to weaken what impulse they have toward self-sufficiency. Yet it is rare for the cycle of violence to be broken *without* outside intervention of some kind.

These myths also blind us to the workings of other broad social and economic forces over which adolescents and their families have little control. They can send us blindly into the houses of families and the psyches of individuals to find answers and offer interventions. But adolescence was invented for specific reasons at a particular point in history; its roots are social and political. So is the violence associated with it.

An Ecological Framework

Violence in adolescence can best be understood in its larger social and historical context. With open eyes, we are obliged to look beyond the individual for both causes and solutions. Intervention requires an assessment of the complete ecosystem of the adolescent of violence and includes four levels of analysis: (1) *individual development* (e.g., parental histories, the adolescent's developmental history; (2) *family system* (e.g., the particular interaction and communication among family members); (3) *community* (e.g., the relationship of the family to local resources, individuals, and institutions); and (4) *social policy* (e.g., the larger cultural fabric into which the individual, the family, and the community are inextricably woven).

At each level of analysis, factors can be found that may make an adolescent particularly vulnerable. For example, in the case of violent delinquency, researchers have found important *individual* variables (e.g., various neurological problems, including epilepsy, hyperactivity, learning disabilities, and head injuries); *family* factors (e.g., erratic supervision, inappropriate and abusive discipline, poor problem-solving strategies, and a lack of follow-through); *community* problems (e.g., differential social and economic opportunities, unavailability of socially approved routes to success, insufficient exposure to mainstream learning experiences, and weak institutions in disorganized neighborhoods); and *social policy* factors (e.g., state and federal policies, which in recent years have cut funds for prevention, at-risk youth, and suitable alternatives to lock-up facilities, while failing to serve the special physical, emotional, social, and educational needs of violent delinquents). All adolescents living with violence—as victims or as perpetrators—are engaged in a process which occurs simultaneously and reciprocally on these four levels. Though they experience violence on an individual level, they are also products of families, communities, and social policy.

There is no golden age of the family gleaming at us from far back in the historical past. Even before the plague of adolescence emerged as a force to be reckoned with, previous generations had their share of misery. But the identity struggle of contemporary adolescents is compounded by our own uncertainty about who they are, and who we want them to become. In premodern society, youth always received an adult identity in the natural course of things. The decisive change, in more recent times, has been the presence of so many alternatives—of career, of lifestyle, of moral and philosophical belief. In ever-growing numbers, adolescents have had to face demanding and sometimes life-endangering choices for which many of them are unprepared. The gap between generations has widened. When childhood and adulthood are defined in such sharply different ways, it is harder, even in the best of circumstances, to move from one to the other. For adolescents of violence, growth itself becomes particularly disjunctive and problematic. It then becomes the job of families, communities, and social policies to help ease the transition and make it possible for adolescents to enter into the freedom and responsibility of adult life.

1

Adolescent Development and Violence

The idea of adolescence as a unique stage in human development is only 100 years old. Yet, since its invention, adolescence has turned out to be a compelling and challenging concept. Social scientists have turned their attention to teenagers and their problems, and research on the typical course of adolescence has proliferated along with ample documentation of "deviant" paths. An understanding of the normal psychological, familial, and cultural influences shaping today's adolescents enables us to look more closely at the effects of violence. What is a "normal" or healthy adolescence? How does violence alter the experience? What are the factors protecting adolescents from violence or making them resilient in its aftermath? Are families of violence different in discernible ways from other families enduring the period of adolescence?

Theories of Adolescence

THE TURMOIL THEORY: HOW MUCH TURMOIL IS NECESSARY?

Theoreticians maintain one of two basic premises when describing normal adolescent development: that turmoil is necessary or that it is not. The turmoil theory of adolescent development proposes that adolescents normally undergo significant disruption in their personality organization. This disruption, in turn, leads to fluctuations in moods, changeable and unpredictable behavior, confusion in thought, and rebellion against one's parents.

Turmoil theorists believe that adolescents need to go through certain struggles in order to separate successfully from their parents and develop their own identity, learn how to relate well to male and female peers, and have a stable personality; if they do not endure such turmoil during the adolescent years, they cannot, by definition, grow into mentally healthy, mature adults. The theory was first described by Hall (1904), who saw *Sturm und Drang* as a universal characteristic of the developmental psychology of adolescents. Hall stated that it was typical of adolescents to oscillate between the extremes of psychological functioning.

Later, Anna Freud (1946) expanded considerably on Hall's work, emphasizing the ways in which the biological changes of puberty create disruption and psychological chaos for the individual adolescent. She suggested that the effect of puberty on the adolescent is comparable to the beginning phase of an acute psychotic reaction. In other words, the weakening of the ego together with increased strength of the instinctual forces make it almost impossible for the adolescent to function in a balanced and harmonious way. Anna Freud set up a "no-win" equation for adolescents: They are either controlled by their impulses, which lead them down the path of delinquency, or overrepressed, which results in symptoms like depression and phobias. In either case, her theories hold that adolescents cannot function well. "To be normal during the adolescent period," she notes, "is by itself abnormal" (p. 275).

Recent researchers have developed similar arguments. Within the psychoanalytic schools of thought, adolescents appear to be quite disturbed as a matter of course. Peter Blos (1967), a major contributor to the psychoanalytic literature on adolescence, wrote, "adolescence is the only period in human life during which ego regression and drive regression constitute an obligatory component of normal development" (p. 172). Blos maintains that, without mammoth internal (and hence external) struggles, the adolescent is not developing properly. In the 1960s, the turmoil theory was reincarnated as the "identity crisis," which became a cliche.

The term "identity crisis" was actually coined by Erik Erikson

(1963, 1968), another major contributor to theories of adolescent development. Erikson notes that the period of adolescence is marked by increased conflict characterized by a normal fluctuation in ego strength. The potential for growth is associated with the intensity of this conflict: The confusion is part of the process leading to identity formation. Erikson (1963) believes that the *primary* task of adolescence is the development of such an ego identity.

> In puberty and adolescence all samenesses and continuities relied on earlier are more or less questioned again, because of a rapidity of body growth which equals that of early childhood and because of the new addition of genital maturity. The growing and developing youths, faced with this physiological revolution within them, and with tangible adult tasks ahead of them, are now primarily concerned with what they appear to be in the eyes of others as compared with what they feel they are, and with the question of how to connect the roles and skills cultivated earlier with the occupational prototypes of the day. (p. 261)

Erickson posits that if adolescents are unable to develop a sense of personal identity out of their role struggles they may then fall prey to the dangers of role confusion. He theorizes that without a strong sense of *who* they are, adolescents become more vulnerable to delinquency, peer pressure, and more severe psychological disturbances.

Such a positive personal identity is, in many ways, shaped by the development of skills that are basic to competent adulthood: literacy, problem solving, abstract reasoning, conflict resolution, intimacy. Without these skills, adolescents are more vulnerable to the alternative paths of confusion, despair, and violence. And some role confusion seems inevitable when there is violence. Without personal safety, the big questions about belonging and the future are luxuries not commonly considered, and vital skills are harder to acquire.

Erikson (1956) views both conflict and mental health as inevitable parts of adolescence. He explains the identity crisis of adolescence as a psychosocial phenomenon tied to a particular culture. As the society changes, so too will the adolescent's search for identity. Like other turmoil theories, Erickson's identity crisis is not bound by static cognitive and biological data. As adolescents change internally, they are also naturally affected by their interaction with their peer group, changes in their family structure and functioning, options for joining the adult world, the larger culture of the time, and so on. As all of these psychosocial factors change, so will the cognitive and biological variables.

Despite its popularity with theoreticians and the popular press alike, the turmoil theory is controversial, and it is not borne out by empirical survey data collected by a wide variety of researchers. For example, Offer and Sabshin (1984) conducted an enormous study of 20,000 middle-class adolescents over a period of 19 years. They discovered that the vast majority (more than 80 percent) of the adolescents studied felt happy, strong, and self-confident, evincing little turmoil or identity crises. The other 20 percent, however, did struggle with personal and social problems. Further, there is little to suggest that adolescents are becoming increasingly troubled. For example, Offer, Ostrov, and Howard (1989) compared adolescent self-image across the 1960s, 1970s, and 1980s, and found a curvilinear effect for these three decades. The adolescents of the 1960s seemed the healthiest (less turmoil). However, adolescents of the 1980s were *better* adjusted than those of the 1970s.

These data are consistent with many other predominantly middle-class samples of different sizes (e.g., Douvan & Adelson, 1966; Elmen & Offer, 1993; Masterson, 1968; Oldham, 1978; Rutter, Graham, Chadwick, & Yule, 1976; Tolan, Jaffe, & Ryan, 1990). It is evident that clinical populations—selected because they exhibit problems of adjustment such as those used by Erikson—may have simply provided a biased sample of the general adolescent population. Additionally, the studies using middle-class subjects suggest that the adolescents who are in turmoil are abnormally, not normally, distressed. At the same time, it must be underscored that the life circumstances described in survey questionnaires mostly by happy, middle-class adolescents may share precious little with other social groups. Before the debate between researchers about what constitutes normal adolescent development can be resolved, changing family structures and other socioeconomic, racial, and ethnic factors must be considered.

While a polarization of these opposing camps has occurred, the extremes point out the range of possibility for adolescents. The brooding idealists and impulsive delinquents who are alienated from the adult community are at one end of the continuum. Yet they may have much in common with the confident, self-satisfied, and happy family members at the other end. At the very least, the varied experiences of adolescents may begin to inform clinical work and social policy alike with what distinguishes different adolescent groups and what leads to greater resiliency and coping, even in the face of stress.

Placing adolescent development in a context that has a broad, normal range of responses is a first step in moving away from harmful myths that perpetuate belief in the extremes. Not having to subscribe to the myth that all adolescents go through major identity crises, or the opposing myth that the American family is happy and untroubled, we may be able to look more closely at the richness of the period of development we call "adolescence." At the same time, we can try to demystify it, and come to accept adolescence for what it is: one of many stages in life from birth to old age.

LIFE-CYCLE THEORIES

As the study of adolescence has progressed, a wide range of specialists have come to realize the necessity of looking at this stage of development in the context of the family. Sociologists first began to visualize the family as a unit composed of individuals undergoing their own life-cycle tasks. Life-cycle theorists maintain that adolescence is a period of identity formation that involves the basic tasks of separation and individuation, but holds no more unique claim to identity formation than any other life stage (e.g., Toews, Prosin, & Martin, 1981). The process of identity formation starts during infancy, when the newborn begins to differentiate from the mother, and continues through old age. What seems unique about the formation of identity during adolescence is that physical development, cognitive development, and changes in social expectations coincide, pressing adolescents to review their previous identifications and begin clearing a pathway toward the future.

Later, life-cycle theorists observed that family members depend on each other to complete their individual life-cycle tasks. The family is the primary group in which most individuals learn the basic

norms of human behavior and social expectations. Within this context, values and attitudes are passed down through generations,
giving individuals a sense of history and continuity. The family
also supports developmental growth by providing individuals with
emotional nurturance. More recently, life cycle theorists have seen
the family as a unit having its own developmental tasks. This view
has led to the theory that the family also has its own life cycle, with
predictable and identifiable transitions. Since the 1950s, perhaps as
a result of this view, the concept that the family is the basic unit of
human development has achieved general acceptance (Carter &
McGoldrick, 1989).

Like individual stage theories of development, family life-cycle
theory addresses the normal developmental processes experienced
by most people as they move from one stage to another. The assumption is that there are tasks at each stage that need to be accomplished, and that the transition from one stage to another is always
accompanied by a normal degree of crisis. For example, in late
adolescence the family task involves preparing the adolescent to
leave home. The "identity crisis" of the adolescent and the "midlife
crisis" of the parents may coincide to make this a particularly painful transition. How the family accomplishes its developmental tasks
and copes with the crises will have a tremendous effect on the
individual development of family members. An important point to
consider when using this framework is that differences in class and
culture, as well as changes in society, will also influence the life
cycle of a family. In other words, child development occurs in interaction with different members of the family and also in the context
of parent development. But the parents' development continues
concurrently with that of their children. Issues of career expectations, marital satisfaction, health, and economic stability all influence how parents view and interact with their children. Also, and
perhaps most important, the manner in which the parents themselves were socialized during their own individual development affects their access to the general instrumental and coping skills
needed to engage successfully in work, marital, and social roles, as
well as the specific skills needed to socialize their children effectively.

As children move into adolescence, they become increasingly

independent and spend more time outside of the home away from adult supervision. They establish new roles, and reconstruct their self-representation in reference to the biological, social, and cognitive changes associated with maturation and culturally normative experiences. During this period, the parents' role becomes increasingly managerial and consultative. Adolescents become more active participants with their parents in negotiating and selecting experiences inside and outside of the home.

Families in which violence of any sort develops—physical abuse, sexual abuse, suicide, delinquency—are, by definition, in distress. While there are many ways that a family can be dysfunctional (indeed, some say it is hard to find one that is not) families of violence work in distinct ways, marked by specific kinds of problems in the development of individuals and of the family group.

As a family moves through adolescence, three aspects of family interaction become crucial to the continued development of adolescents: monitoring, discipline, and involvement. In a variety of studies, violence in the home has been associated with difficulty in one or more of these functions. "Monitoring" is a broad term that includes parents' knowledge of their children's activities, peer associates, and whereabouts outside of the home. Effective monitoring entails the negotiation and communication of clear rules and expectations about *all* areas of the adolescent's life (e.g., curfew, drug use, school attendance and performance, peer selections). Parents must monitor compliance with family rules, and engage in effective problem-solving and discipline when rules are violated (e.g., Snyder & Huntley, 1990; Snyder & Patterson, 1987).

Good monitoring, discipline, and involvement help keep adolescents safe and assist them in learning how to make healthy choices. These parenting functions are important in limiting adolescents' exposure to antisocial opportunities and learning experiences, and in providing opportunities for healthy activities outside the home. However, good monitoring and discipline will also take into account the adolescent's increasing competence and responsibility. This means that parents have to temper their controlling involvement by offering experiences in which adolescents can act independently and exercise their own judgment. Simultaneously, parents must act as positive models by listening to their adolescents and expecting to be heard themselves. The delicate balance of involvement—without detachment or smothering—evolves with age and experience, as parents and adolescents engage in a mutual and developing dance, so that by the time adolescents are ready to leave home they are able to lead competently on the dance floor.

By contrast, poor monitoring, discipline, and involvement—whether by virtue of absence or excess—can lead to serious problems. At one end of the continuum, inadequate parental monitoring is associated with many varieties of delinquent and dangerous behavior (Patterson, 1986). Several longitudinal studies have further demonstrated that parental coldness, passivity, and neglect, and a lack of family cohesion and shared leisure time, are associated with one-time and recidivist delinquency (McCord, 1979; Pulkkinen, 1983). Without the protective parental functions, adolescents are less likely to acquire adequate communication skills, be comfortable with give-and-take, learn how to handle intimacy or take responsibility for themselves. Instead, they become susceptible to the values of violence and short-term personal gain.

At the other end of the continuum, overmonitoring is often associated with suicidal depression (e.g., Cytryn & McKnew, 1980; Garmezy, 1981; Karpel, 1980; Spinetta & Rigler, 1977). Adolescent depression is common in overprotective and emotionally overinvolved families. In abusive families, overmonitoring is used to insure compliance; the family, threatened intolerably if the adolescent challenges parental authority or asserts an independent will, restricts freedoms in a highly punitive fashion (Pelcovitz, 1984). The dynamic in incestuous families can also be defined by overmonitoring and overinvolvement. Fathers or father figures in these families are authoritarian and act in possessive and jealous ways (Finkelhor, 1984; Summit & Kryso, 1978; Tierney & Corwin, 1983). Families that cannot tolerate healthy individuation, or do not know how to ease up on rigid, intrusive structures, may well be setting the stage for violence that is directed toward the adolescent in one way or another.

The life-cycle framework is especially useful for understanding the experiences of the 20 to 25 percent of adolescents and their families who demonstrate serious problems. It provides guidelines for examining the tasks and transformations required of a family with adolescents. The therapist can use this approach to make a clearer assessment of how the family is coping with this stage of development; sharing the life-cycle perspective with families can be an extremely effective method of intervention. For example, the generational conflicts and power struggles that most of these families present as problems while in therapy can be reframed, or seen in the context of normal developmental processes characteristic of adolescence, or of midlife. This may allow the family to view the situation as temporary rather than permanent and hopelessly out of control. By focusing on the tasks that need to be accomplished during these stages, the family can be helped to negotiate new roles and patterns that may lead to developmental growth.

Developmental Tasks of Adolescence

The changes that can take place during adolescence are numerous and have been defined from a variety of perspectives, including biological (e.g., hormonal changes associated with puberty), cognitive (e.g., the acquisition of abstract reasoning skills that are part of formal operational thought), psychological (e.g., stable identity formation evolving from experimentation), social (e.g., identification with a peer group), sexual (e.g., identification of sexual preference) educational (e.g., development of educational and vocational goals), and familial (e.g., leaving home). Each perspective generates its own list of changes that must take place in order for the adolescent to pass on to the next developmental stage. While some of the changes, like puberty, generally happen on their own, others, like the move to abstract reasoning or vocational planning, may not happen at all without some sort of intervention.

Different developmental theories offer their own value systems about what is most important for adolescents to accomplish. For example, Piaget (1968) pictured adolescents as philosophers who ponder their place in the world and struggle with their attempts to make sense of life. By contrast, Jay Haley (1980), a family therapist, sees adolescents as engaged in the primary, painful, encompassing task of developing the skills necessary to separate from their families.

Some theoreticians have attempted to integrate the different perspectives to create a more unified list. Havinghurst (1972) delineates a fairly comprehensive set of tasks. Such a list offers evidence for what a complex and difficult load an adolescent must take on in order to become an adult.

1. Achieving new and more mature relations with age mates of both sexes
2. Achieving a masculine or feminine social role
3. Accepting one's physique and using the body effectively
4. Achieving emotional independence of parents and other adults
5. Preparing for marriage and family life
6. Preparing for an economic career
7. Acquiring a set of values and an ethical system as a guide to behavior—developing an ideology
8. Desiring and achieving socially responsible behavior
(pp. 45–52)

THE EFFECTS OF VIOLENCE ON NORMAL ADOLESCENT DEVELOPMENT

It is possible to speculate with some confidence about the effects of violence on any and all developmental tasks. For example, using Havinghurst's (1972) outline, it becomes evident that violence interferes in profound and far-reaching ways with the nature of adolescence itself.

1. Achieving New and More Mature Relations with Age Mates of Both Sexes. The troubled peer relationships of both adolescent victims and perpetrators of violence have been well-documented. For example, the social effects of physical abuse on an adolescent include passivity and withdrawal (Martin & Beezley, 1977), heightened aggressiveness, and oppositional and defiant social strategies (Kempe & Kempe, 1978). Numerous studies have found that abused children's peer relationships include larger amounts of anger and violence than those of nonabused children (Kinard, 1980; Reid, Taplin, & Lorber, 1981; Reidy, 1977). Researchers consistently note that social competence and peer relationships are particular areas of vulnerability for abused children (e.g., Shirk, 1988). Similarly, sexually abused adolescents also tend to have a range of social difficulties including aggression, depression, social withdrawal, running away, and sexual acting-out (Friedrich, Urquiza, & Beilke, 1986; Herman, 1981). Youthful offenders, whether classified as having solitary-aggressive or group-type conduct disorders (American Psychiatric Association, 1987), can be seen as having significant problems developing new and more mature relationships with peers, given their tendency toward antisocial and maladaptive behaviors.

The social effects of violence on the lives of adolescents have implications beyond the developmental period of adolescence; they also set the stage for difficulties well into adulthood. Although findings vary, previously abused adults (particularly men) have generally been found to have higher levels of aggression and are more likely to commit violent crimes. There even appears to be a linear relationship between the amount of abuse experienced by offenders and the amount of violence they cause (Geller & Ford-Soma, 1984).

2. Achieving a Masculine or Feminine Social Role. Although Havinghurst's (1972) idea is a bit anachronistic by now, the effects of violence on the process of achieving a masculine or feminine social role are still worth a brief analysis. Implicit here is comfort with, and acceptance of, one's sexual orientation and expression. The data on gay and lesbian adolescents are sparse but point to an increase of both physical and sexual victimization within the family as a consequence of their sexual orientations (Martin & Hetrick, 1988). In their study of gay adolescent boys, Hunter and Schaecher (1990) concluded that the earlier one self-identifies as gay, the greater the physical punishment from adults. Perhaps as important, the notion of social roles is a disturbingly patriarchal one, which suggests its own kind of violence. The world of violence is typically one in which perpetrators define feminine and masculine social roles and power relationships narrowly and rigidly. Deviations from these roles, even for adolescents who are heterosexual, can lead to violence. In the most simplistic form, the masculine social role is one of aggressor and the feminine social role is one of victim. In an abusive family, these stereotypes serve only to perpetuate violence and limit more androgynous options for adolescent males and females, both gay and straight.

3. Accepting One's Physique and Using the Body Effectively. Distortions in body image of victims of both physical and sexual abuse are common. It must be difficult indeed to accept and use effectively a body being violated or rejected. Eating disorders, including over-eating, anorexia, and bulimia, are described frequently in the sexual-abuse literature (e.g., Courtois, 1988), and treatment of survivors of both physical and sexual abuse frequently centers on reclaiming the body. As Dolan (1991) notes, "This [establishing a positive identification with one's body] is a particularly powerful therapeutic achievement, which reverberates through many areas of the client's life, most notably affecting her self-esteem, self-awareness, and her ability to be sensuous and sexual in functional, healthy, and personally meaningful ways" (p. 164). Moreover, since adolescents focus so many of their concerns on physical aspects of themselves, it follows that they will have more severe problems using their bodies effectively if they are being physically or sexually violated.

The effects of violence on body image can also be more subtle. Many adolescent survivors describe the ways they are able to "leave their bodies behind" when they are being abused. Numerous retrospective studies have shown that trauma and abuse victims report psychic numbing at the time of the abuse (e.g., Krystal, 1978). Psychic numbing occurs for some adolescents after an overwhelming trauma and involves the experience of having one's emotions deadened and becoming physically disconnected from one's body. Unfortunately, adolescents are not necessarily able to control when they dissociate, and any stress that resembles the original trauma can bring it on. When this happens, it becomes more difficult for adolescents to assess a perceived threat realistically, or to develop other, more effective skills to protect themselves. This self-hypnosis can also be a precursor to more serious adult dissociative states including, in the most extreme form, multiple personalities, each with its own body image.

4. Achieving Emotional Independence of Parents and Other Adults. The achievement of emotional independence from parents and other adults presupposes a healthy dependence in which earlier needs had been met. This is seldom, if ever, the case for adolescents living with violence. To begin with, the family structures in which adolescents become victims or offenders tend to fit extreme types. For example, in many incestuous families there is a lack of generational differentiation; blurred role boundaries allow the victim-daughter to become a central female figure in the family (Lustig, Dresser, Spellman, & Murray, 1966). Mothers of incest victims are frequently described as incapacitated through mental illness or physical disability, or as physically or emotionally unavailable, while fathers are dominant and authoritarian (Finkelhor, 1979; Herman, 1981).

Physically abused adolescents generally come from two types of families: authoritarian or overindulgent. The authoritarian adolescent-abusing family is marked by inflexibility. Family members relate to each other in such an unyielding way that any change is felt as a threat to the survival of the family. The overindulgent abusive family, by contrast, is marked by dramatic inconsistency. Rules change from day to day and are enforced randomly. Parenting functions range from passive and permissive acceptance of the adolescent's behavior to especially punitive styles (Straus, 1988).

Findings within the area of juvenile delinquency similarly depict family dysfunction. Delinquency has been associated with higher rates of marital and family conflict (Gove & Crutchfield, 1982) and low levels of parental acceptance and affection (West & Farrington, 1973). Overall, then, adolescents who live with violence have a particularly difficult task in achieving emotional independence from their parents and other adults. They do not have the benefit of a gradual increase of freedoms and responsibilities, nor do they have the concurrent steady emotional support for the steps that they are taking toward adulthood.

5. Preparing for Marriage and Family Life. Fifth, and perhaps following from the foregoing, an adolescent of violence cannot take even the first steps toward preparing for marriage and family life. The interpersonal legacy of violence for adolescents may remove the possibility of developing responsible adult relationships. This legacy includes: a lack of trust, fear of intimacy, emotional lability, manipulation, substance abuse, depression, and thought disorders. Adolescents growing up with violence not only lack role models for competent partnering and parenting, but generally have before them some of the most disturbed examples imaginable for conflict resolution and intimacy. The intergenerational-transmission hypothesis has some clinical support as well. Indeed, rather than preparing them for marriage and family life, their families of origin may well be training these adolescents to take their victim or perpetrator experiences into their adult lives and future families.

6. *Preparing for an Economic Career.* Adolescents who live on or over the edge of violence seldom see that the rewards of work are available to them. While others prepare for an economic career, these disenfranchised, unprotected adolescents concentrate on survival, which may deprive them of the energy that careful entry into the job market necessitates. Additionally, the job prospects for many of these adolescents are bleak. Because of changes in the labor market, decent paying jobs increasingly require higher education or specialized job skills that many young people have not had enough opportunity to gain. As a result, youths without education beyond high school are finding it difficult or impossible to find stable, full-time work that pays enough to support a family. Minorities and women are at greatest risk of finding only part-time (or sporadic) employment at best, and low earnings. While some adolescent victims, wanting to achieve outside of the home, may find sanctuary in school and jobs, these appear to be part of a finite, resilient subset of victims. Delinquents and other adolescent perpetrators of violence generally demonstrate a minimal or erratic interest in steady, legal employment.

7. *Acquiring a Set of Values and an Ethical System as a Guide to Behavior—Developing an Ideology.* While it is possible to imagine that some adolescents living with violence acquire a set of positive values and an ethical system to guide behavior, these are difficult to maintain in the face of violence. The degree of resourcefulness, resilience, persistence, and perspective displayed by adolescents— how they cope with the violence—may be, in large part, connected to the kind of ideology that they are able to develop. The value system of an adolescent of violence would necessarily include explanations for much tougher questions than other adolescents need to answer. For example: Why is this happening to me? Am I worth caring about and protecting? What do I have to do to survive? What is really important to me? How do I keep growing and learning when I want to shut down? Whether the ideology develops as a result of the violence or in spite of it, it is clear that the ethical

systems of these adolescents do not develop easily, given the lack of persuasive and positive models.

8. Desiring and Achieving Socially Responsible Behavior. Desiring and achieving socially responsible behavior demands both an understanding of social norms and access to the resources to adapt to them. While some adolescents may know that the violence is wrong, many others see it as the only way of being they have ever known, or as the only option available to them. Adolescents who live with violence must figure out how to fit in and belong to a society that is, from their perspective, unable to protect or care for them. Violence pushes adolescents toward the margin. This edge is defined not only by life or death, but also by belonging or being cast aside, by feeling valued or worthless, and by anticipating a future that can be exciting or terrifying. Social responsibility can only emerge as a consequence of one's taking hold of life, and of having a sense of belonging and feelings of worth and hope for the future. In the face of violence, these can be daunting tasks indeed.

The effects of a life shaped by violence reach into virtually every aspect of adolescent development. Yet, even within the potentially devastating landscape of violence, adolescents can sometimes learn the coping skills necessary to escape the violence and make safer choices for themselves.

Coping with Violence

Adolescents who are resilient in the face of abuse appear to have some "protective factors" that enable them to persevere despite chronic and acute stress in their lives (Rutter, 1979). The research on such resiliency can be grouped into three levels: characteristics of the individual, factors within the family, and extrafamilial relationships.

INDIVIDUAL CHARACTERISTICS

Individual characteristics contributing to resiliency in the face of violence include genetics and temperament, gender, age, locus of control, and cognitive coping skills. Research on genetics focuses upon the association between individual genotypes and environmental stressors. Genetics, for example, has been linked with higher creativity in children of mentally ill parents and, to a lesser degree, with criminality as well (Rutter, 1979).

Similarly, temperament, also thought to be innate, can lead to particular responses to stress (Kagan, 1984). Inherent qualities, such as level of energy, lability of mood, intensity of action, persistence, and distractibility, shape infants' responses to situations such as eating, sleeping, and playing (Carey, 1974; Kagan, 1984; Thomas & Chess, 1977). Infants with a "difficult" temperament—irregular, avoidant, intense, and slow to adapt—may be less resilient to stress than those with more advantageous personality dispositions such as social responsiveness, autonomy, and flexibility. Temperamental qualities tend to be enduring. For example, shy, inhibited infants tend to be less resilient in the face of stress than their more outgoing peers, even into adulthood. Although interesting, such innate factors interact mightily with other individual and environmental characteristics, and probably account for relatively little in how adolescents cope with violence.

The effect of gender upon resilience is also complex and, from a clinical point of view, somewhat confusing. However, several studies note that girls are more resilient than boys in the face of stressful childhood situations, including hospital admissions, birth of siblings, and parental discord (Rutter, 1987). With the onset of adolescence, some of these differences reverse; adolescent girls have *more* problems with self-esteem, body image, physical effectiveness, and self concept (Offer, Ostrov, & Howard, 1981). Notably, studies on adult survivors of physical abuse depict more resilient women than men. In her 18- and 30-year follow-up studies of resilient adults, Werner (1989) notes, "Resilient women tend to weather stressful life events with less impairment to their health; they also rely on more sources of support than do resilient men" (p. 78). Most longitudinal studies point to this developmental shift. In the first decade of life, boys are more vulnerable than girls when exposed to severe stressors, but by late adolescence this trend is reversed. Young women then appear to become more vulnerable, especially with the onset of early childbearing. As the work of Carol Gilligan has also demonstrated amply, adolescent girls who were once confident and hopeful frequently find themselves plagued by self-doubt and confusion with the onset of puberty at about age 12 (Mikel-Brown & Gilligan, 1992). By the age of around 30, the balance then shifts back in favor of women. Clinically, of course, this does not seem to be necessarily true, as women survivors appear to seek out treatment more frequently than their male counterparts, and are often quite devastated by their traumatic past, even (and maybe especially, as painful memories return) after age 30.

Gender is also complicated because the types of violent stressors faced by males and females tend to be different. For example, boys get into trouble much more often than girls. Researchers are less likely now than in the past to explain these differences as genetic and look more toward differences in personality and socialization (Dryfoos, 1990). While boys participate in violent and aggressive behavior, girls are more likely to be involved in lesser offenses such as running away. Similarly, adolescent girls are two to three times more likely to be sexually abused than are boys, and are particularly vulnerable to date rape and acquaintance rape. Within the family, the risk of physical (nonsexual) abuse for girls is lower than for boys during the younger years but increases with age. The relative risk reaches a peak during the preadolescent and adolescent years, when girls become more at risk for physical abuse than boys (American Psychological Association, 1993). In general, girls, socialized to remain connected and compliant, endure the stress of feminine victimization. Boys, socialized to control, endure stress associated with the narrow path defined by masculine aggression (Campbell, 1993).

The relationship between age and resiliency is also complicated, especially as it has a confounding effect upon the other variables. Some researchers speculate that the effects of violence are variably troublesome depending upon whether the violence (a) began in childhood and continued into adolescence, (b) began in childhood but became more severe in adolescence, or (c) began in adolescence (Garbarino & Gilliam, 1980; Lourie, 1979). The hypothesis is that the more recent the violence, the more resilient the adolescents will be. Interestingly, Farber and Joseph (1985) attempted to test this theory with abused adolescents and found *no* difference among the groups. All adolescents studied had ego deficits and demonstrated emotional and behavioral reactions that made the groups indistinguishable from one another.

Ultimately, age may interact with resiliency in more subtle ways, taking into account the variety of other factors that may contribute to survival. From a cognitive-developmental perspective, the age of the child at the onset of the violence can lead to developmental differences in the *experience* of violence, different *outcomes* resulting from developmental differences at the time of abuse, and developmental differences in the *expression* of enduring distress resulting from the violence. When it comes to making sense of violent experiences, age is a very sticky variable that may explain the ways in which individuals are traumatized better than the reasons they are resilient.

Research on "locus of control"—an individual's perception of the cause of events—has yielded more consistent results. In the general population, at one end of the continuum, individuals with an *external* locus of control do not think they have much say in their lives, believing instead that luck, chance, fate, and powerful others have more control over events than they do. At the other end, individuals with an *internal* locus of control perceive that they are responsible for all that happens to them. Most typically, someone functioning well has a locus of control that tends to be slightly internal, but can be flexible depending upon the situation. By contrast, most adolescents of violence have dramatically external loci of control, greatly impeding their abilities to take hold of their own lives. It is quite possible that a climate of violence *teaches* an external locus of control, because there is seldom any correlation between an adolescent's actions and the response of others in the environment. Interestingly, adolescents make suicidal gestures when they feel particularly powerless over their lives; in resorting to a suicide attempt they may be trying to take charge of their deaths.

In contrast to the general consensus that violence inevitably leads to an external locus of control, resilient individuals in a number of studies have described their own personal competence and determination as factors that enabled them to cope with the violence (Cohler, 1987; Felsman, 1989; Werner, 1988). It seems logical that some flexibility in attribution is necessary to survive. Feeling blameless about the cause of violence, but capable of ending or escaping it, is probably the optimal locus of control for most victims.

Adolescents who avoid violence or are able to minimize its effects also have other coping skills that their peers do not. Such coping involves three primary components: (1) understanding, evaluating, and reframing the meaning of a troublesome situation; (2) engaging in competent action; and (3) keeping powerful emotions, such as anger or fear, from being too overwhelming.

Understanding, Evaluating, and Reframing

The first coping skill that distinguishes resilient adolescents is really a cognitive one: They are able to think about the violence in a different way. They do not simply blame themselves or feel hopeless, because they can entertain an array of useful perspectives about what is happening to them. Being intelligent and having a good fantasy life distinguishes adolescents who cope well from their traumatized peers in several studies (e.g., Olson, 1992; Zimrim, 1986).

It makes sense that brains and imagination would help someone handle a violent situation. Adolescents living with violence must first and foremost be able to understand that this is only one of many possible ways to live. However, such insight does not easily lead to action. In fact, such a realization may in itself be initially threatening. For example, a sexually abused adolescent may consider stopping the abuse, but be concerned about the possible destructive consequences to different family members, including divorce, foster care, or incarceration.

Once they have the perspective necessary to understand what is happening to them, adolescents can then evaluate the meaning of the violence in their lives—which they usually measure by the intensity of its emotional impact. Many adolescents who have taken steps to end the violence against them describe the variety of ways in which their lives were controlled by it and the stress, uncertainty, and psychological pain it caused. While the initial appraisal of a violent situation can seem threatening, subsequent reassessment over time can change the meaning to one of opportunity and promise. For example, a suicidal adolescent who survives can discover resources and supports in the external environment sufficient to help make life-affirming choices.

In order to reframe the problem of the violence, adolescents have to be able to control the meaning of the situation and contain powerful disruptive emotions. While the history of the violence cannot be changed, its significance in the adolescent's life has to evolve. For example, abused adolescents who become safe need to develop more productive personal stories. While they may have described themselves as powerless victims, they can begin to see that they are now empowered and skillful young adults. This evolution occurs over time. There are many steps involved in changing the meaning of the violence to be able to move away from it: sizing up the situation, examining a range of of alternative possibilities, generating accurate information, developing a workable course of action, making corrections along the way using new information, finding and using available environmental supports, and seeking out new supports as needed. Naturally, effective problem-solving does not occur instantly. Time, persistence, and flexibility are usually required to move away from abusive experiences and acquire and retain an enduring and positive sense of self.

As adolescents mature intellectually and gain more experience outside of the violence, their capacity for conceptual and reflective thinking can improve. However, it is quite clear that violence does not enhance and stimulate abstract reasoning abilities. On the contrary, many studies point to a clear association between cognitive lags and violence of many kinds (e.g., Fish-Murray, Koby, & van der Kolk, 1987; Stott, 1982). Treatment of adolescents of violence must have a strong cognitive-developmental component to enable them to begin taking control of their lives in a reasonable, thoughtful way. They then may gain the ability to see the same situation from multiple perspectives and envision new possibilities for ending the violence in their lives, or for viewing themselves as survivors instead of victims. While a capacity for abstract reasoning is not by itself sufficient to change a life, it is a powerful tool for beginning that often-difficult process.

Engaging in Competent Action

The second coping skill that distinguishes resilient adolescents is a behavioral one: They employ creative solutions to potent problems. They devise a plan to minimize, escape, or end the violence against them. They engage helpful people in tackling their problems with them. Resilient adolescents find other places in which to excel and to feel whole; they attach to someone who thinks highly of them; and they look for the way out and work toward it systematically over time. Resilient adolescents keep the date of their eighteenth birthday in their minds and are determined to get there.

Keeping Powerful Emotions at Bay

The third part of coping well involves employing protective strategies that can control powerful disorganizing feelings such as fear, anger, and guilt. When adolescents are paralyzed by fear or wild with anger, it is difficult for them to work their way through stressful and frustrating experiences. Along with cognitive and behavioral strategies, adolescents must also be able to protect themselves psychologically. Three types of emotional strategies help adolescents manage the potent emotional content aroused by violent experiences: damage control, defense mechanisms, and complex protective reactions.

Damage control is really an initial reaction to violence that enables the adolescent to reduce or minimize feelings of personal discomfort without actively addressing the violence. Exercising, listening to music, talking to friends about other things, crying, and expressing mild anger can all be part of a sequential coping process that allows the adolescent to gain some breathing room before tackling the problem head on.

Defense mechanisms, which are employed by both resilient and nonresilient youngsters, serve the unconscious purpose of altering the emotional experience of the violence by distorting, distancing, or filtering it. A successful use of defenses generally involves a variety of them in different combinations. While there is no way to prescribe defenses for someone, resilient adolescents appear to be able to handle stress by balancing several approaches over time, while their nonresilient peers continue to use the same defense that once worked, whether or not it continues to protect them emotionally. For example, an adolescent who was first abused as a child may have used denial of strong feelings in order to cope. As the years progress, the distressing experiences may be reenacted through more abuse or in symbolic ways—rejection by a boyfriend or girlfriend, for example. The feelings of pain and anger may gain in intensity to the point where they cannot be denied effectively. A resilient adolescent would be able to add other defenses, like intellectualization and rationalization to deal with the new pain. A nonresilient adolescent might, instead, become overwhelmed by the strong feelings inside, and consequently cope poorly by erupting with rage or becoming paralyzed with despair.

Adolescents commonly dissociate in the attempt to survive an overwhelming and potentially psychologically destructive event such as physical or sexual abuse. Unfortunately, such dissociative attempts as amnesia, numbing, and "spacing out" are rarely, if ever, fully successful in the original situation. Moreover, long after the original traumatic experience has passed, the survivor of violence may spontaneously (though unconsciously) reactivate these dissociative defenses in responding to other stress. Even when such defensive responses help the adolescent cope immediately with stress, they do not facilitate newer, more flexible strategies.

Defenses can have growth-enhancing or growth-inhibiting qualities. The ideal defense provides protection, does not greatly distort reality, allows for some expression of feelings and gratification of needs, and does not block the cognitive or behavioral steps that are essential for breaking free of the violence. By contrast, poor defenses prevent fulfillment of needs, involve excessive distortion of internal and external reality, and severely reduce the flexibility necessary to work through stressful conflicts.

Complex protective strategies involve the integration of damage control and defense mechanisms with other behaviors. For example, suicidal adolescents can exercise or practice relaxation techniques when feeling signs of stress. Improved communication skills among family members and productive uses of rationalization and minimization can also enhance their coping. Resilient adolescents use a variety of coping strategies. No one set of protective mechanisms, problem-solving approaches, or decision-making strategies will work in all situations. There are times to observe, times for direct action, and times to set problems aside for a while.

FAMILY FACTORS

The family can serve as both a socializing and protecting environment for the developing child and adolescent. Early familial socialization provides children with the rudiments of socioemotional and cognitive skills that influence the nature of their transactions with peers and teachers. Parents further influence the nature of these transactions by choosing schools, selectively encouraging activities outside of the home, and monitoring the child's peer relationships and school performance. This monitoring function becomes increasingly important during late childhood and adolescence, and serves a protective function, particularly in severely disadvantaged, high-risk environments.

Certain aspects of family structure and demographics may also provide a kind of protection that can help an adolescent cope with violence. For example, variables such as the presence of an intact, two-parent family, economic advantages, smaller family size, and the absence of other family-stressful events have been associated with more competent functioning in children in a number of studies (e.g., Earls, Beardslee, & Garrison, 1987; Werner & Smith, 1979). Even when they are not functioning well, families with more resources can offer more alternatives to an adolescent.

The ways in which adolescents manage their relationships with their families can also provide some protection for them. For example, in studies of resilience in alcoholic (Berlin & Davis, 1989) and divorcing families (Wallerstein, 1983), those who coped well kept emotionally distant from the family and removed the crisis from a central place in their lives. Robert Coles (1989) similarly commented upon the ability of resilient children living in war zones to step back and question their experiences. The ability to see oneself as separate from a physically and sexually abusive family is similarly a vital method of coping (Zimrim, 1986). This adaptive distancing may permit adolescents the perspective required to "take stock" of their situations.

In addition, resilient adolescents are capable of differentiating between the reality that is attributed to them by others in their families and a more functional reality. They do not necessarily "buy" the family's story about them. Zimrim (1986) offers a poignant example of a resilient youngster in her child-abuse study. The boy remembered that his mother would introduce him to guests by saying "'Have you ever seen anything so stupid?' I remained silent, but in my heart I said to myself: It's not me, it's she who is the stupid one" (p. 344).

EXTRAFAMILIAL FACTORS

Instead of relying upon parental approval to feel good, resilient adolescents may be able to find other kinds of relationships and activities that can kindle and maintain their self-esteem. One of the strongest findings in the resiliency literature is the presence of a caring adult in the life of the abused child or adolescent. The involved adult does not have to spend a great deal of time with the adolescent, but the relationship has to be maintained over a period of time (Cohler, 1987; Garmezy, 1981; Steele, 1986; Werner, 1989; Zimrim, 1986). In addition to peers, resilient adolescents turn to neighbors, ministers, elders, and teachers who can provide support not found at home. Werner (1988) concludes that, "Our research on resilient children has shown us that they had at least one person in their lives who accepted them unconditionally regardless of temperamental idiosyncracies, physical attractiveness, or intelligence" (p. 5). Resilient adolescents may be able to find other adults who can offer them some of the important parenting functions they may not receive from their actual parents.

These adolescents also find ways of achieving outside of the home where they are able to compensate for all kinds of bad feelings developed there. For example, resilient children often do extremely well in school or display an enthusiasm for art, theater, or athletics through which they can channel and sublimate their aggressive impulses into areas of high achievement (Garbarino, Dubrow, Kostelny, & Pardo, 1992; Murphy & Hirschberg, 1982; Werner, 1989). Because of their increased independence and ability to get around on their own, adolescents can also take advantage of community resources like the YMCA, church groups, and recreation programs to the extent that violence does not define their lives, but is rather just one element in them.

It is important to note that the construct of resilience is fairly static and usually measured by behavior (e.g., school achievement), the presence of some desirable state (e.g., self-esteem), or by the absence of severe psychopathology (e.g., major depression). It does not take into account that people who cope well at one point may eventually suffer more obviously, as so often seems true clinically. Nor does it measure the other unseen costs of violence that may be relevant despite the person's ability to cope well. For example, survivors may achieve at school or in jobs but have difficulty sustaining satisfying relationships. Violence affects everyone, even those who may appear resilient in its aftermath. Just because some adolescents are able to cope well, or because some families can change to live free of violence, does not mean that they have gotten off more easily than others or that they are better in some way. Pain varies with the individual as do the resources to cope with it. Even adolescents who seem to be handling the violence in their lives relatively well have suffered deeply, and will pay for the violence in small or large ways throughout their lives.

Treatment of Adolescent Victims and Offenders

Therapeutic interventions designed expressly for adolescents are a relatively recent development, probably dating to Freud's treatment of Dora, an 18-year-old girl. Since that time, other psychodynamically oriented approaches, along with cognitive, behavioral, family, and group methods, have been used with increasing attention toward the particular developmental level and contextual experience of the adolescent.

There is scant evidence about the relative efficacy of taking different therapy approaches with adolescents. While ample outcome studies have been conducted concerning treatment with adults and children, comparable research on therapy with adolescents is sorely lacking. The literature that does exist tends to treat adolescent experience and psychopathology in a monolithic way, with little regard for important differences in age, developmental level, background, diagnosis, and the chronicity or severity of the problems that brought the adolescent into treatment. Such heterogeneous samples of adolescents make it difficult to interpret the significance of most of these studies.

Further, though much is known about the effects of violence on adolescents, even less outcome research exists on the preferred treatment modalities for these victims and offenders—with the exception of some useful outcome studies on therapy with delinquents. However, even though the findings have limits, the data that exist on the treatment of adolescents indicate quite clearly that psychotherapy can provide significant, relatively lasting improvement for a range of adolescent groups and problems (Kazdin, 1985; Tramontana, 1980; Tramontana & Sherrets, 1984; Weisz, Weiss, Alicke, & Klotz, 1987).

The social problems surrounding violence in adolescence also contribute to confusion about the best interventions, and their presence suggests emphatically that multisystemic approaches have the best chances of working. Beyond outpatient individual, family, and group therapies are a host of alternative youth treatment services; most are offered in conjunction with some form of psychotherapy and do not necessarily replace more traditional approaches.

Psychotherapy broadly describes a wide range of interventions designed to decrease or eliminate symptoms and maladjustment and to improve adaptive and prosocial functioning. The interventions generally rely on interpersonal interaction, counseling, or activities that follow a specific treatment plan. The focus is on how adolescents feel (affect), think (cognition), and act (behavior). Techniques within and among the vast array of psychotherapeutic approaches can vary greatly, based upon who is identified as the patient (e.g., the adolescent, the parents, the family), the medium of treatment (e.g., talk, play, outdoor challenges), the central therapeutic focus (e.g., the individual, the family, the peer group), and the setting where the intervention is carried out (e.g., clinic, home, school). More than 230 different treatment techniques are currently used for children and adolescents (Kazdin, 1993).

Since the vast majority of these techniques have not been studied empirically, clinicians tend to approach adolescent problems by doing what they have been trained to do, using the strategies they have already used, regardless of any objective criteria for success. Even where data do exist (e.g., individual therapy on its own has not proven effective for delinquents), we persevere, doing the best we can with what we know and what we will be paid to do. At times, our belief systems about what victims and offenders need will prevail even in the face of contrary data. At other times, lacking contrary information and alternative funding, traditional interventions are probably better than no help at all.

INDIVIDUAL THERAPY

This is a broad, inclusive category of treatment that comprises all of the different approaches to meeting alone with an adolescent. Despite the variations in technique, it is commonly accepted that in individual therapy the quality of the relationship between adolescents and their therapists influences the adolescents' emotional and behavioral responses. It is also generally believed that the development of some kind of reflective self-knowledge plays a central role in therapeutic improvement.

Violence in the lives of adolescents in all cases marks a significant disruption in normal development and has a dramatic interpersonal effect. The core experiences of both victims and offenders are disempowerment and disconnection from others. Recovery is thus based upon empowerment and the creation of new connections (Herman, 1992). Such recovery can take place only within the context of relationships; it cannot occur in isolation. Individual therapy, therefore, becomes a very potent healing tool. In the renewed connection with a caring adult, adolescents of violence are able to rebuild the ego structures that were damaged or deformed by the participation in violence. These structures include the basic capacities for trust, initiative, competence, and identity (Erikson, 1963). Just as these capabilities are originally formed in relationships with other people, they must also be reformed through such relationships. Despite particular beliefs about the best way to treat various forms of trauma, it may not, in fact, matter much how the connections are made. What matters is the healing that only such connections will provide.

FAMILY THERAPY

During the past 30 years, researchers and clinicians have increasingly recognized the link between family relations and the behavior problems of adolescents. In cases of violence, families are often implicated by acts of both commission (as perpetrators or violent role models) and omission (through failure to protect or inadequate monitoring of the adolescent). As a result of this recognition, family-based treatment models have been developed for virtually all forms of violence in adolescence. Despite some differences in methods, family therapists share a view of the family as an interactional unit in which family communication is reciprocal and bidirectional. Family therapists deal with the second ecological level and view adolescence as a social rather than a biological or intrapsychic phenomenon.

Family therapy has proven effective for a range of adolescent problems and, compared to other approaches, it has been shown to be equal or superior in effectiveness in several studies (e.g., Fishman, 1988; Goldenberg & Goldenberg, 1985). There are several noteworthy benefits of using family therapy with adolescent victims and offenders. First, problems are typically resolved more quickly than in individual approaches; this makes family therapy more cost-effective as well. Because the course of treatment is shorter, because all family members receive treatment but are not billed individually, and because the recidivism rate is much lower, the family-therapy approach is, generally, a less expensive and more productive use of resources. Another reason why family therapy can be effective is that it involves all of the significant people in the life of the adolescent. When all are so involved, changes are more likely to be maintained because the family system itself and not just an individual is being transformed. Consequently, the opportunities for maintaining new, more productive behaviors are much greater. Finally, family therapy is effective because it actively includes family members in the treatment process. Family therapists do not view families as external irritations, likely to compete with or disrupt the therapy, but as resources to facilitate the adolescent's healing.

Contrary to the well-earned enthusiasm of many family therapists, there are still times when family therapy needs to be simply one of a variety of treatment methods used, when it cannot be the treatment of choice for a period, or when it should not be attempted at all. For example, when family violence of some kind is the presenting problem, the level of individual pathology and family danger can be so great as to limit the effectiveness of a systemic intervention. Even if family members agree to participate together, their safety within and between sessions must be verifiable. In my practice, I will not work with abusive families unless I have some way of enforcing rules that eliminate opportunity for ongoing verbal, emotional, physical, or sexual abuse. For example, I might arrange for the adolescent to live elsewhere and stipulate that both parents must be in group treatment before I will work with all of them together.

Similarly, when older adolescents absolutely refuse to involve their parents (or these parents do not want to be seen), I will not press in a doctrinaire way for family therapy. If only some members agree to come, I will invite the others periodically, but work with whoever is motivated; working with victims and offenders is hard enough without additional interference. It is possible to think and work systemically without the whole system in the room; when someone in a family changes, other members will be affected.

When adolescents have been in multiple placements or are estranged from their families, I may work with whoever has them in physical custody at the time—or I might just help the adolescents play the unfair hand they have been dealt in life, with no involved caretakers at all. In these situations, I may also use the term "family" loosely to apply to anyone around who appears to be fond of the adolescent, and invite such a person or persons in to help support our work together. While I am quite sympathetic to the theoretical notion that families enable or impede adolescents from leaving home in the right way, I am also a pragmatist; if there is not a viable family to work with, I don't hunt one down.

Overall, family therapy must be a serious consideration when violence in adolescence is part of the presenting picture. But, it makes no sense to be rigid about it, and there will always be times and situations working with adolescent victims and offenders when other interventions must be considered instead.

GROUP THERAPY

Group therapy is often the treatment of choice for adolescents because it lends itself naturally to the peer orientation of this stage of development. Moreover, when adolescents are victims or perpetrators, they become marginal in some way; either by the perceived stigma of their involvement in the violence or the increased difficulty they have participating in the mainstream. A structured and supportive therapy group helps adolescents living with violence find the peer connection and empowerment that can be helpful for healing.

Group therapy for adolescents of violence generally addresses three different skill areas in which both victims and offenders usually have deficiencies.

1. *Interpersonal skills.* Without the ability to make meaningful connections with others, adolescents of violence will become increasingly isolated from their peer group at just the time in development when such socialization should be a major focus.

2. *Problem-solving skills.* Violence is often perceived as a single powerful solution that gets in the way of developing alternatives. Not surprisingly, most adolescents living with violence are quite concrete in their reasoning abilities, with attendant adjustment and interpersonal effectiveness sorely compromised. Therapy groups can help members generate multiple solutions to interpersonal problems, anticipate consequences of a particular course of action, and plan out a viable and nonviolent strategy.

3. *Cognitive-coping skills.* Violence easily leads to distortions in reasoning about a wide range of internal and interpersonal problems. Therapy groups can help adolescents analyze their thoughts; label appropriately their self-defeating statements; observe and rehearse new, and more accurate, self-statements; and develop the ability to reinforce themselves privately. The connections with other adolescents enable victims and offenders alike to think about themselves and their lives differently.

There are many ways to understand violence and intervene to stop it. Individual, family, and group psychotherapy provide some solutions for the involved individuals and their families. However, violence in the life of an adolescent is a crisis for development at all levels: as long as communities and the greater social fabric are profoundly associated with violence in adolescence, therapy alone will not be sufficient. Violence is also a social problem, ultimately requiring social and political as well as personal solutions.

2

Suicidal Adolescents

Susan: "You'll be sorry when I'm gone"

Adolescent suicide attempts and deaths continue to pose a growing mental health problem. Each year, approximately 1 million adolescents move in and out of suicidal crisis or experience episodes of hopelessness and despair in which suicide is considered a possible solution (McCoy, 1982). According to the National Center for Health Statistics (1990), more than 400,000 of these adolescents will attempt suicide each year, and approximately 10,000 will be successful.

Suicide for adolescents between 15 and 19 years old is the third leading cause of death, closely behind motor vehicle accidents and homicide. The suicide rate among teenagers has risen more than 300 percent in the past 25 years, and this statistic is probably simply not an artifact of better reporting. In fact, there are maybe 5 times as many suicides as are actually reported and 10 times as many suicidal attempts as completed acts, or so say thousands of local health authorities and coroners. Many adolescent suicide attempts do not result in medical or mental health intervention; many actual suicides are judged incorrectly by authorities to be accidental deaths. So there are really no reliable statistics (Petzel & Cline, 1978). Among reported cases, adolescent girls attempt suicide four to eight times as often as boys, but boys succeed four times more often than girls do (Carlson, 1983; National Center for Health Statistics, 1990). Males tend to use more lethal means than do females. Adolescent boys resort to shooting and hanging themselves, crashing their cars, and jumping from heights; girls typically attempt suicide by using pills or slicing their wrists, means that are less likely to result in death or disfigurement (Davis, 1983).

The Referral

I got a call from an emergency room nurse about the Stark family just as I was packing to go home from the office one evening. At that time, I was working in an adolescent crisis program attached to a metropolitan hospital, and our staff rotated the emergency calls. Since it was my turn to respond, I trotted across the street to the hospital to wait for a pretty, petite 15-year-old girl to finish throwing up a charcoal product that serves as a decisive method of stomach cleansing, and also, though not intentionally, a nasty punishment for taking a drug overdose in the first place. While we waited for Susan to emerge, sober and resentful, I spoke with her distraught mother for a while. Susan's 11-year-old brother, Mitch, wandered in and out restlessly, alternatively visiting the food machines, whining about being bored, and draping himself on his weepy mother.

Ms. Stark told the following story about her family and the events leading up to Susan's suicide attempt. Susan lived with her mother and younger brother; her parents had divorced when Susan was 12 and she had not seen her father for almost a year, although he lived less than an hour away. After she began high school the previous year, Susan became increasingly isolated from her family and critical of her mother, and spent every moment she could in her room. Like many adolescents, Susan had different standards for cleanliness from her mother, and they had weekly arguments about straightening up Susan's room. The day I met the Starks, the same fight had again precipitated a protracted shouting match in which Susan accused her mother of preferring her brother to her, and blaming her (Susan) for the divorce. Susan reportedly ran sobbing into her room. Later, her mother called Susan to supper but got no answer. She found Susan unconscious on the floor with three empty or nearly-empty pill bottles around her. On Susan's desk she found a suicide note: "Dear Mom, I know that you'll be sad to find me dead. You'll be sorry when I'm gone. I hope you'll be happy with no more fights. I love you, Susan." Ms. Stark was particularly concerned about *why* Susan would do such a thing. While the family conflict had been intense at times, it had not seemed to her that Susan would feel she had to kill herself because of it.

In fact, adolescent suicide attempts can have a variety of motivations behind them; often the wish to be dead is less significant than other messages that the adolescent wants to get across. There are at least 10 different kinds of dynamics underlying suicide attempts, none of which is mutually exclusive from the others.

1. Anger Turned Inward. These adolescents are actually enraged with someone or something else but, for a variety of reasons, are unable to express it outwardly. They may fear rejection or retaliation or they may have developed a corresponding sense of self-worthlessness that precludes entitlement to strong feelings. In some families, individuals are given little permission for such powerful expressions, and feelings thus build up with no place to go. For these adolescents, the suicide attempt is really the enactment of hostility aimed elsewhere. Susan's farewell note certainly included some of this punitive intention when she wrote, "You'll be sorry when I'm gone." During later therapy, she actually expressed a murderous rage toward her father for abandoning her. Since he was not around, according to Susan, she took her anger out on her mother and then on herself.

2. Manipulation. Adolescents who cannot get their needs met through direct and nonviolent means may resort to a suicide attempt without necessarily thinking about killing themselves at all. Manipulative suicidal adolescents seek to gain attention, to influence the behavior of others, to send a message, or to punish others—ultimately to gain power in a situation in which they feel powerless. The suicidal act is a dramatic, controlling one that ensures them center stage for a time. Susan's suicide attempt can be seen as being somewhat manipulative; after all, she took the pills before supper, with a sure chance of being found before too long, and following a disagreement in which she felt unheard and unloved by her mother. Her intention was also probably not to die (she had done her homework for the next day, and subsequently, after the suicide attempt, was angry when she was not permitted to go to the movies that weekend as she had planned), but rather to manipulate the status quo in her home.

3. A Cry for Help. The suicide attempt that serves as a cry for help is usually not lethal. Adolescents who attempt suicide for this purpose typically feel much better after therapy begins because they are then finally getting the attention they desired all along (but couldn't ask for in a way they could be heard). A suicidal cry for help is often a last-ditch effort when other methods of finding changes have failed. Of course, since adolescents are not pharmacologists, they cannot gauge accurately the dosage that they need to cry for help but not die. Susan was lucky that the three bottles of pills lying around in the medicine cabinet were not, individually, or in combination, instantly fatal when overingested. In Susan's case, her cry for help was not, ultimately, aimed solely at her mother. As treatment evolved, it became clear that she missed her father terribly, and the post-attempt crisis successfully brought him back into her life for a while.

4. Psychosis. For about 10 to 15 percent of suicidal adolescents, the attempt is apparently more of a desperate means to relieve increasing internal tension and confusion than a reaction to external stress. Loss of contact with reality can be particularly terrifying when adolescents hear voices telling them to kill themselves. Abuse of hallucinogens can also cause an adolescent to become suicidal, making "bad trips" particularly dangerous. When adolescents are suicidal, it is important to find out if a thought disorder or the use of mind-altering chemicals has anything to do with the threats or attempts. Susan's contact with reality was adequate, and she was not psychotic or abusing mind-altering drugs at the time of her suicide attempt.

5. The Suicidal Game. For some adolescents, toying with death is a game reinforced by the attention it attracts from peers and adults. These adolescents are not interested in therapy and do not understand what the big deal is about. Their attempts tend to be obvious and flamboyant—driving recklessly, cutting themselves in an exposed place like the neck or arms, walking on train tracks when a train is coming—and they deny that they are afraid of death in any way, even when confronted with the possible consequences of their behaviors. Their lives may be sufficiently empty that the thrill of walking on the edge seems worth the extreme risk. Susan did not attempt suicide as part of a game with death, and had not evinced any previous self-destructive behaviors.

6. *A Reaction to Loss.* Some depressed adolescents have experienced the death of a beloved relative or friend and feel that life is not worth living without the dead person(s). They may harbor fantasies, either consciously or unconsciously, that after they die they will join their loved one(s) again. Susan's cat had died a month earlier. She grieved mightily for him, believing that only he had listened and understood her. While the deceased friend is more typically human, it is not uncommon for adolescents to have extreme attachments to their pets and experience true loneliness and despair upon their deaths. The death of Susan's cat was not an immediate precipitant of her suicide attempt, but it was a clear factor in her increasing feelings of isolation and desperation.

7. *Life is Too Hard.* The motivation for some adolescents to attempt suicide is to stop unendurable pain and conflict. While death is seen as the only option left, it is really the end of problems—not the end of life—that these adolescents seek. They lack the skills necessary to address their anguish in a more functional manner. As Shneidman (1984) has pointed out, suicide is a coping strategy; its problem, compared to other strategies, is that when it succeeds the adolescent dies. Susan reported that she did feel desperate when she began swallowing the pills. She felt that she had tried everything that she knew to make things better at home, but still felt overwhelmed by the conflict with her mother and the cliques at school. In some ways, her suicide attempt also reflected the need to find sanctuary from unbearable stress.

8. *Rage and Revenge.* Some adolescents are consciously punitive of others. More than just wanting to manipulate or get attention from someone, they seek to teach a lesson, or somehow get even, using their potential death as a club with which to bludgeon others.

Since retaliation is the motive, these adolescents don't actually want to die, but rather to terrify someone. In these cases, the anger is expressed on both sides of the conflict, and the suicide attempt is an escalation of words and actions that are increasingly violent. Homicidal thoughts are also often present—expressed by both the suicidal adolescent and others in the family. Susan's farewell note did have a revengeful turn to it; "I know you'll be sad when I'm gone" is certainly a hostile thought. However, Susan did not want her mother to suffer so much as she wanted to feel better herself, so rage was not really her primary motivation for a suicide attempt.

9. *Imitation and Suggestibility.* If adolescents are already at some risk for suicide, they may be more vulnerable to the news that others—celebrities, peers, or relatives—have attempted or committed suicide. Some studies have found that suicidal adolescents were likely to know or have been in touch with relatives or friends who had been suicidal (Shaffer, 1986). What is noteworthy in Susan's case is that her mother was also feeling depressed and suicidal. It is quite possible that Susan was unconsciously enacting something unspoken for her mother. Certainly the gesture got help for the whole family.

10. *Alienation.* Some adolescents do not necessarily perform a single suicidal act, but rather behave in a chronically disengaged and self-destructive pattern that could at any time result in death. Wenz (1979) demonstrates that social factors like poverty, parental and family conflict, problems with peers, and school difficulties may interact reciprocally with some adolescents' feelings of powerlessness, loss of hope, and isolation. As they become increasingly disenfranchised and disconnected from the mainstream, these adolescents' interest in and ability to protect themselves diminishes. They may then place themselves at greater risk by, for example, abusing drugs, running away, having unprotected sex with a variety of partners, or engaging in thrill-seeking suicidal games. They may also give up and do something overtly suicidal. Susan was clearly not alienated to this degree. Her family and friends were strong enough that her experience of isolation had not severed the real ties that she had. However, if her suicide attempt had not led to a crisis and

change, it is possible that she would have behaved in increasingly alienated ways.

The Suicidal Adolescent

When I first saw Susan in the emergency room, ashen and exhausted, she looked more like a neglected 10-year-old than an articulate suicidal adolescent. A stained baggy sweatshirt hung in folds over her tiny frame and her jeans were ripped in the knees and thighs in the fashion of the time. She shuffled into the room dragging her sneaker laces behind her, frizzy brown hair in a tangle over downcast eyes. The moment she saw her mother, she burst into tears, and threw herself sobbing into her arms. Her younger brother, Mitch, briefly joined them in a family hug while I looked on, feeling a little choked-up myself. I felt as though I was observing a family reunion after a long trip and commented on this as I pulled Susan's chair closer to her mother's and then urged them all to sit down for a little safety planning. Susan quickly agreed that she wouldn't try to kill herself again, noting wryly that vomiting the charcoal had been worse than death and her mother said she would monitor Susan more closely for the next few days until we got to the bottom of things. Obtaining this promise from both parent and adolescent is essential if the adolescent isn't admitted to the hospital. Ms. Stark also planned to rid the house of any unnecessary pills, putting others under lock and key for a time.

Before sending Susan home for the night, I asked a variety of other questions to ascertain whether this was a safe plan. Most therapists develop such a set of questions to satisfy any lingering doubts about suicidal risk. If Susan or her mother had given me vague or inconclusive responses to any of my concerns, I would have recommended a brief stay in the hospital while we worked on individual and family problems. Assessing suicidal risk requires quite conservative standards because the stakes of an incorrect evaluation can be so high. My assessment includes six general areas of inquiry.

1. Lethality. Although Susan had ingested 15 to 20 pills, she did so with a good chance of being found quickly, and with little premeditation about where and when she would kill herself. Further, taking pills is a less lethal means of suicide than many—and she had no other plans for killing herself. Thus, I could begin to trust her assurance that she did not fully intend to die and would not attempt suicide again any time soon.

2. Mental Status. Susan was in touch with reality, understood my questions and gave coherent, thoughtful responses to them. She was not hallucinating and had no history of substance abuse that would raise additional concerns. Since her thought processes and memory were clear, I was reassured that her mental status was adequate for discharge.

3. Continuing Suicidal Intention. Susan admitted that she had thought about suicide many times in the past few months, and had even noted that the bottles of pills were in the medicine cabinet. However, she also felt prepared to work with her mother and me to make things better so that she would not have to resort to a suicidal gesture again. I felt that Susan was at decreased risk for suicide attempts immediately following this crisis and would not try again were she to go home that evening.

4. History of Depression and Suicidality. Susan had clearly been depressed for some time. Prior to her suicide attempt, she had felt increasingly hopeless, despondent, listless, and powerless in her life. However, she had never attempted suicide before, and expressed relief that she and her mother could now sit down and talk. While Susan was at some risk for a future suicide attempt if her situation remained unchanged, she was willing to give therapy a chance. Often after a crisis such as a suicide attempt, an adolescent's depression lifts temporarily as others step in to help out.

5. Manageability of Stress. Susan related numerous factors in her life leading up to the attempt; her fight with her mother had simply been the last straw. She noted that her schoolwork was slipping, and for the first time in her life, she was at risk of failing both math and Spanish. Her best friend was becoming involved with a boy who was part of a group she did not like. Other friends had grown distant, and the boy she had liked all summer pretended the day before that he did not recognize her when she saw him at school. Previously a talented gymnast, she had become too winded from asthma and allergies to compete at the higher levels. Her father never spoke to her and had insulted her terribly by sending her money and a store-bought and unsigned card for her birthday. Her brother played soccer, and her mother took time from work to attend his games, even though she had seldom gone to Susan's gymnastic meets. Susan wanted a new kitten but her mother wouldn't take her to the Humane Society to get one. Susan's list was long, sad, and self-pitying. It was also, for the most part, solvable. I was able to persuade Susan that, together, we would tackle everything we could, and that I would teach her skills to cope with the things she might not be able to change. In a crisis precipitated by a suicide attempt, especially one in which the stress list is this long, it is important to figure out a way to offer glimmers of hope and genuine concern. Susan responded favorably to my encouragement, and agreed to return the next day to "get to work." She did not seem to need inpatient treatment to do this.

6. *Family Supports.* Susan felt abandoned by her father, rejected and neglected by her mother, and competitive with her brother. Patterns of communication between Susan and Ms. Stark were laced with sparks of open hostility and withdrawal. If Susan regressed sufficiently, her mother would nurture her briefly, but felt quickly that Susan was "just trying to get attention," as though attention were something bad to want. I ran the initial session closely, and each was able to respond by making commitments to me, which for the night was sufficient. Without some structural and emotional changes though, I felt Susan would be at risk again in the future.

When Susan and her mother returned the next afternoon (Mitch was playing soccer and Ms. Stark didn't want to disrupt his schedule, despite my request for all to attend), Susan looked much better. She had stayed home from school and appeared clean and rested. Ms. Stark, by contrast, looked drawn and overwhelmed. She began by telling me that she thought Susan should have been admitted to the hospital, and questioning my credentials. Her hostility was intense, and took up a good portion of our first meeting. She was particularly angry that she had to miss work to meet with some "shrink," and, because I had seemed so sympathetic to Susan's stress list, she thought I was insufficiently attentive to the problems *she* had raising an oppositional and unresponsive teenager all by herself. She positioned herself on the far side of the room, across from Susan, who sat mutely on the couch playing nervously with the fringe on a blanket.

By listening carefully and supportively, I was able to diffuse some of Ms. Stark's rage, though it simmered perceptibly below the surface through several more meetings until she began to trust that I was on her side, too. When I discovered that her parents lived on the same block as she did, and had lots of opinions about her mismanagement of Susan, I invited them in, too. This helped me enormously in learning about the intergenerational tensions in this family.

Ms. Stark had one brother, Jason, who had been disowned by their parents while he was in college and protesting the war in Viet Nam. He had also been hospitalized for depression during this period; his parents believed his depression was a ploy to avoid the service. Ms. Stark heard from him from time to time and said that he "lived a drifter's life" on the west coast. Susan reported that Ms. Stark had told her that she increasingly understood why Nana had kicked her brother out of the house, leaving that vague threat to weigh like heavy fog between herself and Susan. At the same time, Ms. Stark was terrified that she too would be abandoned and feared crossing her parents, even when she felt she had a right to stand up for herself. For example, Susan and her maternal grandmother "ganged up" on Ms. Stark when she scolded Susan, increasing Ms. Stark's anger considerably. Unable to argue with her own mother for fear of being disowned, Ms. Stark took out her compounded feelings of betrayal on Susan. Thus, Susan's suicide attempt appeared to be a signal of a lack of family resources as well as personal resources.

Ms. Stark's exhaustion was real and well-earned. She worked full-time and took care of two children and two demanding parents, who insisted she drive them to appointments and grocery shopping, although they could well afford to take a cab. While her parents did give her some economic and emotional support, she paid for their involvement in other ways. For example, they had interfered in her marriage, and had disapproved of Mr. Stark from the beginning. In many ways, they had never really let her go to start her own family.

Susan's parents had met when Mr. Stark visited the area on a business trip from his office in the midwest. At that time, he was a salesman for a pharmaceutical company and on the road a lot. Susan's mother was then working as a waitress in the hotel he was staying in. After a whirlwind courtship, they had married and Ms. Stark had relocated despite her mother's displeasure; daily phone calls maintained what Mr. Stark thought was excessive contact. After Susan was born, Ms. Stark became even more homesick, and pushed her husband to arrange a transfer back east. Six years later, the family bought a house near Ms. Stark's parents in the suburbs of a large metropolitan area. Ms. Stark later believed that this move "was the beginning of the end" of her marriage, although she and her husband had remained together for six more years. Mitch's birth and infancy served to estrange the couple further; Ms. Stark's mother came over to babysit and when that happened her husband did not like to come home. Although she was not consciously aware of it, Susan knew well the pattern her father had developed of disappearing under stress. Mr. Stark's own parents had divorced when he was small, and he saw his father infrequently after that. His mother remarried and had several more children; Mr. Stark called his stepfather "Dad."

Ms. Stark recalled having been shy and careful about who she brought to the house. She had dated a couple of men but her parents hadn't liked them and it was too difficult to sustain a relationship under those conditions while living at home. The distance and speed of the courtship with Mr. Stark made Nana's criticisms vague and inconsequential. Living in the midwest had helped in some ways, but she felt guilty and feared she had abandoned her parents. From many miles away, Ms. Stark tried to portray her husband as hard-working and faithful, though Nana was a tough customer even from afar, and made her daughter fret about infidelity while Mr. Stark was on trips.

The Stark family had difficulty harkening back to a time when things were going well. Ms. Stark said that life had been simpler in the midwest, but she had not been happy then. She had felt overwhelmed raising just one child in a small town. Now, as a single parent with two children, one an adolescent, she was often frantic with her own sense of inadequacy. Susan's suicide attempt was simply another chapter in her story of feeling incapable of managing her life.

The Family of the Suicidal Adolescent

While many families find adolescence to be a lot of work, families of suicidal adolescents appear to have particicular kinds of problems, making them different in some distinct ways. The structure and organization of the suicidal adolescent's family appear to contain a variety of factors associated with family disorganization—poverty, losses, health and mental health problems, unemployment, and chronic marital and family conflict—that are less commonly found in families with nonsuicidal adolescents. Repeated suicide attempts are often associated with enduring family problems that did not change following prior attempts.

A general typology of how families of suicide-attempting adolescents are organized includes seven factors: a lack of generational boundaries, marital conflict, displacement of parental hostility, symbiotic parent-child relationships, inflexibility, vague discipline, and social isolation. While all these factors are not common to all families of suicidal adolescents, they provide a broad context for suicidal behavior.

LACK OF GENERATIONAL BOUNDARIES

Unresolved conflict in the parents' families of origin leads to intense ambivalence toward their children as well as their own parents. The parents of the suicidal adolescent may not have individuated from their own parents and problems of strongly felt and expressed hostility, feelings of deprivation, low self-esteem, and magnified attachments across generations may remain (e.g., Bowen, 1978; Pfeffer, 1981). Such enmeshed relationships create a situation in which separation and individuation are associated with fear and pain in family members. In this context, the suicide attempt may articulate the desire to separate from the clutches of an overinvolved family.

The lack of separation between Susan's mother and grandmother was a point of clear and immediate concern. On the one hand, Susan felt she had no privacy from her grandparents. When her mother complained that Susan never talked to her anymore, she retorted, "So you can have something to talk to Nana about? Get a life." Ms. Stark admitted that she and and her mother were close, but denied that she gossiped about Susan. "When you have kids, you'll see how necessary it is to have someone to talk to," she added. Susan had unusually vivid early memories of her life in the midwest, when she and her mother "were together 24 hours a day, seven days a week." Susan's mother had been more involved with Susan when her own mother was far away. Susan lost her primary importance when they returned east, and Nana was in the home on a daily basis.

On the other hand, though, Susan also benefitted from her mother's connection with Nana. She was adept at playing off her mother and grandmother against each other, the way children in two-parent families often do. For example, at one point Susan wanted to go an expensive concert. Her mother refused to pay; she also told Susan she did not think that it would be appropriate for her to go. Susan then went to Nana, neglecting to say that her mother had essentially denied permission. Nana gave Susan the money and then defended Susan when Ms. Stark expressed anger that Susan had lied to get the tickets. Nana later said that Susan had attempted suicide because her mother never let her have any fun.

As alliances shifted, this triangle of three generations of women turned rapidly. Through her suicide attempt, Susan became dominant for a time and was able to articulate her need for her mother's private and undivided attention. Within several months, Ms. Stark was able to look at her own behavior, and to begin to set limits that were more suitable for Susan's level of development. I tried to push Ms. Stark into becoming a more active parent by having her imagine what kind of relationship she might someday have with Susan, and by asking Susan what she wanted so that things could be better at home. Ms. Stark wanted Susan's friendship and to feel that Susan was glad to be in the home. For her part, Susan wanted her mother to listen to her and to be interested in her without judging, criticizing, or publicizing what she said.

We talked about ways to include Nana while at the same time

setting limits to protect their privacy in other situations. Ms. Stark began to do this well. On one occasion, when Nana interfered with her handling of a conflict with Susan, she told her mother, "This is my daughter and my life; you'll just have to let me make a mess of this myself." Upon hearing that her mother said this, Susan noted wisely, "Yup, it felt better knowing I'd only have to deal with mom's mess. Like in school, sometimes you can just talk to the teacher and leave the principal out of it and it goes better."

MARITAL CONFLICT

In most families of suicidal adolescents, the marital relationship is severely distressed. The choice of a spouse may have been influenced greatly by fantasies and perceptions of people in the parents' own families of origin. Anger is expressed variably; sometimes it is quite open, but often it is indirectly aired. The parental relationship centers around dependency conflicts in which one spouse is either threatened with being hurt or is capable of hurting the other. The threat of separation is always present, and one parent is often depressed (or suicidal). Some adolescents attempt suicide in response to actual or threatened parental loss by divorce, separation, death, or abandonment (Fishman, 1988; Jacobs, 1971; Landau-Stanton & Stanton, 1985; Stanley & Barter, 1970).

At my request, Ms. Stark called her ex-husband and arranged to meet me with him. I wanted to get some more background and also hoped to ask him what the potential for more involvement might be. He was agreeable about attending one or two sessions, and seemed genuinely concerned about Susan.

Mr. Stark remembered that he had never been interested in settling down, but thought he had found the right woman when he met Ms. Stark. He thought his parents had been delighted with his "city woman," but Ms. Stark disagreed. In therapy they recreated old arguments about his mother's intentions when she had visited them. For example, if Mr. Stark's mother cleaned the house, Mr. Stark was thankful, viewing it as a helpful gesture. By contrast, Ms. Stark was angry and embarrassed that apparently her mother-in-law thought she was a poor housekeeper. Ms. Stark claimed that she "never felt a part of their phony jolly midwestern ways."

The Starks reported an unusual level of conflict from the beginning. Mr. Stark's schedule left his wife alone for varying stretches of time; she tended to be resentful when he returned, so his trips lengthened. Ms. Stark noted sadly that she didn't notice that they had become separated for a few weeks after he moved out because she was so used to his absences. Mr. Stark said that he worked too hard to put up with being "hammered at" when he was home. He loved being with Susan, but it became harder to break into the twosome of mother and daughter as time went on, and he admitted he had stopped trying.

The Starks had also developed few skills at resolving conflicts, knowing that sooner or later he would be away again. Mr. Stark believed that arguing was a bad thing and became silent and emotionally distant when his wife was upset with him. She felt that he did not see how angry she was, or for how long, but he stated firmly, "If it hadn't been for the kids, I'd have gotten a one-way ticket back to Iowa a long time before we split; it was hell for me, too." He described what it had felt like coming home to a depressed wife and kids who acted like they didn't know him: "I wanted to have a family to be part of like my [step]dad did, but they didn't seem to care."

Susan did not recall hearing her parents fighting much, noting that her mother might "bitch at him about something, but he'd just be a wimp and apologize." She did remember that they didn't often do things as a family, and had thought it odd that her parents took turns being with her and Mitch. Although she was aware, at some level, of their conflict, she was shocked when her mother told her about the divorce and that Daddy was moving out. She blamed her mother at first, then her father, then herself.

During our individual sessions, Susan began to reconstruct how she had been caught in the middle of their conflict, particularly by her mother's making her a confidante. After the divorce, when she visited her father, he would ask her endless questions about her mother; when she returned home, her mother would grill her there. She ended up feeling that it was her fault when, inexplicably, her mother would fly into a rage when Susan answered a simple question like, "What did you have for supper at Dad's?" She felt even worse when her father stopped arranging visits, and was not comforted when her mother said that he had picked the perfect job for someone who couldn't handle a family.

DISPLACEMENT OF PARENTAL HOSTILITY

Some researchers have noted that suicidal adolescents seem to be responding unconsciously to their families' hostile wishes to be rid of them (e.g., Landau-Stanton & Stanton, 1985; Rosenbaum & Richman, 1970; Sabbath, 1969). In some cases, the parents display aggressive feelings toward their child instead of toward each other. When parental hostility is present, two questions illuminate the suicidal behavior: (1) Who did the adolescent really want to kill, wish dead, or wish to suffer? (2) Who wished the adolescent to die, disappear, or go away? Rejection of the adolescent, which characterizes many such families, can also be manifested by parental indifference and denial of their adolescent's problems.

Susan's retreat into her room was not noticed by her father because he had lost contact with her by the time of her suicide attempt. Indeed, he had noted readily that he was waiting to be transferred out of the state, and that he probably wouldn't see much of his kids after that. Susan heard this as an indication that she was expendable and that he would be able to leave without even a twinge of his conscience if she and Mitch were out of the picture. Of course, her mother noticed that Susan was up in her room more frequently, but she was relieved that Susan was home while not being a bother.

Angry that she had the children without a break, bitter that Mr. Stark could come and go as he pleased without any responsibility, and overwhelmed by Susan's neediness, Ms. Stark harbored many escape fantasies of her own. Consequently, Susan felt rejected by both of her parents, and was enraged that no one was available to protect her. While her parents did not consciously believe that they wished her to die, her problems may have been a constant reminder of all that they were not doing for her.

The parents' feelings of unexpressed anger were reciprocated by Susan. Several months after treatment began, Susan began to verbalize how she felt about her father. "He gets to live in [a nice suburb] and buy himself any toys he likes. We have to live in a dump with mom ragged out all the time because of how much she has to work. If he was dead, we'd get his life insurance policy, which is a hell of a lot more than we get now. I used to be sad that he didn't want to see me and Mitch and pay for the things we needed. Now, I'm just pissed, pissed, pissed. Maybe he should go back to Iowa. Maybe his plane will crash on the way . . . "

SYMBIOTIC PARENT-CHILD RELATIONSHIPS

Suicidal adolescents may have an especially close or symbiotic attachment to a parent, usually the mother (Berman & Cohen-Sandler, 1980). The mother-child bond may have intensified as a result of a shared loss (from death, separation, or divorce) earlier in the life of the adolescent. Because of this intense interaction with one parent, the adolescent has more difficulty developing the skills necessary to function autonomously. For these adolescents, the suicide attempt may be the most obvious method of individuation.

Susan's relationship with her mother had been typically intimate. In her early years Susan even slept with her mother when her father was away on business. After her parents separated, Susan's role as confidante and mediator intensified. Lately, though, because of Ms. Stark's hectic schedule and the level of acrimony when they were together, Susan had seen less of her mother than she was accustomed to, and than she liked. She claimed that she would have liked to come out of her room more if her mother were kinder when she did.

Susan also believed that her mother's allegiances had shifted to Mitch and that she was less important now that he was old enough for her mother to confide in. But when Susan accused her mother of favoring Mitch, Ms. Stark looked incredulous: "I bend over backward to make things even with these kids. I feel like I do everything for Susan, and Mitch gets what's left over. He never complains, so I feel even worse. But Susan has always been the love of my life. I can't believe she doesn't know it." She reminded Susan of how embarrassing it had been for Susan when her mother attended gymnastics meets; she felt unwanted there. Susan denied feeling that, citing times she had asked her mother to come but work had been more important. With my help, Susan was able to articulate her sense of loss about spending so much less time with her mother. We set up weekly dates for just the two of them to spend time together, relaxing, shopping, ice skating, or engaging in some other activity they decided upon. At the same time, we began to clarify the importance of privacy and separate lives for each of them. It is difficult for many families with adolescents to achieve a balance between closeness and individuation that meets everyone's changing needs. For families having difficulty tolerating separation, this is an even more important task.

INFLEXIBILITY

The families of suicidal adolescents tend to relate to each other in such an unyielding way that any change is felt as a threat to the survival of the family. This produces intense anxiety and associated regression. Achievement of personal goals becomes equated with separation, desertion, or untimely death (Pfeffer, 1981). As a result, family preoccupations with these issues, especially with death, can be prominent. The adolescent who is caught in the rigidity of this system may attempt suicide both as a means of escape and as a means of effecting a family reorganization that permits the family to remain together in a more tolerable and flexible system.

Susan's family was inflexible because it was caught in outmoded survival patterns of behavior more suited to a family with younger children. Members were unyielding because they did not know other ways to behave. As with many families, even ones that have navigated childhood proper without hitting the shoals, adolescence poses new currents, winds, and rocks. Education, modeling, skill development, and reinforcement of efforts to listen and change were all required to replace old responses with new ones. Instead of saying "No" and "Because I said so," Ms. Stark had to learn that she could negotiate at times with Susan. For her part, Susan had to learn to request discussions and set times to have them with her mother. She also had to accept that arguing her point of view might not change her mother's position.

Troubled listening and communication patterns also reflect this inflexibility. The Starks had reached an impasse with the old long silences and shouting matches. They benefitted from learning how to listen actively, using "I-statements," brainstorming, and arriving at solutions together. In my office, we practiced these new skills. As Ms. Stark began to feel more competent, she was able to view Susan's needs as more tolerable, and less threatening. As Susan developed more effective strategies for being heard, her feelings of hopelessness abated entirely.

VAGUE DISCIPLINE

Parents of suicidal adolescents commonly handle their offspring with a less overt investment of time and with fewer clear limits than other parents. Often they respond with silence and withdrawal when they are dissatisfied. An adolescent may view this as indifference or as hostility. Some researchers have noted that this parental group remains remarkably bland and does not react with what would be normal anger, worry, fear, or confusion (e.g., Petzel & Riddle, 1980; Yusin, Sinay, & Nihira, 1972). This lack of parental presence can be compounded when a parent is physically or mentally ill and the adolescent is forced into a caretaking role. Such role reversals compromise the tasks of adolescence, and cause feelings of aggression to be turned back on the self. In these cases, discipline is even more difficult for the adolescent to understand or manage. In general, parents of suicidal adolescents do not provide the kind of clear and consistent involvement needed by their offspring.

The problem of vague discipline haunted Susan. She did not really know what the rules and expectations were for her behavior. It took many weeks for us to review and clarify them. In families with a history of extreme closeness like Susan's, it is common for rules to be tacitly understood rather than stated clearly. But if adolescents are to separate safely, they need to know precisely what is being asked of them and what will happen if they comply or do not. Ms. Stark did not want to be pinned down to particular consequences, and Susan balked when curfews, grades, and privileges were discussed. Sometimes I seemed to be the only one in the room working on the problem. For example, I'd ask, "What time does Susan need to be in on school nights?" and hear from Susan that she didn't usually go out and from her mother that she *couldn't* go out. Then, after further probing, I'd learn about four times in the past two weeks when Susan had arrived home at nine or ten o'clock, once to be chastised by her mother, once to be grounded for the weekend, and twice without consequences. Susan felt the lack of structure meant the odds were in her favor; she did not find my line of questioning useful. Ms. Stark stated that she felt attacked by me and asked, in mock alarm, "What am I supposed to do, call the police?" Coming up with a consistent policy was clearly arduous and never fully realized. I had to be satisfied that my point was understood, and to accept that Ms. Stark was overwhelmed and following through the best she could.

I emphasized that there is an important difference between rigidity and clarity. Families can be very rigid about their expectations for how members behave while at the same time keeping members guessing about what will happen if they make an error. So, for example, Ms. Stark had a rigid rule in her own mind: No going out on school nights. However, Susan did not know about this rule; were she to guess about it based upon her mother's actions, she might conclude that the rule was: No going out on school nights some of the time. She knew she had a good chance of going out without penalty. In the end, Ms. Stark needed to know that she could retain veto power over plans, but that Susan was old enough to be able to make her case if she handled herself responsibly.

SOCIAL ISOLATION

It is interesting to note that in families with suicidal adolescents family members feel quite isolated, even though their history suggests unusual closeness. As personal and family resources become depleted, the quality of connections becomes more tenuous and fragile. Wenz (1978) describes this sense of isolation as a "family anomie syndrome" (p. 45). He found that the high-suicide-risk youngsters he studied tended to be part of family structures characterized by (a) a high degree of disorientation from cultural and family norms, and (b) feelings of family powerlessness. The whole family was found to be anomic, not just the adolescent. In these cases, the suicide attempt was an accurate enactment of everyone's feelings; the adolescent may have perceived correctly that the family was unable to provide satisfactory alternatives to it.

Both Susan and Ms. Stark spoke of loneliness. Ms. Stark had only a few friends and had not dated since her divorce, despite being asked out a few times. She felt close to her own mother, but perceived her as all-powerful. She saw people around her having more of the American dream than she did. She worked all the time, took no vacations, had a suicidal child, and had undergone a descent into poverty that seemed inescapable. Susan had a few friends but considered herself to be the kind of person that only has one best friend at a time. When such a friend became involved with a boy, or with other friends, Susan was devastated. She did not observe her mother handling social situations any better than she did.

The link to natural resources in the community is central to the treatment of all adolescents of violence, and not just the suicidal ones. Violence is, by definition, isolating. Therefore, individual and family therapy need to be complemented by other services and activities that help family members reach out constructively and learn new coping skills. Both Susan and her mother appeared surprised when off the top of my head I was able to suggest several activities for each of them to do together and separately that would help them branch out socially. But they were responsive to some of my ideas. Ms. Stark joined a community chorus and became an active fund-raiser for it. She also attended a few meetings of Parents Without Partners. Susan went to an allergist who got her breathing clearly enough to resume gymnastics. Together, they joined an ongoing communication group sponsored by the local "Y" for parents and teens, which alternated weekly with separate adolescent and parent support groups. Reducing social isolation by connecting the Starks to the community was an important part of treatment. It is one of the simpler, more practical ways to aid families with suicidal adolescents.

Resolution

I saw the Starks for more than a year, with the visits becoming less frequent after six months. Mr. Stark became more involved with his children for a time, even taking them to DisneyWorld that winter vacation. His commitment began to diminish again as the family functioning stabilized. Susan realized that she had to accept that he would be there in a crisis (which was more than some fathers she knew of) but he would not necessarily be a part of her day-to-day life. Interestingly, she worked to keep her father around for her brother, even setting up times for them to be together, noting humorously, "A guy needs a dad. I mean, I do too, but poor Mitch is surrounded by PMS all the time. He should get a break."

Ms. Stark's mother, Nana, continued to be an important source of loaded support. I enlisted her as a consultant from time to time when I felt stuck, and invited her in to help me out. This strategy worked well; it kept her from getting in the middle of conflicts and at the same time maintained her respected position in the family. For example, one day Susan and her mother were engaged in a particularly protracted and obscure battle about who had left the dishes in the sink. Nana and I watched the argument. As long as they were listening to each other, I refrained from interrupting. When the discussion escalated into a shouting match, I called for silence, and turned to Nana, asking what she observed going on. She thought a moment, and in a quiet voice befitting an esteemed elder, replied, "They're saying that it is hard sometimes to be in a family, but that they love each other and want to keep trying, even though they're not so good at the details." (I'm no fool; I ended the session there.)

With Susan and her mother, I kept the focus on communication skills, adolescent development, and family needs. Ms. Stark was increasingly receptive to my help as she saw Susan feeling better and venturing out of her room more. She also liked feeling more in control of her own life and being supported about expectations she had for her children's behavior. I helped with practical matters like chores and rules, and also provided a mediating role when the conflict between them caused old patterns to reappear. They learned, for example, to ask for a "rewind" when they began on the wrong foot. Either of them could ask for it, and then the discussion would begin again. This simple strategy diffused many hot spots before they ignited.

Many of my meetings were spent alone with Susan, who grew in every way during the time we worked together. We tackled her problem list, and dealt with new crises (like a pregnancy scare) as they arose. We found a local college student willing, for a small fee, to tutor her and chauffeur her after school so she could pick up her grades and attend gymnastics practice and meets. With this support, Susan passed the year easily, and began the next year unassisted and confident. Through gymnastics, she met a few new friends, and began going out with the brother of one of them. This relationship was ultimately a painful one for Susan; he was older and had troubles of his own. However, she weathered the rejection and loss without suicidal thoughts, and was able to express her anger and disappointment directly. She also got a new kitten. These functional changes were important, and every bit as valuable as the therapeutic relationship itself. Over the course of our contact, and through the many changes she made, Susan learned to care about herself and to make self-protecting decisions. With her suicide attempt, Susan had not been trying to die. Rather, she had been trying to rid herself of a life that was too hard. She welcomed one she could manage, and learned to take great pleasure in it. At our final meeting, she showed me a medal she had recently won on the balance beam. She noted with a sly grin, "I've become much better balanced, haven't I?"

3

Runaways

Michelle: "You'd leave too if you was me"

Some studies using predictive sampling techniques estimate that one out of every eight adolescents between the ages of 12 and 18 will run away from home at least once (Young, Godfrey, Matthews, & Adams, 1983). The National Network of Runaway and Youth Services believes that the best annual estimate of adolescent runaways is between 1.3 and 1.4 million (Bucy, 1985). It is impossible to record the actual number of runaways with complete accuracy because of the range of definitions, reporting conditions, and sampling techniques used. What is certain is that many of these youngsters are at risk in their homes as well as on the streets; recent accounts describe that close to 80 percent of runaways in shelters are trying to escape physical, sexual, psychological, or emotional abuse (Farber, McCoard, Kinast, & Baum-Faulkner, 1984). However, the street is no sanctuary. After one month, half of the runaways will have had to resort to prostitution or other crime to support themselves; by the time they have spent six months on the street, it will become nearly impossible to rescue them and interest them in continuing their education, looking for employment, working on family

54

problems, and giving up drugs. Running away is a dangerous last resort for vulnerable and victimized adolescents. These runaways will be revictimized daily as they fend for themselves by stealing, drug dealing, and prostitution (Langway, 1982; Satchell, 1986).

The Referral

A seasoned child protection services worker called me one sunny fall day to persuade me to take on a repeat runaway who did not want to see a counselor. She had been rounded up by the police early the preceding morning and had a family, in the worker's ironic words, that was "a complete masterpiece, a real work of art" (code words for disorganized and uncooperative). Having an inexplicable weakness for adolescent girls who don't want counseling, I couldn't refuse. The worker's parting words after I asked her to have Michelle's mother call me were, "Good luck getting paid for this one!" Later that week, prepared for the worst, I was surprised to see a family of six quiet people sitting politely in the waiting room ten minutes early. I tried to avoid being lulled by appearances, knowing that families of runaways are in distress almost by definition.

Michelle, an obese, awkward youngster, lagged behind the others as they came into my office, and then shuffled along hesitantly. Her long, straggly brown bangs hung over her eyes and several dozen bracelets jangled loudly as she selected the remaining chair close to me. When she looked up at her mother, her eyes were a startling pale blue, though she kept them downcast, staring at her lap for most of the first hour. Although I had gotten a summary of events from the child protection worker, I asked the family for some background information and the details of what had brought them in. Her stepfather, Mr. Davis, spoke first; I sensed Michelle's annoyance with that by the agitated clanging of bracelets to my left, though she did not look up or say anything.

Michelle Moore, a 14-year-old high school freshman, was the third child of her mother's first marriage, which had ended in divorce when Michelle was four. Her mother, a receptionist for a construction company, subsequently married Mr. Davis, a construction foreman, and had one more daughter, Danielle, age nine. Michelle's oldest sister, Kathy, age 20, no longer lived at home but was worried about Michelle and attended several of the sessions. Her brother, Pete, age 17, and a senior in high school, was planning to move out after he graduated that spring, speaking vaguely of joining the army. Michelle's biological father had remarried and moved away. He had not had contact with the family for several years. This seemed to suit Michelle at the time of our work together; she was confident that she could find him if she wanted to.

Three days before we met, Michelle had disappeared after school. Her frightened mother had called the police, and they conducted a search around the area. At one o'clock the following morning, the police found Michelle three towns away, in a pizza parlor, with two young men in their early twenties. She was known to the area police because of previous runaway episodes, and was located more quickly than is usual in such cases.

Michelle would not speak, so I asked her permission to hear what her family thought about recent events. She shrugged but did not say no. I persevered to learn that her family had many ideas but no certainty about why Michelle kept running away. Her stepfather thought that she was having trouble at school. He noted that she had had several unexcused absences, and had come home in tears a few days earlier after being teased on the school bus. Her brother said that she had been fighting with her mother a lot, and that she hated her stepfather and didn't want to live under the same roof with him. Danielle, the younger sister, thought that Michelle was a snob and was always complaining when she was at home. Kathy, the older sister speculated that maybe Michelle wanted to see a boyfriend. I noted that her departures were mysteries for them and asked about the other times she had left home without permission.

Ms. Davis recalled that this was the fifth time that Michelle had run away this year; most recently they hadn't found her for six days, during which time she had been to New York City and back. The other absences were briefer and more local; she had stayed at friends' houses a couple of times, slept in the park once and spent a night in the home of a man she had met whom she had been forbidden to see. Each time, she had promised to stop running away and had agreed to speak to the school counselor but had remained silent during the subsequent meeting. The New York City trip had been the most frightening for the family, although Michelle had returned in good spirits. She had gone with friends to see a rock concert and had met some people there who let her stay with them. Michelle had told her mother that the new friends had persuaded her to return home and had paid for her bus ticket. She had scoffed at her mother's concern for her safety.

Young adolescents, especially ones who are being abused at home, have great difficulty judging how risky their behavior can be. I agreed emphatically with Ms. Davis about the danger of New York City's streets, and noted my conviction that luck rather than skill had enabled Michelle to return home safely from the city. I wondered about what would have happened if she had not gotten help returning. Though I did not yet know Michelle's reasons for running, the pattern of departing and the distance traveled raised my suspicions about abuse of some kind.

At the time of the New York City incident, about three months before our meeting, Ms. Davis had seriously considered getting help for Michelle, or having her sent to the regional facility for delinquents. She had called child protection services to determine her options. They told her she could call the police and go through a "ChINS: Child In Need of Supervision" process, which would involve child protection and a probation officer who would help the family manage Michelle's runaway behavior. They also recommended family counseling. Michelle had been upset that her mother wanted to send her away and, along with everyone else in the family, was unenthusiastic about therapy. Ms. Davis had not followed up on any of these ideas once it seemed that Michelle was settling back down. She noted that she only wanted peace in the house, and was fearful about what Michelle would do if she felt her mother was backing her into a corner.

This time, however, Ms. Davis was unwilling to wait any longer, and was seeking advice about whether Michelle "needed to be sent away or locked up or what." However, with child protection involved, she was bound to keep Michelle in therapy as part of any intervention they might offer. As with all types of violence in adolescence, there is a window of opportunity to intervene with the family. It is open widest when the family realizes it is in crisis and when external pressure is bearing down. As the crisis resolves, the window tends to close rapidly, sometimes on the fingers of the meddling therapist. Michelle's family arrived for treatment in crisis; I felt pressure to move quite quickly, expecting that they all might settle back into their old—and for Michelle, unhappy—patterns of family behavior. I sensed that we were looking out of this window together, though I did not know for certain what it was we were seeing.

With a brief history in hand and anxiety in my heart, I asked the rest of the family to leave so I could speak to Michelle alone. Before they left, I set up another meeting for Michelle and her mother in a couple of days, and arranged for Michelle to stay with Kathy for a couple of weeks. While Mr. Davis was unhappy with this plan, saying Michelle needed to learn to stay at home, I was able to make it clear that I saw this as a temporary arrangement and would work for her return once it could be established convincingly and safely. I reasoned that Michelle would have difficulty being at home until she had acquired some skills for dealing with the stresses in her life in ways other than running from them.

I looked for any signs of interest Michelle might offer in connecting with me. I asked about the bracelets, and about the rock group she followed (confessing that I had also been a Grateful Dead fan before I passed over into the world of responsible adults). Michelle continued to be silent, though I saw her glancing sideways at me a few times, and she nodded occasionally in response to questions indicating that she was listening. Still, I realized that she was being incredibly self-protective about something. Growing increasingly suspicious about abuse of some kind, I felt obligated to reveal to her the consequences of any disclosures she might make. I assured her I would only recommend out-of-home placement or hospitalization if she was unsafe in any way in her home or had plans to hurt herself. Pushing harder, I told her that I knew that she must have had some good reasons to run and place herself at as much risk as she had done. I expressed relief that she was safe now and told her my job was to help her learn how to feel more in control of her life. I assured her that I wouldn't let her return home if she felt in danger there. I asked her if she could tell me anything at all about what had happened. After letting me sweat it out and do all the work for 15 minutes, Michelle's only comment to me was, "You'd leave, too, if you was me." She would not elaborate on this point.

Most adolescents who run away do little to plan where they are going or the details of how they will manage once they get there. Like Michelle, they just decide one day that they don't want to go home, or be home, and they leave.

Many, also like Michelle, run away and return home several times. This chronic running away pattern holds particularly true for adolescents who run away from abusive homes (Janus, McCormack, Burgess, & Hartman, 1987). The forces that compel an adolescent to run away are significant, as are the reasons they have for returning home.

The Runaway Adolescent

Different researchers have attempted to categorize the various motives that adolescents have for running from home and the types of runaways that are ultimately found. In one such typology (Roberts, 1982) organizes runaway behavior along a five-point continuum ranging from 0 to 4:

0 *Nonrunaways.* These adolescents manage conflicts with their parents without runaway behavior. They can satisfactorily negotiate their requests to travel or stay out.

1 *Runaway explorers/social pleasure seekers.* These adolescents want to travel or participate in activities against the wishes of their parents. Typically, they are girls interested in dating or attending parentally disapproved events. They do not stay away long, and they frequently leave notes informing their parents where they have gone. Other researchers (e.g., Lappin & Covelman, 1985; Miller, Miller, Hoffman, & Duggan, 1980; Nye, 1980) have described the relatively small group of runaways (about 20 percent) who leave to meet new people and challenges more than to escape what they have left behind. They may be bored, angry, or unmotivated at home, but their primary concern

is getting to more interesting and exciting places. They enjoy an adventure, and may take off on a lark even though their home life is relatively stable.

2 *Runaway manipulators.* These runaways seek to put an end to conflict at home by frightening their parents into submission. When they cannot negotiate a satisfactory compromise about rules and expectations that they feel are unfair, they run from home hoping that their parents will then worry sufficiently so that when they call, the parents will relent and agree to anything to get them back again.

3 *Retreatists.* For this group, life at home includes a high level of family conflict, perhaps including some violence. The adolescents may also have significant problems with school, and peers and drugs. Running away is an attempt to escape all that is going wrong. Their expectation is that life elsewhere has to be better. Nye (1980) notes that this group is the largest; it describes about 75 percent of adolescent runaways.

4 *Endangered.* These adolescents are fleeing verbally, physically, and sexually abusive homes. They feel that they need to leave to save their lives. They make up a small but significant proportion of runaways (about 5 to 10 percent of the runaway population) and may believe that they have the least to risk by trying the streets. In one study of runaways who left home and found their way to youth shelters (Farber et al., 1984), 78 percent of the adolescents self-reported physical or sexual abuse against them as their primary reason for leaving home. In addition to "endangered" runners, they have also been variously called "terrified" runners (Greene & Esselstyn, 1972), "victim" runners (Miller et al., 1980), and, at the extreme end of abuse and neglect, "push-outs," "exiles," "castaways," and "throwaways" (Janus et al., 1987; Miller et al., 1980; Nye, 1980; White, 1989).

Some researchers argue that the endangered/push-out group is much larger than is commonly believed, and may actually describe

40 to 50 percent of runaways (Adams & Gulotta, 1983; Langway, 1982). Counting adolescents on the streets at any given time is a nearly impossible task, and those that choose to repeatedly return or stay there are clearly saying that this life, with all of its danger and uncertainty, is preferable to a home where their family at best seems nonsupportive and rejecting, and at worst, homicidal. They are the repeat runaways, who, without intervention, will join the swelling ranks of homeless and missing adolescents whose numbers may easily exceed 1 million (Dryfoos, 1990).

When I met Michelle, she was well on her way to joining this endangered group. I learned this two weeks after our first meeting, as Michelle slowly, carefully, and tearfully, shared her story with me. She had finally told Kathy, who had given her an ultimatum: Someone, Michelle or Kathy, would do the talking, but I was going to find out. For three years, her stepfather had been sexually abusing her. He had used vague threats of family destruction (with particular emotional harm to her mother) if she told anyone, and purchased lavish gifts for her to maintain her compliance and secrecy. At first, the special attention he paid to her felt complimentary, especially since she had felt he preferred his biological daughter, Danielle. Michelle had been glad she was chosen to go to job sites or on weekend errands with him alone. At first, he had fondled her and had her "sit on his lap." Gradually, he had become more threatening, and forced her into sexual acts, including masturbation and fellatio. When she tried to resist being alone with him, her mother had intervened on his behalf, urging her to "keep Papa Tommy company,"

Each time Michelle felt overwhelmed, hopelessly trapped by Mr. Davis and the abuse, she fled the home. Once out, she became more optimistic about her ability to protect herself, and vowed to herself that she would make the abuse stop when she returned. Janus et al. (1987) note that this repetitive running away from an abusive home reflects a limited idea of how to generate alternatives; the same troubled solution is attempted over and over again. Time away from a painful, confusing environment may also be accompanied by a gradual forgetting, disbelieving, or questioning whether the environment at home was really as bad as remembered. In Michelle's case, such contradictory perspectives appeared to be assisted by her feelings of power and freedom on the street. She reasoned that if she could handle herself so well on her own, she really should be able to manage her "asshole stepfather." Once back, however, she blamed herself doubly for her weakness in not standing up to him and for having thought she had any control in the first place.

Michelle's activities outside the home when she was on the run only served to compound the trauma for her. She pursued older boys and young men and had been sexually involved with several who were in their late twenties. She unconsciously sought to rework the incestuous trauma by mastering her feelings about it with other men. Not surprisingly, she was quite vague about what happened when she ran, saying she was drunk or stoned or just "brain dead" when she was out there, and didn't remember much. Certainly her substance abuse and adrenal rush could cloud memories for her. However, this kind of dissociation seemed to be part of a larger response to being traumatized. Michelle's running away was particularly concerning because she was an abuse victim.

The issue of blame is an important one for all abuse victims, but especially for those who have become runaways. Incest is, at its foundation, a violation of trust and power. To keep the abuse secret, to feel compelled to continue in the abusive relationship, and to refrain from acting out against the abuser, adolescents must be manipulated into believing that they are full participants in the incest. Like Michelle, they may feel exploited but their experiences are disqualified by their perpetrators, and they are led, increasingly, to feel responsible for the abuse.

By the time I met Michelle, her thinking and reasoning were confused indeed. She had embraced a paradox, which had enabled her to survive though at significant personal cost. On the one hand, because she was just a young teenager, she was unable to have an obvious effect on the unpredictable and frightening events in her life. On the other hand, however, any danger she was in at home or on the street was her responsibility to handle, and only she was to blame if she then felt exploited. Unfortunately, Michelle could not come up with any alternative solution to her dilemma save to leave home, placing herself in danger—frequently sexual—and then, as though she had mastered the fear, to return home again.

My job was first and foremost to break the runaway cycle by stopping the abuse. This time, Michelle could not return home until her stepfather left it. Disclosure to her mother and to Child Protection Services would set into motion major personal, familial, and systemic changes, including, quite possibly, protracted out-of-home placement and court proceedings. Her stepfather could end up in jail, and she could be disowned by her family. Other siblings might also come forward with disclosures of their own, and newspapers might pick up the story. Friends might stop speaking to her if they heard she had had sex with her stepfather. Her mother could fall apart. All the possible outcomes from disclosure make it a daunting task for most adolescents.

To understand what this process would mean for Michelle, I needed to have a broader knowledge of her history and resources. I explored with her each of four aspects of her situation that might affect both her methods of coping with the incest itself and her subsequent adjustment to the changes to come: preabuse factors, the traumatic events, how Michelle managed the period of nondisclosure, and the implications of disclosure.

PREABUSE FACTORS

Although difficult to assess, it is helpful to get a sense of how the runaway was functioning before the incest began. The adolescent's individual and family history contributes to safety planning in important ways. For example Michelle and her mother had been closer before Mr. Davis entered the home, and had become increasingly estranged since the abuse began. Michelle reflected sadly that her "mother has no idea of who I am, she doesn't know me at all. I feel invisible, which ain't so easy for a fat person to do." She expressed a yearning for a lost relationship; in fact her running served as a metaphor for her desire to have her mother find her and bring her closer. Each time she returned, she felt her mother make an effort to talk to her. Unfortunately, once reassured, Ms. Davis would again become busy with her work and other commitments.

Another factor, Michelle's level of cognitive and personality development, also provided information about how to explain events to her, as well as areas of particular vulnerability. Michelle's reasoning was quite concrete and more like that of a younger child. It is impossible to determine whether the abuse impeded her intellectual development by throwing up emotional interference or whether her limited understanding of herself and events in her life made her more vulnerable to abuse in the first place.

Some children appear to have a "steeling" quality (Garmezy, 1983) that gives them a kind of temperamental resistance to stress and enables them to cope in spite of significant environmental strain. Such youngsters might not be as unbalanced by the factors that appeared to have made Michelle vulnerable even before the abuse. These included the multiple disruptions of divorce, father absence, several moves, and birth of a favored sibling. In fact, these traumatic events appeared to have set Michelle up for both subsequent abuse and running away. Michelle craved attention and nurturing, which made her stepfather's careful plan attractive to her. He skillfully played upon her particular dependencies and loyalties, blending these with threats about what disruptive and unhappy events would happen if she told anyone. It does not seem likely that she had much ego strength to resist the abuse. She was not one of those people who, as Finkelhor (1984) suggests, are naturally protected from abuse by a "front of invulnerability." Little about her conveyed that she would not go along with abuse or keep it a secret; in fact, she was easily intimidated. In short, she was a prime target. Despite momentary feelings of triumph over danger, over the longer view Michelle's activity on the streets actually served to reinforce this sense of herself as someone who lived dangerously all of the time.

Michelle's family structure and functioning, which included an absent father, a dominant stepfather, a busy mother, and and a cute little half-sibling also placed her at greater risk for abuse. First, the loss of contact with her biological father increased the importance of "Papa Tommy" for Michelle. Indeed, she spoke nostalgically about the fun they had going on expeditions together before the abuse had commenced. Second, Mr. Davis's lack of early involvement with Michelle may have further weakened the incest taboo for him. Stepfathers are more frequently sexually abusive of their stepchildren than biological fathers are (Finkelhor, 1984; Herman, 1981; Poznanski & Blos, 1975). Third, Michelle's need to please and protect her mother made it more likely she would do as she was told. Ironically, the runaway behavior was actually an attempt on Michelle's part to maintain the secret of the incest so her mother would not "go crazy" or throw Michelle "out on her big ass," as Mr. Davis had predicted might happen. While Ms. Davis could not initially see how Michelle's running away, which panicked her so, was a behavior Michelle employed to *protect* her mother, this was my contention from the outset.

I also wanted to learn about any other kinds of trauma to Michelle that had taken place prior to the sexual abuse in her earlier years. I knew that unsubtle, direct questioning might yield inconclusive, false, or hostile responses, but I also wanted her to know that I was ready to hear about anything in order to better understand what was happening for her. As Yvonne Dolan (1991) has noted, "To fail to have the client adequately share the details of the abuse may not only play into the secrecy and stigmatization so often characteristic of sexual abuse, but also lead to the client's feeling discounted and inadequately supported" (p. 25). With a young adolescent as skittish as Michelle, I walked a fine line between being an available and straightforward ally and just one more intrusive traumatizing adult. While Michelle reported no other abuse, she had been deeply affected by the many changes in her life; the significance of the abuse was compounded because it felt like another major loss for her.

Background information is important because it sets the stage for the kind of new learning that has to take place in order to break the cycle of abuse and running. If Michelle had had a long traumatic history, her ability to trust and to begin to take charge of her own life would be even more severely compromised. In such a situation, I would expect that the development of our therapeutic relationship might take many months, and that the content of our time together would be less important than the fact of my involvement as a stable, consistent, and nurturing person in Michelle's life. In general, when I know that running away is the culmination of long-term abuses, I pace the treatment more slowly, handling present dilemmas as they arise while slowly building an alliance with the adolescent. In Michelle's case, I was able to proceed more quickly once I gained her confidence that I was going to hang in there with her. She was quite open to being helped. She knew she needed it.

THE TRAUMATIC EVENTS

The way an abused runaway manages to make sense out of what is happening is highly influenced by factors that define the traumatic events themselves. These include, for example, the identity of and relationship with the offender, entrapment, the offender's access to and control of the victim, the number of occurrences, sexual activities, and methods of maintaining secrecy about the abuse. In addition, the runaway needs to make sense out of any additional traumatization that occurred in the course of running away. While incest cases require special consideration, all abused runaways need to come to terms with facts of the violence against them.

However, incest often carries with it an especially complex series of cognitive and emotional shifts (Burgess & Holmstrom, 1978). In cases like Michelle's, where the adolescent has not had to endure anything as blatantly wrong as physical pain, the struggle to find meaning involves pouring out a witch's brew of ingredients as disparate as pleasure and terror. Intense feelings of specialness and privilege are countered with equally severe experiences of betrayal and emotional blackmail.

Michelle's relationship with her stepfather was not the only one to be compromised because of the abuse. The loss of trust in Papa Tommy occurred gradually; along with it, her willingness to trust other men, other people, and then, ultimately, herself eroded. For all abuse victims, the loss of trust leads to a period of heightened vigilance in which the victim has the hopeless task of remaining alert to every possible—real or imagined—assault on the self. Scanning all relationships for suggestions of abuse makes intimacy impossible. This vigilance also ultimately decreases the victim's feelings of control over her life, because there is really no such thing as being prepared for abuse.

Michelle's relationship with her mother was also damaged severely because her mother typically insisted that Michelle spend time with "Papa Tommy" even when Michelle protested. This made Michelle feel invalidated. Furthermore, her mother did not seem to exert much effort in getting to the root of what was troubling Michelle. Her decision to minimize Michelle's distress by labelling it the behavior of a typically angry teenager, coupled with her dislike of conflict, made Ms. Davis look the other way and try to smooth things between her husband and daughter. Ms. Davis' needs for peace and normalcy gave Michelle messages that her pain was not important to her mother. Michelle then reasoned that *she* was the problem, and ran off to some place where she could get drunk, overeat, and have unprotected intercourse. These self-destructive reactions to abuse and feelings of being devalued are very common.

In addition, Michelle's feelings of being out of control made it difficult for her to take responsibility for anything she did. For example, at one point during our contact, we discussed how she was feeling about an upcoming interview with the police. Michelle expressed a desire to run away again. After exploring this, I asked her to assure me she would not do so, and she replied, "I could tell you I won't go, but my feet may have a different opinion."

THE PERIOD OF NONDISCLOSURE

During the period of abuse, an adolescent is necessarily coping in a variety of ways. The psychological impact of the trauma is typically exacerbated by the need to maintain a secret. Runaways are further endangered because the very methods that they employ to manage the abuse often revictimize them. Thus, adolescents like Michelle are really enduring three distinct types of violence: incest, secrecy, and street life.

Most abused runaways suffer from classic signs of post traumatic stress disorder (PTSD). It is usually helpful to discuss this diagnosis with adolescents to whom it applies, because it normalizes their experience and reassures them that they are not alone in their reactions to the abuse. The American Psychiatric Association's (1987) Diagnostic and Statistical Manual of Mental Disorders says that this diagnosis can be made when the following four conditions are met:

- There is a "psychologically distressing event" (p. 250) that would evoke significant disturbance in almost anyone.

- Victims reexperience the trauma in their minds through

recurrent dreams, nightmares, flashbacks, and recollections of it.

- Victims experience a numbing of responsiveness, feelings of dissociation and reduced involvement with the outside world, detachment from others and from their own inner experience, withdrawal, restricted affect, and a loss of interest in daily events.

- Victims may also experience a wide variety of other reactions or symptoms, such as sleep disturbance, difficulty concentrating, memory problems, irrational guilt, extreme alertness to danger in the environment, an exaggerated startle response, and increased reactions to other events that symbolize or resemble the traumatic event.

After meeting with Michelle and learning about her history and how she had coped with it, I felt confident in making a PTSD diagnosis. At the same time, I realized that she also suffered from limited coping and problem-solving skills, school failure, and an unforgiving self-image. During the three years in which her symptoms of PTSD had developed, the practical consequences of this diagnosis also emerged. For example, her preoccupation with the abuse impaired her memory and concentration. This, in turn, made the acquisition of math and reading comprehension skills nearly impossible. Her hypervigilence taxed her friendships sorely, as she was alert to any microscopic insults and could become quite upsetting for seemingly small or trivial reasons. Indeed, when I ended a session a few minutes late with the client before her, Michelle would enter my office forlorn and angry, making sarcastic comments to me, to which I responded by asking how it made her feel—hurt? mad? sad?—when I kept her waiting (I also apologized). Invariably, she would deny my shrink talk, but would relax soon thereafter. Accustomed as she was to betrayal, she was ever on the lookout for signs that I did not actually care about her as much as I purported to.

Although Michelle and I developed an important relationship, we did very little in the way of traditional insight-oriented therapy. Instead, the content of our time involved very concrete activities and highly practical troubleshooting. I persuaded Michelle to stay after school and meet with her teachers to get extra help. I had Kathy take her to the stationery store to purchase a homework assignment book. Once Michelle understood that she had PTSD, she was more amenable to the idea that she needed to write down nightly assignments instead of relying on her memory. She wanted to have a better social life, so she practiced calling friends up using my plastic play-therapy phones. I enacted a variety of responses that allowed her to recognize and manage her reactions to her peers. For example, she had to handle the chance that they might not be free at the time she wanted to see them, or sound as happy to hear from her as she hoped.

All the while, we worked directly on managing PTSD: creating safe places in her mind, learning relaxation and breathing techniques for feelings of panic, orienting to the present, noticing change no matter how small, and using supportive relationships to help her manage present fears and anxieties. Abuse and PTSD interfere mightily with the development of skills all adolescents must have to navigate school, friends, and family. The acquisition of such skills is every bit as important as the awareness provided by traditional psychotherapy, if not more so. Moreover, without these skills, abused adolescents like Michelle will have compounded difficulties following disclosure.

THE PERIOD OF DISCLOSURE

Disclosure refers to the time that the abusive events are made known to others in the family and community. The potential outcomes of disclosure are many and varied. At one extreme, the responses can be cooperative and thoughtful, with the best interests of the adolescent in the foreground. Healing can be facilitated by immediate belief of the truth of the report, prompt legal response, and support from others in the family. At the other extreme, the families can be ambivalent or even condemning of the adolescent, and the systems can move in slow and contradictory ways. When adolescents are unsupported following disclosure, they are likely to become more symptomatic (e.g., depressed, suicidal, anxious), avoidant (e.g., abuse drugs and alcohol, dissociate), aggressive (e.g., delinquent, paranoid), or disorganized (e.g., psychotic). For this reason, the movement from nondisclosure to disclosure is a powerful event which can have a dramatic effect on the outcome for the adolescent.

As disclosures go, Michelle's experience was a relatively positive one. At Michelle's request, I had her mother and Kathy attend a meeting with Michelle, a child protection worker, and me. Together, we shared the necessary information with Ms. Davis and requested that the other children spend a few days out of the home while she and Mr. Davis made plans about what they wanted to do. Initially, Ms. Davis was in shock. We were careful to go slowly with her but even so, her eyes glazed over, and she shook her head saying, "no, no, no, it can't be."

She made the transition to understanding when Michelle crumpled to the floor and buried her head in her mother's lap, sobbing, "I'm sorry Mommy, I didn't want to do this to you, but I couldn't stop him and he had to stop." While Ms. Davis silently stroked Michelle's hair, I outlined the connection among Michelle's school and social problems, running away, trouble communicating, and oppositional attitude, and the abuse, emphasizing that there was no doubt in my mind that Michelle was telling the truth. I tried to seed the suggestion that eventually the family might be able to get back together, if that is what everyone wanted, but for now, either Mr. Davis or the children would have to leave. The child protection worker asked Ms. Davis to review her options, and inquired about Ms. Davis's safety in her home without the children.

After weeping silently for a few minutes, Ms. Davis spoke in a quiet voice, looking down at Michelle despairingly, "I'll do whatever I have to for my baby. Tommy will be out today. Don't be sorry, Shelly, it's all my fault. I only wish you had told me. Honestly, I never knew a damn thing. How could he . . . ?" Her voice trailed off. Kathy said that Michelle could sleep on her couch for a while more until things settled down, and asked her mother whether Danielle might go to an aunt's; Pete could easily find a friend to impose on. They discussed which extended family members had to be told the truth and which shouldn't. Together with the child protection worker, they made arrangements for what would happen during the next several weeks with the legal and social service systems. Michelle had been adamant all along that she did not want to press charges against her stepfather but wanted him to get help for himself. Acknowledging this desire, the child protection worker gave Ms. Davis the names of appropriate support-group leaders for her and for Mr. Davis, recommending them strongly. The police would have to file their own report.

For Michelle, the worst was over, and she was able to express much relief that her mother had believed her and that adults were planning on her behalf. Her acute fears about the repercussions of the disclosure continued to linger for several weeks. She wondered what Papa Tommy would do to change her mother's mind about supporting her, and worried about the police interview. She was terrified about her classmates' finding out and embarrassed about the family gossip she was sure would heat up the phone lines once a particularly talkative aunt found out. However, she managed a small grin when I praised her up and down for how well she had managed the disclosure, and nodded in assent when I asked her if she agreed with my assessment.

The Family of the Sexually Abused Runaway

Once disclosure has been successful and the adolescent is safe and supported, work with the family can begin. Initially, I prefer to work without the perpetrator although, down the road, if the family wants to be together and he has been in group therapy of his own, I will agree to include him. While I make an effort to listen to the wishes of different family members who may want him to partici- pate sooner, I believe that I must work first and foremost as an advocate for the emotional and physical safety of the adolescent. Especially when the victim is also a runaway, I want to ensure that she has sufficient personal resources available to her so that she can employ them instead of running away, should she feel at all unsafe. In dealing with PTSD it is important to realize that just the *idea* of seeing the perpetrator can produce physiological responses to trauma as real as if the abuse were recurring. In the realm of family work with incest, I am centrist in my approach; I neither routinely include nor exclude perpetrators, but wait and see what evolves for the adolescents during their individual therapy.

Historically, there has been much more speculation about the contributory role of the adolescent and the mother in incest cases than about the circumstances that cause an adult male to sexually abuse his own daughter. When adolescents run away, attention of family and professionals is diverted onto them; their actions initially appear more troubling than troubled. Incestuously involved adolescents have also been blamed for their seductive advances toward their fathers or father-figures, or described in terms of their deficits: needy, dependent, overly compliant, and helpless. Mothers of incest victims have been described as incapacitated through mental illness or physical disability or as physically and emotionally unavailable (Finkelhor, 1984; Herman, 1981). While these descriptions have not changed much in the last decade, the emphasis on *who* is responsible has shifted somewhat.

Families as a whole have also been implicated in incest and running away. For example, some theoreticians believe that, because of blurred role-boundaries in the incestuous family, mothers allow their daughters to become central female figures in the family (e.g., Lustig et al., 1966). Mirkin, Raskin, and Antogini (1984) similarly describe three ways that the female runaway functions in her family: parenting, protecting, and preserving. These authors note that normal hierarchy is reversed in the family by the way in which the adolescent "parents" her parents and siblings. She serves as a protector of the parents' marriage, allowing them to avoid underlying conflict by focusing on her misbehavior. In addition, she preserves the family organization at the preadolescent level of development. Both incestuous and runaway families have been further described as unusually anxious about separation and loss, and their rigid requirements of interdependency keep them trapped. The adolescent cannot negotiate greater distance and autonomy to accommodate her own emerging needs. Running away from incest can force parents to behave like supportive adults by coming to look for her, while at the same time bringing in outside intervention for the whole family (Karpel, 1980; Mirkin et al., 1984).

These descriptions do not explain why incest is not disclosed immediately or why some families respond nonsupportively to their adolescents once they disclose it. Even worse, perpetrators are often let off the hook. Ultimately, explanations about the adolescent's role, the mother's complicity, and the family dynamics shed little light on why the incest occurs in the first place. As Sink (1988) has noted, families do not cause incest. Rather, they must react to it, and many are ill-equipped to act effectively either to confront the abusing person or to protect the child.

Overemphasizing the roles of adolescents and families can thus only be expected to obscure the perpetrator's responsibility for the abuse. Incest, first and foremost, is an abuse of power. Men who are incestuously involved with their children view their rights of authority and ownership as superseding any other rights. Incest does not stop simply because women and children want it to. Rather, offenders must be persuaded to change their sex-role attitudes and behaviors.

Finkelhor (1984) has proposed a model that places the onus more fully where it belongs. He suggests that in order for incest to occur, four preconditions must be met:

1. *Motivation.* The motivation to sexually abuse a child includes emotional congruence (sexual interaction with a child fulfills an important emotional need); sexual arousal (realizing that the child can be a source of sexual gratification); and blockage (other sources of sexual gratification are less available and satisfying).

2. *Disinhibition.* The second precondition of abuse is the perpetrator's ability to overcome internal inhibitors, including social, moral, and psychological taboos against incest. Without motivation to abuse, disinhibition alone is not sufficient to create a perpetrator. But with motivation, disinhibition can result from alcohol, impulsivity, or mental or emotional impairment.

3. *Access.* The motivated and disinhibited perpetrator must also be able to find an unsupervised and vulnerable victim. The more access that he can have, the more likely that he will abuse. While protection of adolescents will reduce their availability for abuse, it does not by itself reduce the problems of motivation and disinhibition.

4. *Overcoming resistance.* Adolescents vary widely in their ability to resist abuse. Some appear relatively invulnerable,

while others are sufficiently needy and dependent that they go along with a powerful adult. In many cases, the abuse occurs without the use of force to gain the adolescent's compliance and secrecy. Abusers adeptly manage the adolescent's immaturity and insecurity, mixing well-timed bribes with threats that harm or distress will result from disclosure.

Therapy for the Family of the Sexually Abused Runaway

Group treatment for perpetrators is the most effective means for addressing all of these preconditions (e.g., Sonkin, Martin, & Walker, 1985). The perpetrator must learn to take responsibility for his behavior and find ways to gain control over it. At the same time, his access to children must be limited to closely supervised meetings. Along with group treatment, but not as a substitute for it, I sometimes recommend individual or family therapy for a perpetrator. Mr. Davis was manipulated into participation as a condition of seeing his biological daughter. Later, he realized that he needed to be there. Initially, very few perpetrators are willing participants in a therapy that holds them accountable for their actions. Just getting them to commit to group therapy can be a very important step for them and for their families.

Once the incest has been disclosed, and a plan for managing it is in effect, attention can shift to understanding the family interactions that have endured despite the disclosure, and building new skills so members may grow past this developmental impasse. The dysfunctional communication patterns that led to both the secret of the incest and the running away require particular attention. To ensure that new family patterns replace the old, I typically direct the family therapy down five general paths.

DECREASING EMOTIONAL INTENSITY

For families to change and communicate better, the intensity of feelings aroused by the disclosure has to decrease sufficiently so that reason and compassion can prevail. For Michelle's family, the first three weeks of therapy were awash in confusing and painful feelings. Michelle's double whammy of running away and revealing her secret had naturally aroused a smorgasbord of powerful negative emotions like anger, hurt, rejection, and disappointment among the different family members. To bring the family back to a semblance of calm, I encouraged family members to slow down, take things a day at a time, breathe deeply, use their heads, and spend time pursuing small, safe pleasures. Based on my knowledge of other cases, I was able to reassure them that the family was not always going to hurt as much as this. Until people could listen to one another without sobbing, screaming, or wailing, there was little else that could be accomplished.

IMPROVING COMMUNICATION

All families that experience the secrecy of incest and dangers of running away are, by definition, weak in the area of communication skills. Fortunately, these are easy to teach and learn if family members are willing to practice, and they can be demonstrated routinely in family therapy sessions. Active listening is central to successful child-rearing and can make the difference for adolescents; even when they are not able to do as they like, they still know that they have been heard. It is not just the adolescent who needs this validation. Often the mother has also been abused and needs to feel defended or feels paralyzed by guilt. It is also possible that the mother may be too lax about any guilt she may bear over being an accomplice to the abuse. Frequently such women have no capacity for self-assertion or for maintaining boundaries, or even for simply saying "No." Like their daughters, they must come to realize that they have options other than coerced silence. Further, they must learn to put the right priority on their children's well-being and to defend not only themselves but their children.

While Ms. Davis had not been physically battered by her husband, he controlled her with an intimidating anger. She went to great lengths to sustain peace and not upset him. Ms. Davis avoided conflict by working long hours and sending Michelle on errands with her husband when he wanted company. The disclosure forced her to evaluate both her own compliance with his tyranny at home and her level of denial of her daughter's distress. My willingness to listen to her and help her sort through her own experiences provided her with some of the support she needed to begin to take care of Michelle and listen more carefully herself.

REESTABLISHING LOVING FEELINGS

Although the family is under a great deal of stress and may be preoccupied with hostility and confusion, strengthening the positive emotional connections after disclosure is vital for all members. Michelle and her mother had been raging at one another for so long that they needed to rekindle the special feelings they had shared many years earlier. Ms. Davis needed to be reassured that she was a good parent and could learn how to love Michelle more effectively. Even though it is not usually thought of as a skill, family members need to relearn how to demonstrate caring for one another. Even the positive side of the ambivalence toward the perpetrator needs to be emphasized some of the time. For example, there were many wonderful things that Mr. Davis provided for this family. Especially in light of Danielle's utter devotion to him, we had to honor what we could about the positive ways in which he had parented all four children.

INCREASING YOUTH INDEPENDENCE
AND RESPONSIBILITY

This can be one of the most difficult steps for many families caught up in a struggle for power and dominance over their teenager's behavior. The goal is to increase youth responsibility and decrease parental overprotectiveness; the way to do this is to move away from a parent-centered decision-making style toward one in which the adolescent is also an active participant. It's a strategy not of permissiveness but of using the opportunity to provide adolescents with help as they learn to establish values, set personal limits, and make their own thoughtful decisions. When conflicts arose, I engaged Ms. Davis in exercises to establish her own clear reasoning (is it safe, is it affordable, is it at a suitable time, etc.) and ways to present her thoughts to Michelle.

CONSTRUCTIVE PROBLEM SOLVING

Families need to learn to define problems creatively and stay with a discussion of options long enough to find areas of consensus or possibility. This can only occur when family members have active listening skills and feel loving toward each other. In learning to arrive at mutually satisfactory solutions, the family creates options where there were none before. For example, Michelle previously had seen no option for managing stress other than to run away and escape. Through therapy, she learned how to stand up for herself, negotiate, find people to talk to, and look for alternatives to running away.

The ultimate goal of family therapy is to establish a family system in which the adolescent does not have to run away from home but can *walk* away from home at the appropriate time. Family therapy can end when options are opened up not only for the adolescent but for the parents as well. All families need to have available to them a variety of alternatives for managing stress, as well as negotiation skills. In families where incest and running away have been problems, having more options enables the whole family to grow past the pain and dysfunction.

When Ms. Davis went home from the disclosure meeting, she called her husband at work and demanded he meet her for an urgent conversation. Although he first denied any wrongdoing, Ms. Davis persisted with him, begging him to tell the truth if there was any chance he wanted the family to survive. Mr. Davis then reluctantly acknowledged that some of the abuse and bribery had occurred. He moved out later that week, but did not go into group therapy immediately. Michelle had decided that she did not want to see or speak with him until he apologized to her. Two months later, with the understanding that he might be able to increase his visits with Danielle and decrease his involvement in the legal system, he entered into the offenders' program offered by the local community mental health center. The terms of his subsequent probation strongly reinforced his participation in group therapy.

Michelle returned to her mother's home five weeks after therapy began, by which time she felt that she would be safe there. After Mr. Davis had been in group therapy for three months, she commenced weekly hour-long visits with him in the child protection office. He wrote her a long heartfelt letter filled with shame, remorse, and love. This persuaded her that he was working on his problems, too, and she discovered she actually missed him. Mr. Davis was not allowed to call the house once Michelle was in it, but he stayed in touch and remained an important person for the other family members as much as he could. He contributed economically and, to the best of my knowledge, seldom missed a supervised visit with any of the children. Notably, he respected the restraints put on him, and even wrote me a letter thanking me for my help with Michelle. The threat of incarceration may have loomed over him, or he may have genuinely decided to make changes; either way, his efforts were concerted.

I saw Michelle for two years; we terminated therapy because I was leaving the area. I might have continued for six months to a year more if I could have. Yet I felt cautiously encouraged that her life was back on track. Predictably, the early events in Michelle's healing proceeded quickly and smoothly. Once convinced of her safety, she made great personal gains. She began to develop real self-confidence and find pleasure in trying things new and challenging, even if trying meant she might fail. She discovered that she had a real talent for working with young special-needs children and began volunteering in an early intervention classroom. As her own schoolwork improved, she earned her way into college preparatory classes. She established two fairly stable friendships, and sang with her mother in church on Sundays. When we parted, Michelle was ready to try some of her new skills unaided, reassuring me that she would seek therapy at another time if she felt she needed it.

However, I remained concerned about her hypervigilance, her relationships with boys, and the legacy of the abuse that haunted her in her dreams. She refused to confront the role her weight played in her management of stress and her lack of self-esteem. Too often, she continued to blame others for her problems and to "run" from them psychologically unless she was carefully assisted in looking at her responsibility for herself. She preferred to avoid conflict, much as her mother had. Michelle's journey toward taking charge of her life had certainly begun, and would likely continue well into adulthood, when she would truly be out on her own, in the right way, at the right time.

Michelle sent me cards occasionally for a couple of years after we stopped seeing each other. She wrote that her family was working toward reunification; her mother had begun dating Mr. Davis again. She felt all right about it, especially since her mother was now in a "no bullshit" support group of her own. Her parents were also in couples counseling with a professional I respected highly. I confess that I very seldom feel certain that a perpetrator will not offend again, even with the finest that therapy has to offer. However, I did believe that Michelle now knew that she could say "No," and that Ms. Davis would no longer look the other way. In other words, if all the family were in agreement, the plan seemed like a good one to me.

One Christmas, Michelle sent me her school picture. As it fluttered out onto my desk, I recalled her huddled presence the first day we met: toes pointed inward, those clanging bracelets, the transparent eyes peering from a frizzy awning of bangs, that silence concealing despair and hope. Now, in the picture, her pale-blue eyes startled me as they stared so confidently back at the camera. I was delighted to see such a photo, and sat back in my chair to admire her strong, courageous smile.

4

Delinquents

Richie: "I'm not afraid of dyin'"

The term "delinquent behavior" refers to illegal activities that are committed by a child or an adolescent. Such activities include a vast range of behaviors which, at the low end of seriousness, include status offenses *(for which adults would not be arrested or prosecuted): truancy, running away, alcohol use, incorrigibility, and curfew violations. As Farrington (1987) has noted, almost all adolescents will commit one or more status offenses before they are 18 years old. At the other end of the continuum,* index offenses *reflect serious criminal activity that can do irrevocable harm to victims and communities: violent offenses such as homicide, robbery, rape, and aggravated assault, and property offenses like burglary, larceny of more than $50, auto theft, and arson (Federal Bureau of Investigation, 1987). Between these extremes are a wide variety of* general offenses, *some mildly violent (e.g., hitting a parent or peer). Other such activities include the sale and use of illegal drugs, damaging property, petty larceny, buying stolen goods, prostitution, breaking and entering, disorderly conduct, panhandling, and joyriding.*

What information we have about juvenile delinquency in the

80

United States is based on public documents and population surveys. Male adolescents account for a disproportionately high percentage of the serious and violent criminal behavior in our society. During 1986, for example, youths under the age of 18 years accounted for 15.4 percent of arrests for violent crimes, and 33.5 percent of arrests for property crimes (Federal Bureau of Investigation, 1987). Moreover, researchers have found that a relatively small subset of adolescents account for a large percentage of adolescent crime, and that the antisocial behavior of these offending adolescents is statistically stable (e.g., Henggeler, 1989).

Millions of American youngsters commit minor offenses all of the time, and a sizeable number get arrested. More than 1.7 million arrests occurred among 10- to 17-year-olds in 1986 (Flanegan & Jamieson, 1987). More than half a million of those arrested were age 14 or younger (46,000 were under age 10). Of those arrested, 1.3 million ended up as formal cases in the juvenile justice system. More than half a million of these cases concerned serious crimes; in fact, the number of index offenses actually committed may be 10 times larger than the number of cases that are discovered and end up in juvenile court (Dryfoos, 1990). Approximately 6 million 10- to 17-year-olds reported that, within a 1-year period, they had participated in an act that was against the law; of these, 3.3 million were age 14 or younger. Of those arrested, fewer than 5 percent end up in custodial facilities. In 1985 there were 88,414 adolescents in short-term and long-term juvenile custodial institutions, such as training schools, group homes, and camps in the United States (United States Census Bureau, 1987).

Juveniles also end up in adult courts and prisons in large numbers. In 1986, an estimated 4,000 adolescents were tried as adults, either because they were "not amenable to treatment" and "not fit and proper subjects" for rehabilitation, or because they posed too great a public threat to remain within the jurisdiction of the juvenile justice system. These youths were then committed to adult prisons for an average term of 6.8 years (Schwartz, 1989). Adolescents do not have to be adjudicated as adults to be incarcerated with adults; more delinquents wind up in jail than in custodial institutions. For example, an estimated 92,856 juveniles were admitted to adult jails in 1986 (Schwartz).

The Referral

The Child Guidance Clinic, in which I worked for a few years, had a contract with the local juvenile court. We evaluated and treated any delinquents they sent us, wrote up our findings for their vast closed files, appeared in court, and appreciated knowing that guards assigned to arrange for the safe return of their charges were seated just outside the meeting-room door if we needed them. Ankle manacles ensured that no one would run too far too fast. On paper, the kids always seemed crazy and dangerous. Rattling down the hall, they sounded menacing (indeed, those of us involved with the delinquency project developed a certain tough reputation in our clinic because of the sound of chains jangling in the halls outside our offices and the beefy guards stationed nearby). But, almost invariably, once the kids began talking and drawing, they were transformed into lost toddlers, requiring oceans of support and encouragement to overcome debilitating self-doubt, and battling an environment that demanded levels of personal judgment and responsibility that far exceeded their cognitive and emotional development.

On occasion, very infrequently, I would see kids who were truly scary. Lacking insight, relatedness, warmth, or empathy of any kind, such individuals needed more than any rehabilitation program could offer. With little doubt in my mind, I would recommend that these youths be tried as adults, and I entertained no illusions about my abilities to intervene for them. But until I had had an adolescent in my office for a couple of hours, I did not necessarily know what was beneath the uniformly tough facades these kids offered me. The testing and their reactions to my attempts at kindness would serve as windows into the child underneath.

Richie Nelson entered my room, plopped down and tipped back in his chair. "How ya doin'," he said before I had a chance to welcome him. He popped on his Walkman headphones and began bopping up and down in his seat. A short, slender 16-year-old, he had hazel eyes that were constantly in motion, darting around the room. He pretended not to hear me when I asked him to remove the Walkman. He had been with me less than a minute, and I was already feeling aggravated. He asked if he could smoke a cigarette, and when I told him "No" and, again, to "take off the Walkman so we can talk," he let me know he was annoyed with me, too, by swearing audibly under his breath.

Although I had the referral information provided by the court, I asked Richie for his version of his history, looking for discrepancies in the accounts and checking on those. I was not trying to trip him up but, rather, attempting to get a grasp on how he understood the events leading up to his arrest. However, I also wanted to see if the violence of what he had done meant anything to him; when he minimized it, or denied that his victim had been harmed, I pushed the limits of that account, looking hard for traces of empathy and remorse. I knew that Richie's own life had been tough and I wanted to hear about how he understood its effects on his present situation.

Richie's father had left the family when Richie was a toddler and had been only erratically involved with him since then. Richie saw his father when he wanted to, but he claimed that his stepmother was "a real bitch" and he had not wanted to live with them. Richie's alcoholic mother had evidently had a hard time managing Richie and his three older brothers over the years. By his own recollection, he had been in 11 different foster homes and residential schools, some for as briefly as a few days, and one, on and off, for four years.

He had been first removed from his mother's custody when he was 18 months old. At that time, he was sent to live with his maternal grandmother; sometime during his second year, his mother and three older brothers also moved in with the grandmother. By the time he was six, his mother was having increasing difficulties managing his activity level, soiling, sleep disturbances, and "lying." He was also reportedly engaging in dangerous activities like dangling out of a second-story window and climbing high fences to jump from.

Ms. Nelson and Richie were referred to the child guidance clinic by the school. Richie's kindergarten teacher had witnessed struggles between Ms. Nelson and her mother over how to manage Richie, and she thought that this conflict was causing Richie to act out. When Ms. Nelson expressed exhaustion and doubt about whether she could handle Richie anymore, he was sent to a residential school for emotionally handicapped children. He did well there, and after two years his mother removed him. However, Richie did not last long in her custody. Her alcohol abuse interfered with her ability to get him to school and appointments, and his behavior again began to spiral out of control. He was placed in several different foster homes before being sent to another residential school for almost two years until he was 10. Again, he made relatively more gains there than he had at home or in foster homes but, again, his mother managed to remove him. She took him to Las Vegas to start a new life. Six months later, they returned, and Ms. Nelson requested that he be placed in foster care. She said that he was "hyper, a liar, and a crook," and hoped someone else could straighten him out.

After bouncing between different foster homes and his mother's home, Richie found a foster family that could manage him. When a reunion with his mother did not succeed, this foster family was willing to take him back. Interestingly, he had maintained contact with this family even though he had again been at home with his mother for almost a year before his current crime. All of the agencies involved had been hopeful that his mother would be better able to handle him now that his brothers were out of the home and he was the only child she was responsible for. By Richie's account, his mother cared little about how he spent his time as long as he didn't get into trouble. When I asked him about curfews, school expectations, chores, and the standard middle-class concerns for young 16-year-olds, he laughed, saying "I ain't no baby." Developmentally, I had him pegged for about an eight-year-old; I may have been generous in that assessment. He was clearly unable to assume responsibility for himself, and unwilling to admit it, with little knowledge of what responsible behavior was.

A few days before I met Richie, he and a friend had waited for Sunday Mass to conclude so they could rob someone leaving church. Richie claimed that it was his friend who had knocked down an old man, and that he had only checked the pockets for cash. His lengthy record of crimes prior to this assault included multiple car thefts, check forgeries, breaking and entering a neighbor's home, and destroying property in his school at a time when he had been suspended. This was the first crime against a person he had been caught committing. He admitted that there had been one other attempt, in which his victim had turned out to have a switchblade.

When I asked him about it, Richie pulled up his shirt to reveal a long scar across his abdomen. I gasped in amazement. He shrugged nonchalantly, saying, "I'm not afraid of dyin'; it's no big deal."

The prosecutor in this case wanted to transfer Richie to adult court where he would be punished for his crime, and possibly deterred from repeating it. My evaluation would serve as additional evidence for or against such a waiver into adult proceedings. I informed Richie very carefully about the point of our time together. While I realized that honesty might not be his long suit, I wanted him to know that I could put anything he said and did into my report. At the same time, I also encouraged him to be cooperative, so that I could say some good things in it.

The Delinquent Adolescent

A wide array of adolescent characteristics have been associated with delinquency. These include cognitive factors, social competence, and personality variables that cluster to form particular subgroup classifications. Yet it is virtually impossible to understand delinquent adolescents without paying simultaneous attention to the family, peer, and social structures around them. Any linear description of these factors should not overshadow the important ways in which individual and systemic variables overlap and correlate.

COGNITIVE FACTORS

In a large number of studies, the IQs of delinquents are lower than the IQs of their nondelinquent peers (e.g., Hirschi & Hindelang, 1977; Quay, 1987; Wilson & Herrnstein, 1985). This difference seems to be independent of social class and race (McGarvey, Gabrielli, Bentler, & Mednick, 1981) and does not seem to be affected by any propensity of less-intelligent adolescents to be caught more readily by the police (West & Farrington, 1977). Evidence also suggests that the association between delinquency and IQ is independent of the degree of family pathology (Walsh, Beyer, & Petee, 1987) and of adolescent personality variables (Hanson, Henggeler, Haefele, & Rodick, 1984). Some researchers even believe that a

high IQ serves to protect at-risk adolescents from engaging in delinquent activities (e.g., Kandel et al., 1988).

Delinquents often have a significant discrepancy between their
scores on the verbal and performance sections of intelligence tests;
Quay (1987) offers ample evidence to demonstrate that the overall
association between delinquency and IQ is more specifically linked
to the relatively low verbal IQ of juvenile offenders. This discrepancy has also been linked to convictions for violent crimes (Holland,
Beckett, & Levi, 1981), and the degree of seriousness of delinquent
activity (Walsh, Petee, & Byer, 1987). Such a significant discrepancy
between the sections of the IQ test is also suggestive of learning
disabilities. Indeed, the work of Dorothy Lewis and her colleagues
strongly indicates that organically-caused learning disabilities
are widespread among delinquents (Lewis & Balla, 1976; Lewis,
Shankok, Pincus, & Glaser, 1979).

Low verbal abilities and learning problems are also associated
strongly with other factors contributing to delinquency. For example, academic difficulties can be expected when such deficits are
present. These in turn can lead to a host of school problems that
culminate in delinquent acting out. Similarly, poor verbal skills are
also associated with all sorts of psychosocial difficulties, of which
delinquency is just one form (Quay, 1987; Rutter & Giller, 1984).
Finally, low intellectual abilities impede the timely development of
abstract reasoning skills, problem-solving and other higher-order
processes. Some researchers speculate that the absence of abstract
reasoning abilities is more closely connected to delinquency than
simply low intelligence (e.g., Henggeler, 1989).

Richie had previously taken the IQ test five times as he moved
around among schools and placements. He approached the materials like a veteran. However, even given his previous exposure, his
test results with me were quite consistent with the other assess-
ments and the data available on delinquents. On the IQ test I admin-
istered, an average score is 100. His verbal IQ was 85, which is in
the low average range, and his performance IQ was 118, which is in
the high average range. Any discrepancy exceeding 20 points is
significant. On the reading test, he performed like a fourth grader.
His visual organization and visual memory were better than aver-

age, but his verbal skills were seriously lagging, and his learning disability had clearly not been addressed adequately.

From the beginning of school, Richie had demonstrated both learning and attention problems. The lack of a consistent and supportive environment no doubt magnified his difficulties, as he moved from place to place and school to school, making one troubled adjustment after another. By the time I met Richie he had not formally dropped out of school, but he seldom attended, and he had clearly not learned much in years. Richie had adequate intelligence for learning, but he was severely disabled. By junior high school he had begun to avoid school, where he must have felt he was exposing himself to the humiliation of repeated failure.

Another kind of cognitive deficit that many researchers have found in delinquents is an underdeveloped ability to reason about moral situations (e.g., Gibbs, 1987; Jurkovic, 1980; Kohlberg, 1969). This deficiency impedes delinquents' understanding of right and wrong and limits their appreciation of the rights and feelings of others. Delinquents are amenable to breaking the law because their thinking tends to be egocentric and pragmatic; they weigh their actions solely in terms of advantages and disadvantages for themselves. By contrast, their nondelinquent age peers are generally better able to appreciate the perspectives and feelings of others, anticipate adverse self-judgment for breaking rules, and do not want to "disappoint" their friends and family (Arbuthnot, Gordon, & Jurkovic, 1987; Blasi, 1980; Kohlberg, 1969). Arbuthnot et al. also concluded that the association between moral reasoning and antisocial behavior is not mediated by age, social class, or severity of offense. Delinquents generally reason about their behaviors the way a four-year-old might.

It is also possible for a delinquent to see a conflict from another's perspective, while not caring empathically about it on an emotional level. While empathy seems to play a significant role in the inhibition of aggression (Feshbach, 1983), studies of the association between empathy and delinquency have been inconclusive (e.g., Henggeler, 1989; Lee & Prentice, 1988). It makes sense, however, that the development of both moral reasoning abilities and empathy could reduce delinquent behavior.

Richie tended to simplify the offense that he had committed and to minimize his role in it. He cited the reduction of charges as proof that he wasn't as guilty as originally believed. He denied planning the robbery in advance, as the police had reported, and said he went along with his friend without thinking through what might happen. He explained that he needed some money to buy food because he was hungry, and that "those old folks are rich." My initial sense, perhaps based more on his small size than on what I was hearing, led me to believe that Richie's manner reflected childish impulses covered thinly by an overdeveloped bravado, and little more.

However, I got only a bit further when I tested the limits of how Richie reasoned about his behavior. Initially, he seemed to show little if any appreciation for the human implications of his recent offense. He looked puzzled when I asked him if he thought he had a right to someone else's property, and glanced away when I suggested what it must have felt like for the old man. After a brief silence, he again said, "I didn't think about it." I urged him to do so now. He did this reluctantly, like a student trying to tell the teacher the right thing: "Well, I really don't think the guy was hurt, if that's what you're asking, but maybe he was pretty scared by us." As the interview progressed, Richie tried harder to tell me what he thought I wanted to hear, participating as he knew he was expected to. However, while he expressed concern about going to jail and a desire to stay out of trouble, he did not offer a convincing account of how he would manage that, or of how he understood what had happened. I was concerned about his impulsivity and lack of reflection. The egocentricity remained even when Richie knew he should speak empathically. Yet I retained some sense that his cognitive skills were underdeveloped, rather than irrevocably calcified at this immature level.

SOCIAL COMPETENCE

Many areas of social development have been addressed by delinquency research, including social peer interactions, social cognition and social problem-solving skills, self-esteem, and behavioral norms and standards. Despite rather equivocal findings in all of these areas, a general picture persists of the delinquent as someone who lacks social and problem-solving skills, suffers from feelings of inferiority, and adheres to a system of behavioral standards which vary widely from those held by the law-abiding citizen.

In recent years, there has been growing recognition of the significance of childhood social relations for adult mental health. Unpopular children, for example, are more likely to be disproportionately represented later in mental health settings (Berndt, 1988; Cowen, Pederson, Babigan, Izzo, & Trost, 1973). Unpopular children are also more likely to be delinquent later (Parker & Asher, 1987; Roff, Sells, & Golden, 1972). In fact, the consequences of rejection by peers may be even more harmful to healthy development than the consequences of low achievement that have been documented so widely.

Some researchers even go so far as to postulate that delinquency is the product of situation-specific social-behavioral skill deficits. (e.g., Freedman, Rosenthal, Donahow, Schlundt, & McFall, 1978). In a variety of studies, these researchers distinguished delinquents from their nondelinquent peers by measuring the adolescent's level of verbal response to a role play presenting different problems in social interactions. Other researchers, using other measures, have been less confident about the deficient social skills of delinquents particularly when the mediating effects of verbal ability and IQ are considered (e.g., Curran, 1979; Henderson & Hollin, 1983). Interpersonal aggression can be a relatively adaptive and functional response to certain situations in different sociocultural contexts. For example, inner-city males are frequently put in the position of choosing either to defend themselves or be victimized by more aggressive peers. Such adolescents may behave in ways that seem adaptive at the time, and within the milieu or culture in which they live, but make them look deficient on measures that are developed to assess them outside this context.

Richie's opportunities to develop social competence had been compromised along the way by multiple school and residential placements, poor models within his family upon which to fashion his own behavior, and limited exposure to alternative modes of self-expression. On the streets where he lived, Richie seemed to be adapting to the expectations for his behavior, and he claimed to have many friends. While his social skills were clearly underdeveloped when it came to interacting with the mainstream, he lived in an environment where, until he got caught, it could be argued he had been managing adequately.

Social cognition develops through social interaction; we learn about relationships by participating in them. Accordingly, one might expect that delinquents who have deficits in social skills will also have difficulties solving social problems. Yet this expectation does not appear to have much empirical support. In one of the few studies that compare the problem-solving skills of delinquents with those of nondelinquents, Hains and Ryan (1983) found that the delinquents did not demonstrate deficits in their knowledge of viable solutions to problems. Rather, they were less likely to recognize the need to consider these solutions fully. Again, researchers appear to have failed to consider the powerful influences of situation and attitude that determine how a delinquent may think about a particular social event.

Social cognition appears to be another underexplored area of delinquency, a situation perhaps exacerbated by the lack of a developmental perspective in research, and the current emphasis on searching for deficits. What I found with Richie is that his reasoning was *distorted*, but not necessarily *deficient*. For example, he argued that, since he did not actually knock down the old man, he was somehow less at fault than his compatriot. This sort of reasoning, from a developmental perspective, is perfectly normal for a five- or six-year-old. But it also may be normal for someone who has had to live in a world qualitatively different from most boys his age. Richie's social reasoning, however twisted, may reflect accurately his experience of relationships.

PERSONALITY VARIABLES

Some researchers have concluded that low self-esteem also contributes causally to delinquency (e.g., Gold, 1978; Goldsmith, 1987; Kaplan, 1980). They argue that adolescents who have experienced relatively little success may engage in delinquent behavior simply to increase their self-esteem. While delinquents do view themselves as less competent and successful than their age peers, there is little evidence to suggest that such low self-esteem actually *causes* delinquency. Rather, it is more likely that other variables, like troubled family relationships, poor school performance, and low intelligence (all of which have also been linked to delinquency) also contribute to low self-esteem. However these problems are interactive. For example, low self-esteem can lead to school problems (or vice versa) and, taken together, these can contribute to delinquent behavior.

Richie's personality testing suggested that his view of himself was quite poor. His human figure drawing of a big muscle man with little mitten hands and a vacuous pumpkin face suggests that his tough, cool facade covered a more empty and helpless young man underneath. Richie's capacity for developing relationships may have been limited by his sense of himself as an unwanted child in a hostile and capricious world. For Richie, making sure he *looked* like he was coping adequately may have seemed necessary for survival. Getting caught in a crime probably threatened his self-esteem and shook his self-assurance significantly more than committing it in the first place.

This issue of getting caught ties in closely with the concept of alternative behavioral norms and standards that delinquent subgroups may hold despite the dominant culture around them. Clearly, they live by different rules and measures of success. (Not getting caught is part of being socially competent as a delinquent.) And behavioral norms inform all other components of social competence; for a delinquent, these would include peer interactions, problem-solving skills, and self-esteem. The mutual rejection of legally participating in society binds delinquents together. The support that delinquents get from one another is not matched by encouragement anywhere else in their lives—and this may reinforce the delinquent lifestyle.

There is ample evidence that delinquents come from homes lacking in affection, consistency, and supervision (Adams & Gulotta, 1983; Fischer, 1983; Hirschi, 1969; Patterson, 1982). Theoretically, delinquents then turn to peers for the guidance about how to behave that their parents do not provide. A lack of affection in the home and inadequate parenting also result in hostility, arrested psychosocial maturity, and deficits in empathy that further propel the adolescent into delinquent behavior. Without sufficient support and encouragement at home, delinquent adolescents get stuck in the childhood stages of impulsive behavior and preadolescent moral development. They then find peers who are similarly socially delayed.

As tidy as the reasoning appears to be, this individual- and family-blaming body of literature falls short in some important ways. First, while such dysfunctional homes may compel a child to turn to peers for support not found from parents, most children raised by marginal parents do not become delinquent. In fact, out of all the adolescents in conflict with their parents, only two or three percent turn out to be serious repetitive delinquents. Second, such a model turns the focus onto individuals, utterly ignoring cultural and economic factors which probably play an important role in maintaining most delinquent behavior. Third, it suggests that all delinquent behavior is somehow the same; the arrested development is caused by family problems, which in turn leads the delinquent to join a peer group that shares an alternative value structure. By inference, then, the problem can be solved individually, in the spirit of the medical model, by treating adolescent and family so they become more functional. There is, however, little in the treatment literature to support this notion. Delinquents coerced into treatment are usually not highly motivated clients, to say the least, and may say what they sense people want to hear yet change as little as possible.

When Richie lived in residential treatment centers, he made the greatest gains of his life. Such programs have very clear behavioral expectations, while making fewer demands than families so far as developing intimacy and trust are concerned. Richie's family had not functioned well for him. His father essentially abandoned him. His mother's limited ability to care for and protect him had been demonstrated repeatedly over the years. The school system had also let Richie down by allowing him to slip through the cracks during his many moves, and by keeping him in an academic track that lacked vocational planning or special services for his learning problems. When I met Richie, he couldn't read or write well, and had no ambition for what he might do with his life. No one was expecting much from him, either. Until he got caught, he was just another petty adolescent criminal and prankster on the streets, simply drifting his days away. Consequently, a supportive residential culture made a lot of sense for Richie; it was probably his only opportunity to grow up and learn how to support himself legally. He needed to get off the streets, but incarceration in an adult jail would have been death for this immature boy. Within the safety of such a residential treatment program, he might begin to take hold of his life.

Typology of Delinquent Adolescents

Delinquency researchers have also explored those characteristics of adolescents that make them part of groups sharing the same personality structure. One of the most interesting typologies was developed by Offer, Marohn, and Ostrov (1979) in an inpatient setting. They conducted a five-year research program with 55 delinquent adolescents and were able to fit these subjects into four types:

1. *The impulsive* delinquent shows more violent and nonviolent antisocial behavior than do the other types of delinquents. He is considered quite disturbed by his therapist, socially insensitive by his teachers, and unlikeable and quick to act by most hospital staff members. Yet he seems to have some awareness of his need for help. His delinquency derives from an overly powerful propensity for immediate action.

2. *The narcissistic* delinquent sees himself as well-adjusted and not delinquent. Parents and staff, however, recognize his difficulties in adapting, and characterize him as resistant, cunning, manipulative, and superficial. He denies problems, only makes an appearance of engaging in therapy, and exaggerates his own self-worth. His delinquent behavior is also cunning. He tends to use others to meet his needs—especially to help regulate his self-esteem.

3. *The empty borderline* delinquent is a passive, emotionally empty, and depleted youngster who is not well-liked, is sometimes an outcast and at other times is needy and

clingy, and whose future seems pessimistic. Such adolescents behave delinquently to prevent psychosis and to relieve themselves of internal desolation.

4. *The depressed borderline* delinquent shows initiative in
   school, is liked by the staff, and tries to engage therapeuti-
   cally with staff members. Relationships with parents lead
   to strongly internalized value systems; these delinquents
   show a considerable amount of anxiety and depression,
   from which delinquent behavior serves as a relief.

Within these four psychological classifications, Richie most
closely resembles the impulsive type of delinquent. His delinquent
behavior can be seen to have occurred in the context of a long
history of attention and learning problems and consistently immature reasoning about his behavior. From this perspective, Richie
was oriented to short-term goals toward which he acted precipi-
tously, without regard for the long-term consequences. However,
while behaving quite impulsively on his own, he behaved less impulsively when participating in a structured program. Similarly,
other factors in his environment could increase or decrease his
impulsive acting out.

This typology of diagnosed inpatient adolescents suggests that
delinquency can be understood as a psychological construct. In another kind of classification system, Quay (1987) stresses that delinquents are not so homogeneous as simple pathology models might
suggest. For example, Quay argues that most adolescents commit
criminal acts at some point in time. Consequently, acquiring the
status of an "official" delinquent involves a considerable element of
chance. Quay notes that the vast majority of delinquency research
comparing delinquent with nondelinquent groups misses this important point. In light of the heterogeneity of official delinquents, he
proposes a set of dimensions of behavior that exist on the same
continuum as other kinds of childhood and adolescent difficulties:

1. *Undersocialized aggression.* These adolescents display a repetitive pattern of destructive and aggressive conduct in
   which the basic rights of others are violated. They have

also failed to establish a normal degree of affection, empathy or bond with others, even with other delinquents. As delinquents, their relationships are opportunistic and shallow, and they act first and foremost for themselves.

2. *Socialized aggression.* These adolescents also display a repetitive pattern of destructive and aggressive conduct in which the basic rights of others are violated. However, they have clear evidence of being able to form attachments to others, have enduring friendships, and show concern for the welfare of their friends. As delinquents, their peer group may share their deviant values.

3. *Immaturity/attention deficit.* These adolescents display signs of developmentally inappropriate inattention, impulsivity, and hyperactivity. They tend to sound like younger children in their reasoning ability, and to commit delinquent acts without thinking through the consequences of their actions. Clearly, this describes Richie nicely.

4. *Anxiety/withdrawal.* These adolescents tend to manage stress through internalizing and retreating from social contacts. As delinquents, they may cope with anxiety by behaving in antisocial ways to relieve their feelings of internal pressure.

These two subgroup classification schemes are different from each other but share a similar assumption about the direction for treatment. In Richie's case, intervention would have to follow a protocol that made sense for impulsive and immature adolescents. Ample research indicates that a structured and undistracting learning environment is best for hyperactive adolescents like Richie.

The Family of the Delinquent Adolescent

Much has been written in recent years about the kind of family that produces a delinquent adolescent. These studies fall into four rough groups: family affect, family control, parental psychopathology, and broken homes. The studies that have been conducted have serious methodological problems (see Henggeler, 1989, for a comprehensive review). Briefly, these problems include the limitations of adolescent self-report data, poorly standardized instruments, and the intrusiveness and distortions inherent in family observations. Despite the studies' methodological flaws, it appears that families of delinquents do have particular kinds of difficulties.

FAMILY AFFECT

One of the most consistent findings in the study of the association between children's behavior problems and family relationships is that troubled families demonstrate relatively low warmth and affection and relatively high conflict and hostility (e.g., Doane, 1978; Jacob, 1975; Walsh & Scheinkman, 1993). Within delinquency research, few findings are cited as frequently as the high rates of marital and family discord (e.g., Gove & Crutchfield, 1982; Grogan & Grogan, 1968; McCord, McCord, & Zola, 1959; Tolan & Mitchell, 1990) and low levels of parental acceptance and affection (e.g., Dentler & Monroe, 1961; Glueck & Glueck, 1962; Gold, 1963; Nye, 1958; Tolan, Cromwell, & Brasswell, 1986; West & Farrington, 1973). Research further suggests that adolescents without close family bonds are more likely to become involved in delinquency than adolescents with close family relationships. Once these adolescents start experimenting with delinquent behavior, they are more likely to continue if they develop ongoing associations with a peer group of delinquents (Hurley, 1985).

However, family relationships are bidirectional and reciprocal. Difficult children and adolescents place considerable stress on the family system. Further, the broader issue of resources must also be raised. Parents with sufficient economic and social supports are better prepared to endure the stress of raising demanding adolescents, and to meet their needs for warmth and affection.

Richie's relationship with his parents was troubled from the beginning. His father's departure and his mother's poverty and alcoholism only exacerbated his learning and attention problems. His mother was further overwhelmed by becoming the sole caretaker of four boys close in age. Even without that upheaval, Richie would have been a harder-than-average child for anyone to raise, but his special needs for love and encouragement were clearly not met by his mother. Her difficulty in making an emotional commitment to him was demonstrated by his long-distance journey through the foster care system and her periodic decisions to take him from placements in which he was doing well. Most recently, he had been merely boarding in his mother's apartment; they seldom saw each other. They did not eat meals or plan activities together; she was not monitoring his school attendance except to be angry with him when she was contacted by his counselor for truancy. When asked about how people in his family took care of each other, Richie did say that the Walkman he carried was a gift from his mother, and that she bought him clothes when she could. But there was no sense of that deeper attachment which keeps adolescents connected to their parents even in the face of conflict. This impoverishment of affectionate ties made Richie more susceptible to delinquency; he did not feel he belonged anywhere, or particularly deserved to be safe and cared for.

FAMILY CONTROL

Another dimension, family control, has also been the topic of extensive research in delinquency. Lax and ineffective parental discipline was linked with delinquent behavior in many early large-scale studies. These studies concluded that parents of delinquent children, compared to parents of nondelinquent children, are more likely to engage in erratic supervision and inconsistent and inappropriate discipline, and less likely to know where their children are or who they are with when they are not at home (e.g., Craig & Glueck, 1963; Hirschi, 1969; Nye, 1958; Patterson, 1982; West & Farrington, 1973). In a review of the literature, Snyder and Patterson (1987) concluded that families of delinquents have generally used ineffective disciplinary strategies both prior to and following their adolescent's delinquent behavior. The reviewers also concluded that good supervision enables parents to respond more appropriately to adolescent misbehavior and minimizes the adolescent's contact with troubled peers. Parents of delinquents seem to lack positive family management skills, and thus lean heavily on aversive discipline. However, they are also inconsistent—sometimes punitive, sometimes threatening punishment but not following through, and sometimes unresponsive (Straus, 1984). The data are actually remarkably consistent; poor behavior-management practices in families of adolescents place these youngsters at risk for the development of delinquent behavior (e.g., Loeber & Dishion, 1987; Patterson, 1986).

In Richie's case, his mother had difficulty managing his activity level and oppositional tendencies from a very early age; she first secured therapy for him when he was six. However, she did not become more skilled or confident in handling him as time passed, alternating (in Richie's words) between "hitting me with the iron cord" and "being too out of it to care." Additionally, when he was in residential or foster care, she did not improve her parenting skills, and so he was as troublesome as ever when he returned to her. With the onset of puberty, his antisocial behaviors became even more of a problem for her. Indeed, she appeared to have given up any effort to supervise him, leaving him to fend (poorly) for himself. All the evidence indicated that Richie's mother could not control him, which placed him at high risk, indeed, for further delinquent behavior if he were to remain in her care.

PARENTAL PSYCHOPATHOLOGY

Researchers have also explored the ways in which the problems of parents contribute to delinquency in their offspring. Such problems include, for example, criminal behavior, substance abuse, physical and sexual abuse of their adolescents, and many forms of mental illness that can compromise the necessary parenting functions of monitoring, discipline, and involvement.

One of the most consistent findings in the literature is that delinquency is associated with parental criminality. In many studies, adolescents whose parents engaged in marginal or criminal activity were found to be at high risk for delinquency (e.g., Canter, 1982; West & Farrington, 1973). It is possible that a combination of genetics and environment may account for this finding. If aggressive parents are genetically more likely to have aggressive children (Trasler, 1987) this may be further exacerbated by the antisocial behavior displayed by the parents. However, the effects of modeling may be less important than the fact that such adults may also lack skills for more effective communication and control of their offspring.

Parents who are alcohol or drug abusers also produce children more vulnerable to delinquent acting out (Dryfoos, 1990). These parents tend to perform their parental functions erratically, and may be abusive or neglectful. Such a connection also points to the fact that parents who abuse drugs and alcohol are more likely to have children who do the same. In these families, the relationship between delinquency and substance abuse is complex, and not simply causal. Overall, it can be argued that the effects of parental substance abuse create a home environment that contributes to both drug use and delinquent acting out.

The relationship between child abuse (physical and sexual), neglect, and delinquency has also been explored extensively (e.g., Benward & Densen-Gerber, 1973; Brown, 1982; Lynch, 1978; Reidy, 1977). Incarcerated delinquents report excessively high rates of physical abuse, abandonment, severe parental punishment, and neglect (Dryfoos, 1990), as do adolescents reporting delinquent acts in nonclinical surveys (e.g., Brown, 1984). Some studies of female delinquents find a high incidence (over 50 percent) of having experienced sexual abuse among the girls (Benward & Densen-Gerber, 1973; Jones, Gruber, & Timbers, 1981). Parents who resort to violence to control their adolescents also lack important skills. Stressed beyond their capacities, they become abusive, which in turn conveys powerfully negative messages to their children. Delinquency may be connected to abuse in other important ways. Beyond the modeling of aggression to resolve differences, abuse itself limits an adolescent's ability to weigh options and develop a positive sense of self. Indeed, it is plausible to suggest that abuse breeds delinquency as swamps breed mosquitos.

The role of mental illness in parents of delinquents has also been explored. However, the findings do not suggest clearly why the parents' problems would lead to delinquency as opposed to other behavioral or emotional difficulties. For example, Stott (1982) describes how maternal depression was associated with delinquent behavior in some of his subjects. However, maternal depression has also been implicated in the full gamut of child psychological disorders, and is not particularly predictive of delinquency.

Richie's mother was not a criminal, but she was an alcoholic with a history of depression. She abused her children when they were smaller; now she appeared to wash her hands of disciplining them in any way at all. In fact, she was neglectful of them. It does not seem to make much sense, however, to focus exclusively on Ms. Nelson's psychopathology, since doing so only provides a narrow, more limited way of describing the broad problems of affect and control in Richie's family. It also effectively absolves Mr. Nelson of any responsibility for nurturing and supervising his son. In sum, the diagnosis of a parent has to be less significant than how all family members have managed their lives together.

BROKEN HOMES

Deviations from the "typical American family" with two parents have also been implicated repeatedly. The "broken home" has become something of a cliche in delinquency research, and is generally used to refer to a structure where the mother is a single parent (i.e., "father absence"). This ignores the array of other possibilities (mother absent, stepparent, guardian), the various reasons for parental absence (divorce, death, incarceration, disappearance), the length of parental absence, and the amount of contact with the noncustodial parent. Without any understanding of these mediating variables, the literature on the effects of family structure on delinquency must be viewed cautiously.

However, when studies attempt to delineate the functional determinants of the association between broken homes and adolescent antisocial behavior, they turn up some noteworthy findings. In one large national study, results showed that youths in mother-only households were more likely than youths with two natural parents to evidence deviant behavior and to make decisions without parental input (Dornbusch et al., 1985). Similarly, Steinberg (1987) found that adolescents living in mother-only homes, and homes where the mother had remarried, were more susceptible to negative peer pressures and engaged in more deviant behavior than their counterparts in homes with two biological parents. These studies suggest that when adolescents are more autonomous, less involved with their parents, and more susceptible to peer pressure, they are also more likely to participate in delinquent activities. However, several other studies have found that delinquents experience these kinds of relationship problems in intact biological families as well (e.g., Borduin & Henggeler, 1987; Cernkovitch & Giordano, 1987). In general, it appears that unmet parental roles—monitoring, involvement, and discipline—are more likely to be associated with delinquency than other variables (including broken homes).

Richie's delinquency was probably associated with an array of family variables in addition to his own individual difficulties. As described above, delinquent behavior is linked with low levels of family affection and high levels of family conflict, ineffective, inept, or abusive parental control strategies, and psychological problems in the parents. In addition, delinquency seems to be more prevalent in broken homes, though largely because of the functional characteristics of such homes. Such a general summary of family factors will serve as a description of Richie's life, with one necessary addition: His entry into the foster care system was also an important correlate with his delinquency (Fanshel, 1978). Multiple foster placements serve to exacerbate any problems a child has and to create additional difficulties particularly when little changes at home.

In addition to reviewing the records and test materials, I also spoke to Richie's individual and family therapist before making my recommendations to the court. The therapist had met with Ms. Nelson a handful of times over the year that Richie had been back with her. His portrayal of Ms. Nelson did little to increase my hopes that Richie would improve with her. Given Richie's age and their history together, I could not, in good conscience, recommend that Richie remain in her care. I believed that she had done the best she could, given the struggles of *her* life, including her alcoholism, the difficulty inherent in raising a hyperactive child, and the grinding effects of poverty. Given all of this, however, she could not offer Richie the limits and safety he was so obviously unable to provide for himself.

Moreover, Richie's weighty history of deprivation and broken bonds with parents and other caretaking adults had taken its toll on his ability to feel he could rely on anyone. When I asked him how he would prevent himself from acting out in the future, he responded, "I can take care of myself, like I always have." This pseudo-independent stance was, in my eyes, a defense against a tremendous need for nurturing, stable relationships. There was little in his testing materials to suggest that he truly felt he was that tough. In one of the few nonviolent stories he told to accompany picture cards, he said, "This little boy is hungry and he's gonna sit here and wait for his momma to cook him some lunch. But she ain't around, and he's gonna be hungry and mad." I also didn't buy Richie's "I don't care" stance when I pressed him about his various failures in placements and relationships. This was clearly a last-resort defense, not a fixed character trait. His connections to his therapist, his most recent foster family, and even to his mother and father, were present, however tenuous, despite the fact that he tried to be cavalier about them.

My recommendations were based upon my conclusion that Richie's growth had proceeded slowly and that his character development would need a safe, supportive environment in which to continue; it had clearly not yet solidified. Richie needed the chance to demonstrate that he could benefit from a secure residential and educational program. His history of being able to respond to therapeutic programs in the past indicated that this option should be pursued again. In such a longer-term, secure setting, Richie would be able to work on his angry and bitter feelings without becoming a danger to himself or others. At the same time, he could receive the special educational services and vocational training he needed. I did not want to exclude either of Richie's parents, and I recommended that they be involved in family counseling as well.

At the hearing on Richie's case, my recommendations were approved. He was placed in one of the better residential treatment programs in the area. In court, he seemed calmer than I remembered him. I knew he was relieved that he would not be going to be treated like an adult and incarcerated. Perhaps he was also comforted that adults around him were behaving responsibly and caringly on his behalf. When Richie was 18, he returned to the custody of his foster parents, who had maintained contact with him while he was in residential care. They supported him emotionally and financially while he completed job training in a small-engine repair program. At his most recent review, he was working part-time and had not been rearrested.

5

Adolescent Sex Offenders

Paul: "You don't know what it feels like to be me"

Adolescent sex offenders may number in the tens of thousands, though official estimates vary widely depending upon the source of the data and the sampling methods. For example, it is generally believed that arrest rates underestimate the scope of the problem since disbelief and shame on the part of the young victims and the victims' and offenders' families alike discourage the use of the juvenile justice system. However, the existing statistics do offer one important perspective. Based on data from the Federal Bureau of Investigation (1987), it appears that adolescents under the age of 18 years accounted for 15 percent of the arrests for forcible rape and 16 percent of the arrests for other sexual offenses (excluding prostitution). These data include younger adolescents as well. From 1976 to 1986, the national arrest rate for 13- and 14-year-olds accused of rape doubled, from 20 arrests per 100,000 to 40 per 100,000. For the lesser catagories of sex offenses like exhibitionism, grabbing, fondling, and other similar attacks, the arrest rate for 13- and 14-year-olds increased by 80 percent over the last decade, while the arrest rate for 12-year-olds increased by 60 percent. The offenses vary widely. In their study of approximately 300 juvenile sexual offenders, Fehrenbach, Smith, Monastersky, and Deisher (1986) found that 59 percent had committed indecent liberties (typically fondling a younger child while baby-sitting), 23 percent had committed rape (37 percent with peer or adult victims), 11 percent had exposed themselves, and 7 percent had committed noncontact offenses such as voyerism and stealing underwear. Reviewing current studies of victim reports, which probably represent the most reliable index of adolescent sexual-offense rates, Davis and Leitenberg (1987) report that adolescents are the perpetrators in 34 to 60 percent of all sexual abuse cases. Several studies indicate that 56 percent of the reported cases involving sexual abuse of male children are perpetrated by teenagers (Rogers & Tremaine, 1984; Showers, Farber, Joseph, Oshins, & Johnson, 1983). Extrapolating from national survey data, Ryan (1991) estimates that in 1986 more than 70,000 boys and as many as 110,000 girls were victims of adolescent sexual offenders. Studies that are based on self-reports (e.g., Elliot, Huizinga, & Morse, 1985; Murphy & Stalgaitis, 1987) tend to grossly underestimate the magnitude of the problem because of the stigma attached to offenders and victims alike.

In reviewing retrospective self-reports of convicted adult sex offenders, many studies concur that over half of such adults began committing sexual offenses prior to age 18 (e.g., Abel, Mittelman, & Becker, 1985; Freeman-Longo, 1983). The actual number of sexual offenses and victims is difficult to assess. However, Abel et al. (1986) reported on 240 adult offenders who described the onset of deviant sexual behavior prior to age 18; they had recalled some 581 attempted or completed acts against an average of 380 victims apiece. Finally, whether incidence and prevalence rates are based on arrests, self reports, or victim reports, about 95 percent of adolescent perpetrators are males.

The Referral

While I worked in the delinquency project, I was offered many unusual and difficult treatment cases. Because I had the luxury of good colleagues and informed supervision, I was able to take on cases I would pass up later in situations without the same supports. When Paul Peterson's mother called me, sobbing, and four other calls about Paul followed closely behind, inquiring when I would see him, I knew that this would be "one of those" cases. Ultimately, Paul and his family were referred to me by the local child protection agency, his parents, their lawyer, his mother's therapist, and the police. The involvement of so many overlapping systems is quite common in adolescent sex offender cases.

Ms. Peterson's call was painful. She was extremely emotional and had difficulty providing information to me. She had not yet told her husband, and she was almost as concerned about his reaction as she was about what Paul had done. She also felt that her neighbors would spread the bad word about Paul and that the family would be driven from the neighborhood even while Paul was sent to jail. Her sense of crisis and doom were overwhelming, and I could do little to reassure her because I did not have enough information; for all I knew, her concerns could have been legitimate. It did not take long to understand that this was a true emergency for this family. Even before I fielded the subsequent calls, I scheduled an appointment with the family for the following day.

The day before Ms. Peterson contacted me, a neighbor had called her at work, quite distraught, saying that they had to meet urgently. An hour later, Ms. Peterson met her neighbor and her neighbor's husband and learned that Paul, who was 15, had tried to make their six-year-old daughter perform oral sex upon him and had, the previous week, masturbated by rubbing against the child. Ms. Peterson told me that, during the first incident, she had gone to visit an ailing relative for a few hours; on the second occasion, she had agreed to go into work on a Saturday to help her boss finish a project. She wanted me to know that she usually supervised her children more closely.

While trying to comply with Paul's requests that she tell no one, the little girl had begun asking her mother odd, precocious questions about erections and semen. She had, additionally, become more timid about playing outside. Naturally concerned, the neighbors gradually coaxed the story from their child, and promptly reported Paul to the police and child protection. At the recommendation of child protection, they had also taken their daughter to the pediatrician and, on their own, planned to contact an attorney if Ms. Peterson did not act quickly to get help for Paul.

Ms. Peterson had waited for Paul to come home, and confronted him with the neighbors' story. He initially denied it, but quickly became highly anxious and embarrassed; he wouldn't answer many of his mother's questions, but he agreed to counseling and assured her he would cooperate with child protection and the police when he was questioned by them. He did reveal that he had been poring over a hard-core pornography collection he had found in the back of the garage his family shared with their downstairs neighbors. At first fascinated but frightened by it, he had soon taken to spending as much time as he could examining the explicit photographs. Paul told his mother that these magazines had made him act out sexually.

Ms. Peterson said that her marriage was not a happy one—her husband had left her many times. She feared that he would blame her for Paul's behavior if she told him, and worried that he might depart again because he couldn't tolerate "this sort of thing." I assured her that he would surely find out because the police and child protection were involved, and stressed that she needed to include him in Paul's counseling. I let her know that I expected to see the whole family at our appointment the next day. (Paul had an 11-year-old brother, Joe, whom I also wanted to meet.) Even though I was sympathetic to her distress, I did not want to begin working with this family in any kind of secrecy or implied collusion with anyone. Since I believe that family secrets can create an environment ripe for all sorts of adolescent violence, I jotted a note to myself that Ms. Peterson had asked me about "keeping a secret" in her initial phone call. I sensed that this family had many profound secrets its members were trying to conceal.

The subsequent phone calls I received that day were largely consistent with what Ms. Peterson had told me. Child protection needed my assessment for their report, and were particularly concerned, as is sometimes the case, that Paul might be a victim as well as an offender. They planned to meet the six-year-old victim later in the week. The police were going to interview Paul and his parents later that afternoon, and also wanted a copy of my report. Ms.

Peterson's therapist put herself at my disposal so we might assist this family in a consistent manner. Ms. Peterson's lawyer called just to tell me he would be involved if the case went to court, and also that he wanted any written material I might have. Clearly, in order to help Paul and his family in any lasting way, I had to demonstrate from the outset that I was cooperative and would work actively with all of the different systems. Doing this amounts to a lot of time on the phone, and more than the usual written documentation, but can help organize and focus the treatment so that it can proceed more smoothly.

The Adolescent Sex Offender

Paul and his family were in the waiting room for half an hour before our scheduled appointment. His brother, Joe, read a copy of *Sports Illustrated*, and the others sat in gloomy, nervous silence. I asked to meet with everyone at the outset, and said I would reserve some time at the end of the session to speak privately with Paul.

Paul did not look like his petite, slender parents and wiry brother. He was a short, husky boy with cropped brown hair and thick glasses. He did not look like the other teenagers in his suburban working-class community, either. Nor, as it became apparent quickly, was he an ordinary delinquent. Paul's attire was conservative; he wore a button-down shirt and khaki pants which bunched at his waist and flared around his ankles. In the slang of his classmates, he was more nerd than prep and had been ostracized by his peers for years. When we spoke alone, Paul revealed that he had many intellectual interests, including science fiction, *National Geographic*, and the history of the Civil War. He preferred classical clarinet and chess to rock music and sports. When we spoke of his interests and areas of success, he was able to extend himself outside of his agonizing awkwardness for brief periods. He even became mildly animated describing his passion for gemology and the prized items in his stone collection. But during the earlier discussion of the events that had occasioned our meeting, he kept his eyes downcast and mumbled brief answers, which, to his father's obvious annoyance, he often needed to repeat for clarity.

I began the hour by asking whether everyone had enough information about what had happened. Joe squirmed in his seat and said,
"Yeah, Paul sexed with Katie, right?" I asked if that was what his
parents had told him. He looked at his mother, and asked for confir-
mation, which she offered. Mr. Peterson seemed agitated and irate
as he clenched and unclenched his jaw. Brusquely, he asked me
what I planned to do. He said that he and his wife had participated
in counseling in the past and that it hadn't helped at all. His wife
responded by reminding him that he had only attended two sessions
and had argued with what the therapist had said. She also recalled
for him what their attorney had said: If Paul wasn't sent to the local
juvenile detention facility he would be ordered into therapy anyway
when he appeared in court.

I let them settle down again before summarizing for them my
plans for conducting an evaluation of Paul and the family; I explained that I would turn my findings into a report for guiding
therapeutic decisions and for legal and social service planning. I
told them that we needed as much information as possible to be
sure that we were helping Paul in the best way we knew how.
We spent the next half-hour discussing Paul's development and the
family background. Now, with the clarity of hindsight, it became
quickly evident that Paul had, all along, been at risk for becoming
an adolescent sex offender. He shared many characteristics with
other young perpetrators, including social isolation, troubled peer
relationships, difficulty expressing feelings, and confused thinking.

SOCIAL ISOLATION

Paul had been an outcast during all of his life. The activities he
enjoyed tended to be solitary, and his social life was limited and
superficial; he had always preferred playing with the younger children in the neighborhood. His mother said he had been a moody
child, and would sulk for hours up in his room when children his
own age rejected him. (Paul corrected her by saying he would go
read, and she conceded that this was probably true.) While he
claimed to have a few friends, Paul had not tried to spend time with
them outside of school, and his parents noted that when the phone
rang it was always for the gregarious Joey.

Such isolation appears to be typical of adolescent sexual offenders. Several investigators have also concluded that they tend to have pervasive emotional and interpersonal difficulties. In studies of incarcerated offenders, adolescent rapists are described as loners with poor social skills and difficulties with impulse control and the expression of anger (e.g., Deisher, Wenet, Paperny, Clark, & Ferenbach, 1982; Groth, 1977; Shoor, Speed, & Bartelt, 1966; Van Ness, 1984). Henggeler (1989) further notes that, comparing assaultive and nonassaultive delinquent and nondelinquent groups, adolescent sexual offenders evinced greater anxiety and higher rates of ruminative-paranoid symptoms (i.e., feeling estranged in their relations with others). Perry and Orchard (1992) also describe the sex offenders they studied as reluctant to establish intimate relationships, for fear of being controlled or taken advantage of, and preferring the company of much younger children.

Troubled Peer Relationships

Paul's social isolation was closely tied to how different he was from others of his age in the community. His skills for making and sustaining friendships had never been developed, and he seemed genuinely bewildered by the social whirl at the large metropolitan high school he attended.

Although evidence is sparse, there is a general consensus among researchers that adolescent sexual offenders have difficulty maintaining close interpersonal relationships (e.g., Davis & Leitenberg, 1987). Deisher et al. (1982) concluded that approximately two thirds of adolescent sex offenders have no close friends and that nearly one third have no friends at all. Ryan and Lane (1991) suggest that this lack of peer support increases the likelihood of multiple sexual offenses and that adolescents without friends are at greatest risk of re-offending.

Affect

Paul was completely unable to put feelings into words. He was willing to go along and agree with suggestions like: "Did you feel confused?" "Do you think she felt scared?" "Were you angry about that?" Yet, the more open-ended "How did that feel?" type of questions were mystifying to him, and he would simply shrug anxiously when I asked about feelings in this way.

Toward the end of our first meeting, I tried to get Paul to speculate about how he got into all of this trouble. He was silent for a moment, and tears welled up in his eyes. Then he replied softly, "No, I can't explain it to you. You don't know what it feels like to be me." I gently suggested that he also seemed at sea about *who* he was right now. I asked him if he wanted to explore with me what it felt like to be him, noting that he probably had both good and troublesome feelings. Without pausing, he agreed to meet again.

Like Paul, most adolescent sexual offenders tend to have difficulty identifying, labelling, and communicating their feelings. They usually cannot identify feelings in others, and, consequently, have difficulty being empathic. This inability to discern their own emotional needs and to be sensitive to the feelings of others allows them to continue to offend—because they do not understand the emotional reasons for their offending behaviors and are not stopped by concern for their victims. One of the goals of therapy, therefore, is to help offenders develop empathy for their victims. The first step in this process usually involves teaching offenders how to identify and communicate their own feelings. Ryan and Lane (1991) describe six categories of feelings that juvenile sexual offenders need to learn to label: (1) helplessness/powerlessness/lack of control; (2) degradation / humiliation / embarrassment; (3) fear / distrust / guilt/blame/shame; (4) victimization/persecution; (5) lack of empathy/bonding; (6) affective memories/connectedness. It appears that sexual offenders share a serious problem of extreme emotional constriction.

COGNITIONS

Although psychological testing revealed that Paul's IQ was 140, which meant that he had very superior ability, his capacity to reason about and understand his sexual acting out was extremely limited. Paul used denial, minimization, and intellectualization to defend himself from the stress of his overwhelming sexual and aggressive feelings. Without close monitoring and structure, Paul retreated into a fantasy world fueled by pornography and his own vivid imagination. In sessions with me, Paul's facility with ideas and range of opinions ground to an anxious halt when I initiated any discussion of the family or of his offenses. He said, "I don't like talking about this because I don't know why it happened. The answer is probably deep inside of me somewhere, but I just don't know what it is or how to find it there." Paul knew precious little about sexuality and reproduction. Until he read a book his mother brought home, and we discussed the information in it, he had never heard about masturbation, nocturnal emissions, or sexual intercourse, other then what he had overheard on the playground and had gleaned from the confusing photos in the sexually-explicit magazines. (Like many children of an earlier generation, he had first viewed breasts in *National Geographic*.)

Paul's confused reasoning was grounded in both pure ignorance and distorted beliefs. He explained that he thought of the little girl he had attacked as his friend, even though he was much older than she. He had been feeling tense when he was with her and believed that she would want him to feel better. He had not considered that she might be frightened, or that his actions were inappropriate in any way, only that she was going to help him "feel better."

Like Paul, adolescent sex offenders frequently exhibit a variety of inaccurate and irrational errors in how they think about events in their lives. Typically, their cognitive distortions arise from inaccurate perceptions, assumptions, and conclusions about the world. Irrational beliefs or thinking errors shape the sex offender's perceived need for power or control and justify his abusive sexual behaviors.

The cognitive elements in juvenile sex offending are pervasive; they include virtually every thought that supports or allows the progression toward sex offending. Sexual offenses are planned actions and not simply the result of impulsive, uncontrollable urges of adolescent boys. However, Paul, like most adolescent sex offenders, had great difficulty describing the steps that led to the decision to offend. Paul needed to take responsibility for his thoughts and fantasies before he could develop compensatory skills for the prevalent distortions and confusions. This involved a slow and painful dissection of his world view, his reality testing, and his problem-solving approaches.

Typology Of Adolescent Sex Offenders

Many descriptions of adolescent sex offenders assume that they all belong in one category, or that adult classification systems are sufficient. Recent researchers have attempted to develop typologies of adolescent sex offenders that describe the variation within the group and classify youthful offenders as distinct from the adults they may become. O'Brien and Bera (1986) propose one such typology; it is useful for treatment and placement decisions because it describes seven types of specific motivations and developmental deficits that need to be addressed.

1. *Naive experimenter.* This type tends to be young (under 14 years) with little history of acting-out behavior. He is sexually naive and engages in only one or a very few sexually exploratory acts with a younger child (2 to 6 years) using no force or threats.

2. *Undersocialized child exploiter.* The undersocialized child exploiter evidences chronic social isolation and social incompetence. His abusive behavior is likely to be chronic and includes manipulation, rewards, or other enticement. He is motivated to offend by a desire for greater self-importance and intimacy.

3. *Pseudo-socialized child exploiter.* This type has good social skills and little acting-out history and is apt to present as self-confident. He may himself be a victim of physical or sexual abuse. He is likely to have been sexually offending for years. He tends to be motivated by a desire for sexual pleasure through exploitation, typically rationalizes his assaults, and feels little guilt or remorse.

4. *Sexual aggressive.* The sexually aggressive offender comes from an abusive chaotic family. He is likely to have a long

history of antisocial acts, poor impulse control, and substance abuse. His sexual assaults involve force. He is motivated to offend by a desire to experience power by domination, to express anger and to humiliate his victim.

5. *Sexual compulsive.* These adolescents come from families
that are usually emotionally repressive and rigidly enmeshed.
His offenses are repetitive, often of a compulsive nature,
and are more likely to be hands-off (e.g., peeping or exposing). His motivation for offending may be the alleviation of
anxiety.

6. *Disturbed impulsive.* This type is likely to have a history of
psychological disorder, severe family dysfunction, substance abuse, and significant learning problems. His offenses are impulsive and reflect periods of diminished contact with reality.

7. *Group influenced.* The group-influenced offender is apt to
be a young teen with no previous delinquent history who
engages in an assault in the company of a peer group. The
motivation is apt to be peer pressure and the desire for
approval.

Paul's profile was consistent with some of the characteristics of a
type 2 (undersocialized child exploiter) and some of a type 5 (sexual
compulsive) sex offender. In the context of a repressive family structure, which contributed to his high level of anxiety, his social isolation and social incompetence limited the outlets for his feelings.
(The chronicity of his behavior became evident when, eight months
after the first disclosure, he was accused of, and admitted to, a
similar offense against his six-year-old cousin, whose home he was
visiting.)

The Family of the
Adolescent Sex Offender

Mr. and Ms. Peterson met when he was in the military and a friend
of his was dating her sister. A torrid long-distance romance, punctu-
ated by short visits to her town, resulted in Ms. Peterson's preg-

nancy with Paul. Subsequently they got married. The marriage was troubled from the beginning, and Mr. Peterson left and returned three times before Paul was three years old. While he separated from his wife several times more after that, he threatened to leave even more often, packing his bags on several occasions each year. The boys were aware of most of these episodes; the volume of their parents arguments and the small size of their apartment, left little doubt about what was happening.

Mr. Peterson also conducted multiple affairs during the first 12 years of the marriage. On one occasion, he was caught by Paul and Joe; they recognized the family car while walking home from the school bus, and looked in to find their father embracing someone. Mr. Peterson then told his wife, promising to stop. He admitted to many other instances of infidelity but claimed that he had not thought about how his behavior might hurt his family. The boys believed that their father was now faithful to their mother, but she did not—a point of ongoing stress in the marriage.

Mr. Peterson admitted readily that he had difficulty being close to people, even his own children, saying he was not accustomed to it. He had come from a small Calvinist farm community in which work and silence had been rewarded. He had been unable to talk to Paul about reproduction, sexuality, friendships, dating, or any of the emotional topics important to an adolescent boy. On occasion, Paul had asked his father a few questions about sex, but had gotten vague answers and avoidant responses like "I'm too busy now, we'll talk about it later" or "Go ask your mother." In truth, his father was not much more available on less-charged topics. For example, he had encouraged Paul's interest in American history by giving him books he had finished, but he had never discussed them with Paul. Mr. Peterson worked two jobs, which ensured that he saw little of his wife and children.

Ms. Peterson's family of origin was a large, meddling Italian clan, most of whose members lived within walking distance of the Petersons. And, although Ms. Peterson waited several months to tell me, her now-deceased father had sexually abused her and two of her sisters. The traumatic effects of her own abuse may have made it more difficult for her to think about her son's sexuality. She particularly resented her husband's lack of support in this delicate area.

Overinvolved with her own family, she also understood little about the process of individuation. She appeared to view Paul's movement into adolescence as similar to her husband's infidelity—as another kind of betrayal.

Paul's offense, which at one level signalled his adolescence and individuality, also had the paradoxical result of bringing the family back into an intimate, preadolescent arrangement. By demonstrating his inability to handle independence, he created a situation in which his parents had to closely monitor his life, revoking all the privileges he ostensibly wanted. At the same time, his sexual acting out and secrecy mirrored all too closely his father's own transgressions and the serious communication deficits in the Peterson marriage.

While the Petersons had not been able to negotiate well before Paul got into trouble, the situation intensified after he was adjudicated delinquent and placed on three years of probation. Mr. Peterson missed many family therapy appointments with weak excuses; it seemed he could not handle the troubling feelings that therapy aroused in him. At the same time, he became even less involved in his family life, and again talked about separating. Ms. Peterson reacted differently. She cut back on her work schedule, and became extremely vigilant about both boys: where they were, what they were doing, and who they were with. She never missed an appointment. She continued to put pressure on Mr. Peterson to participate, but he resisted both passively (forgetting plans) and actively (adding to the hours of his second job to compensate for her lost hours).

Therapy for the Family of the Adolescent Sex Offender

The Petersons shared many characteristics with other families of adolescent sexual offenders. Several researchers have noted similar problems including, for example, emotional impoverishment, lack of appropriate affect, dangerous secrets, distorted attachments, and, frequently, a history of disruptions in care and functioning (e.g., Ryan 1991; Thomas, 1991). The adolescent sex offender often acts as a receptacle for negative feelings in the family (especially shame, guilt, and anxiety). His sexual offending may become the presenting symptom in a long history of family difficulties.

Family therapy, therefore, needs to bring family members together into a more realistic and productive pattern of communication. To this end, I emphasized eight areas of concern in my treatment of the Petersons.

AGE-APPROPRIATE INVOLVEMENT

The physical, emotional, psychological, and/or sexual boundaries in the adolescent sex offender's family may be blurred or nonexistent.

In the Peterson family, Ms. Peterson's own history of incest gave her a very conflicted understanding of how to nurture her boys as adolescents. She tended to remain emotionally and instrumentally involved with them, much as she had been when they were younger. For example, she still selected her sons' clothes and decided which outfits they would wear each day by laying them out the night before. Even before the disclosure of Paul's problems she had monitored the boys quite closely considering their ages and the general safety of the neighborhood in which they lived. She blamed herself for Paul's transgressions, because she had gone against her own judgment and let the boys persuade her that she could go to work on the weekend without sending them to stay with a relative. They were expected to come right home from school, and could not play in the park, or go to the town pool on their own, as was common for their age peers. Consequently, Paul had not developed his own controls. He relied heavily on the infantilizing rigidity of his home to organize himself. He got into trouble when his parents went to visit relatives, or were at work more than they had been scheduled to be.

ISOLATION

Some families of adolescent sex offenders perceive that the outside world is so hostile that they must close themselves off from it. This can lead to family secrecy, loss of reality checks, and a lack of support systems in the community.

Mr. Peterson's family lived in another part of the country; he seldom saw or spoke to them. He had no real friends, and was not interested in socializing; he even bowled alone. Friends from his days in the Marines had gradually slipped away, and he had not replaced them. Ms. Peterson's free time was taken up by her demanding mother and various other relatives. While she had a couple of friends at work, the crisis with Paul led her to realize that she had no one, save her therapist, to whom she could speak about serious matters in her life. As an incest survivor, she had grown used to feeling isolated and different, and was quite shy about how to approach people on a deeper level. Her marriage had taught her little about sharing and reaching out, since any intimacy was followed rapidly by conflict.

Isolation of family members can also be exacerbated by multiple family secrets. The juvenile sexual offenses may be only the most recent cause of family shame and embarrassment. In fact, the secrets that exist within these families are often pervasive and may span generations. The proverbial "skeletons in the closet" typically include more than just sexual abuse. Denial may have obscured many forms of dysfunction, including substance abuse; physical and emotional abuse; criminal records; mental illness; physical infirmities; and social, marital, and vocational failures (Imber-Black, 1993). Not only are such secrets kept within the family, they may be kept from other family members. Like Ms. Peterson's incest, and Mr. Peterson's affairs, Paul's sexual offenses would not have been disclosed by him to anyone. It is not only the punitive judgment of others that is feared but also the secret itself. Like many families of adolescent sex offenders, the Peterson family appeared to be superstitious and rigid in the belief that secrets will be more painful and powerful if they are acknowledged or discussed. Such families believe that secrets are dangerous not in the keeping but in the telling.

Joey's openness and warmth were a mystery to his relatives. He was the only one in the family who knew how to make and keep friends, and his ability amazed everyone else. While they belittled him for being a mediocre student, or "the party animal of the family," his easy grin and goofy goodwill were important glue for these isolated, hurting people. When Joey missed family sessions, things seemed heavier and more hopeless, and the focus was relentlessly on Paul.

EXTREME EXTERNAL AND INTERNAL STRESS

The adolescent sex offender's family typically has a large number of intra- and extra-familial problems, such as debt, illness, legal difficulties, and extended family conflict. Constant exposure to such stress weakens family resources. Coping mechanisms may be poor or maladaptive.

For the Petersons, chronic marital stress was compounded by financial difficulties necessitating that Mr. Peterson work two jobs, and by Ms. Peterson's continued entanglement with her family of origin, whom her husband disliked intensely. Given the degree of tension in the home, even before Paul had offended it was not surprising that the ensuing crisis was not resolved easily.

Mr. Peterson decided to move out about seven months after I met the family for the first time. I had seen him five times, and had noticed that in each meeting he seemed more withdrawn and depressed. No one was surprised when he took his belongings to a studio apartment a bus ride away; he continued to see the boys on the Sundays he wasn't working—about twice a month. Paul had noted that his father wouldn't look him in the eye or speak to him much anymore, and felt that his father had broken the fragile tie that connected them.

That spring vacation, a month after Mr. Peterson had moved out, Ms. Peterson took the boys to visit relatives, and Paul again offended, this time against a young cousin, by masturbating with her on his lap. She disclosed this to her mother (Ms. Peterson's sister) immediately, having been educated just a week earlier in school about "good touch and bad touch." The family chaos that ensued brought Mr. Peterson back into the fray, but I decided that Paul needed to be hospitalized to be safe from both his own internal confusion as well as the fury of his home. Paul's transgression was also in direct violation of his probation; we were able to get the court to approve this decision without delay, in so doing also ensuring the safety of the community for a time.

INTERGENERATIONAL SEXUAL AND/OR PHYSICAL ABUSE

Adolescent sex offenders and other family members may have been victims of abuse or may have been abusive, sometimes dating back generations. It is not uncommon for the offender to have been abused by older family members and for his parents to have been victimized as well.

Ms. Peterson's own sexual abuse became a focus of her individual therapy as she tried to understand how her history could be repeating itself. Her survivor's tendency to blame herself also made it more difficult for me to place the onus on Paul to accept full responsibility for his behavior. There was no evidence that either parent had sexually abused Paul, although Mr. Peterson had used a belt on his bare bottom to punish him when he was younger. Such physical violence had been commonplace on the farm where Mr. Peterson was raised, and he was amused at my concern over this history, noting scornfully that "this was candy camp compared to what we got for half of what Paul did." His extramarital affairs served further to provide the message that the family was not a safe haven for its members.

IMPAIRED COMMUNICATION STYLES

Communication patterns in families with an adolescent sex offender tend to be indirect, with feelings and thoughts expressed through behavior or in such obscure ways that family members often misunderstand one another.

It rapidly became evident to me that Paul was not alone in finding it difficult to express himself directly and put feelings into words. Indeed, hearing of Mr. Peterson's mute helplessness as he packed his bags, only to unpack them a few hours later, I saw a close parallel to Paul's bewilderment. Ms. Peterson noted that Paul and his father were "two peas in a pod; they're my strong, silent types. Joey is more of a chatterbox like me." While Ms. Peterson was better able to say what was on her mind, her messages were often lost in her rather dramatic presentation.

A vivid example of this evolved in a family meeting in which Paul had been doing well and the focus shifted to Joe, who had, the day before, stopped after school at a baseball card store, which made him about a half an hour late getting home. In the session, Ms. Peterson resumed raging at him (as she reportedly had the previous day) saying how irresponsible he was, and, weeping, asking rhetorically what had she done to deserve two such thankless children. When I asked Joey why he thought his mother was so upset, he said, shaking his head, "She likes to yell at us." I suggested to him that his mother actually had reason to feel frightened when he was not home on time without calling. He looked amazed, and said he did not think she should be. I turned to Ms. Peterson, and asked for clarification: "Were you worried when Joey wasn't home by 3:15? I know I might have been if that was the plan." She responded tearfully, "Of course. It is such a dangerous world out there and I would die if anything happened to [him]." She later confessed that she was additionally concerned about Joe's also becoming a sex offender. Both the fear of his being victimized and of his possibly offending were real for her and important for Joe to know. We established that he would call or plan ahead if he wanted to go with some pals to the card shop on the way home. In similar situations, we practiced matching up feelings with speech and behavior, while beginning to set up more age-appropriate expectations and consequences.

Even Mr. Peterson made some headway. After Paul went into the hospital, his father returned home. He came into one of our last couples sessions proudly relating that, after a bad day at work, his wife had nagged at him about something. He said he had thought to himself, "This is too much, I can't stand it," and had taken his suitcase out of the closet and tossed it on the bed. For the first time, however, he had looked up at his wife and asked her, "Do you think I should go, or do you want me to stay and try to talk about this?" She had given him a hug and taken the suitcase from him, impulsively throwing it out the window. They were able to laugh about this, and to begin to work on the most basic of intimacy issues: finishing an uncomfortable conversation.

CONFLICTING MESSAGES FROM PARENTS

In adolescent sex offender families, parental roles can be a caricature of themselves. For example, one parent may be extremely involved with the children while the other parent is completely disengaged. With such extremes of involvement, the sex offender's parents are likely to be less emotionally supportive or nourishing than more moderate levels of functioning might make possible.

The Petersons presented a classical model of a distant, emotionally unavailable father and an intrusive, overcontrolling mother. My initial efforts to rectify this imbalance were met with such unhappiness by both parents that I realized I had to change my expectations dramatically. Instead of demanding that Mr. Peterson stay involved, I continued to invite him and to let him know that he was an important player in Paul's life. At the same time, I worked with the ever-available Ms. Peterson on what she might do to parent her boys more effectively, given the possibility that her husband would never do much more than he was doing currently. I gave her the message that we wouldn't spend a lot of time waiting around for him to decide he wanted to be more involved; we had plenty of work to do without him. The children needed her to think through her methods of controlling their behavior. Her idea of limits and expectations made little sense to the boys. Paul had seldom tested her rules, preferring to be at home anyway. It was Joe who had argued for more freedom, and he felt the greater injustice when his mother returned home to monitor his every move.

Ms. Peterson's improving ability to set age-appropriate limits and speak more clearly also had a salutary effect on the marriage. Instead of leaning out of the opposite sides of a capsizing boat, they gradually moved in a bit—and the boat was therefore able to float more easily. The positive consequences of these minor shifts were most quickly noticed by Joey, whose frenzied goodwill was taking a toll on him, as it might on anyone feeling the need to be cheerful all of the time. A few months into treatment, by which time Ms. Peterson was beginning to let him select his clothes and expecting him to make his own school lunch, I asked him if he had noticed any changes at home. He thought a moment and replied somberly, "Mom isn't on my case all of the time anymore, and I can go skateboarding if my chores are done. When I get home, it's like calmer or something." While these minor adjustments did not affect Paul directly at the time, they ultimately made his home a safer and clearer place for him, too.

EMOTIONAL DEPRIVATION

Emotional needs for nurturance and closeness are typically not met in families with an adolescent sex offender, and parental skills are limited in this area.

Paul's feelings of estrangement from his family were profound. He saw his mother's involvement as something she did for herself and not for him. She did not understand him, or any of his interests, and they had had a long history of her "cleaning up" his projects in his room, throwing away valuable stones and magazines. This he felt, rightfully, was a violation of his privacy. Mr. Peterson, who might have been able to understand Paul, was not interested or available, further contributing to his son's lack of connections at home. Without parents who actively supported his unusual interests, Paul became even more of an outcast in his community. More importantly, he felt devalued in his isolation. No one was able to take care of him in the ways he felt he needed.

Early in the therapy, I had Paul meet an elderly psychiatrist friend of mine who knew a lot of American history and also happened to play passable clarinet. I hoped not only to get a consultation from my colleague, but also to provide Paul with an adult who shared some of his enthusiasms. Their relationship turned out to be an important one for Paul and, when they passed each other in the halls of the clinic, they invariably became absorbed in an intense dialogue about something Paul had read or thought about.

While our individual and family therapy sessions also offered Paul the unusual experience of being nurtured and respected, he most clearly began to internalize and consolidate these experiences after he had been hospitalized for a few weeks. He confided in me, "The group confronts you when you're full of shit, but they want to see you succeed and feel better. These kids are sort of like my family now." Paul was able to develop relationships outside of his family that better met his needs for nurturance and closeness. As an older adolescent, he had to come to terms with the limitations of what his parents could offer him, and to learn the skills he needed to assure that his emotional needs would be met elsewhere. While he loved his parents and Joey, he could not make and sustain connections with them that would provide him with an internal map of how to interact positively in the world. Neither his mother's anxious hovering nor his father's remote disapprobation offered viable solutions to his problems in identifying and describing his own feelings or the feelings of others. Like many juvenile sexual offenders, Paul needed to reach beyond his family to begin to heal.

ABUSE OF POWER

In families of adolescent sex offenders, family members, particularly parents, do not know how to use power, and often react to external stimuli instead of an internal value system. Behind such abuse of power are feelings of powerlessness. For example, Mr. Peterson's strict and punitive childhood gave him a tremendous, fearful respect for those in authority over him; at the same time it provided him with a limited model of how to behave when he was himself an adult and expected to be powerful. He acted externally like someone with power, but could only sustain this facade by keeping himself at an emotional distance from his family. Behind this mask was a man who felt utterly disempowered when it came to his wife and children. Ms. Peterson's own feelings of powerlessness were closely connected both to the intrusive, dominating relationship she had had with her own mother, as well as her history as an incest survivor. Without feeling empowered inside of herself, she substituted a high level of vigilance to compensate for her terror about keeping herself and those she loved safe.

Empowerment must be based in reality. Empowered parents feel in charge of, and responsible for the care of their children, responding to the changes in their children's development with changes in the ways they manage the family. When parents feel powerless, they will either abdicate responsibility (while reserving the right to make punitive judgments), as Mr. Peterson did, or involve themselves in power struggles designed to keep the children behaving as though at a younger age, as Ms. Peterson did.

Parental problems over empowerment can unconsciously encourage or support offending behaviors. For an offender, feeling helpless and out of control can trigger an assault. When families are out of control, an adolescent has no external boundaries to guide the control of his behavior. While Paul and his family were in weekly therapy with me, I was able to assist them in, and model for them, age-appropriate ways of setting limits and developing expectations for the boys' behavior. During this time, Ms. Peterson acted in an increasingly empowered manner. However, when her husband moved out, she leaned on me to assist her in following through on decisions she had made.

Without my weekly monitoring, Paul again lost the sense of external support he required to stay in control, and he reoffended when the family took a two-week vacation. It seemed to me that all of the Petersons needed a safer situation in which to practice empowerment. With Paul in the hospital, his parents were able to take an unhurried look at their dysfunctional patterns, and to work together to take charge of Joey (who was turning into somenthing of a live wire as he approached his own teen years). Similarly, Paul was able to benefit from the extremely structured hospital routine to begin to find ways to learn how to control himself.

I saw Paul on several occasions in the hospital and I was pleased to see him befriending one or two boys of his own age as he learned how to put feelings into words. I also worked with Mr. and Ms. Peterson, who agreed to give their marriage another try. Without Paul in the home, they were able to relax more and take time to look at their own troubled communication. Along with the hospital staff, I prepared the family for Paul's return. I agreed that he would be well-served by an offenders group that they offered once he was discharged. However, as the time approached, we all decided he would be better helped by entering a residential treatment program instead of going back home when his hospital stay was over. He did not reenter his community again for more than two years. At age 17, Paul knew that if he reoffended he would probably be treated as an adult, so he had more at stake in staying with his program.

When I ended my work with the Petersons in the summer, the family had changed in some important ways. Paul was living in the residential treatment program, where he was likely to remain for some time. However, he had earned ample privileges there, and spent many weekends at home. He had earned a reputation as a chess whiz among some of the boys and delighted in teaching them what he knew. He had also begun lifting weights, and even his father noticed his new upper body strength with admiration. Mr. Peterson had moved back home and appeared determined to stay there. However, the marriage still had more than its share of rough spots, and his work schedule continued to limit the time he felt he could spend resolving conflicts. He did not increase his involvement with his family as much as I hoped he would. When Joey was caught selling baseball cards to younger children the week before we ended our therapy sessions, I feared this would precipitate a full-blown family crisis. Instead, happily, Mr. and Ms. Peterson decided together how to discipline him, and only mentioned the situation to me in passing.

At our last session, Ms. Peterson brought in a cake to give me as a gift. I suggested that we treat it as a birthday cake for the family, noting that we should celebrate their new abilities to function as a family and to handle adolescent boys. With a twinkle in his eye, Joey added, "This family needs some of those trick candles that keep lighting just when you think you're done." Mr. Peterson retorted, "Even those candles would stay out with all the hot air in this room blowing on them."

I felt encouraged that, together, this family would be better able to blow out the inevitable trick candles and other mishaps it encountered along the way. Their greater cohesiveness, along with the other supports Paul was developing, vastly decreased the likelihood that he would reoffend. I am never certain about these things, but as I wrapped up the remaining cake at the end of the day, I felt hopeful.

6

Physically Abused Adolescents

Dawn: "Maybe it's my fault; I don't really know"

The special problems of abused adolescents have only recently begun to be addressed, despite evidence that adolescents constitute a significant and increasing proportion of child-abuse cases. According to the American Humane Association (1986), of known child-abuse cases 24 percent concern 12- to 17-year-olds, making adolescent abuse twice as prevalent as abuse of children under 6 years old. These statistics suggest that adolescents may be more vulnerable to abuse than infants and small children. The National Incidence Study *revealed that 192,000 American adolescents were known to be maltreated in 1980 (National Center on Child Abuse and Neglect, 1981), and most studies estimate that the actual incidence is much greater than reported (e.g., Finkelhor, 1986; Schillenbach & Guerney, 1987).*

The consequences of adolescent abuse are also severe: 24 percent of fatalities and 41 percent of serious injuries reported in cases of child abuse occur to adolescents between the ages of 12 and 17.

Cases of adolescent abuse involve girls twice as often as boys, whereas there is a more equal balance between the sexes among cases involving preteens. The National Incidence Study *concluded that adolescent girls are one-third again as likely to be abused as girls under age 12. It is evident that teenage girls are at risk for physical and sexual abuse to a degree not fully appreciated in either the clinical or the research literature on child abuse.*

The Referral

One morning, before I had even settled at my desk, I received an urgent call from a high school guidance counselor. Through this conversation, I first heard about Dawn Demato. Dawn, a 15-year-old sophomore, had arrived late for school that day, with thick make-up on her face. Since she had turned 12, Dawn had been known in school for carrying a large pocketbook filled to the brim with blushes, lipsticks, mascaras, and eyeshadows, each with an array of brushes with which to apply it; she spent parts of her free periods reapplying colors to her face on the outside chance that they had begun to fade or smear.

On that day, however, despite her expertise with make-up, a large purple bruise was clearly discernible on Dawn's cheek. The counselor had asked her about this as she had about other injuries in the recent past, and had once again received unconvincing and evasive answers. Dawn had wriggled uncomfortably in her chair and concentrated on picking nail polish off her pinky instead of answering questions. When the counselor had persisted, Dawn had suggested that she had bumped into her closet door in her dark bedroom. However, the guidance counselor had then recalled for Dawn past conversations, including one about a dislocated shoulder a month before (Dawn had explained that injury by saying she had been play-wrestling with someone and it had just "popped out") and a black eye just two weeks ago (Dawn had described this as a "car-door injury"). I later learned that Dawn had concealed many other bruises and lacerations to her neck and torso under her hair and clothing over the past year.

Dawn continued to deny that her facial bruise had been inflicted by anyone but she had agreed to return to her counselor's office during a study period later that morning to talk some more. In the meantime, the guidance counselor wanted some advice from me about how to proceed. I suggested to her strongly that she needed to make a report to child protection services; she made the call, without enthusiasm, to an intake worker immediately after we hung up. There are many reasons why suspected abuse is unreported.

1. *Fear of What Protective Services Won't Do.* Guidance counselors like Dawn's, and others who are in a position to report, often feel that the situation is ambiguous and the evidence insufficient, and that an initial investigation followed by inadequate involvement with the family might create more problems for the adolescent than it solved. In many states, overwhelmed child protection workers will tend to concentrate on the more vulnerable (younger) children, and on sexual-abuse cases; it can be difficult to get protective services for physically abused adolescents. (In Dawn's case, after investigating, a social worker from child protection "kept the case open" for six months, but provided no additional services to the Demato family.)

2. *Maintaining a Special Relationship.* Adults who help adolescents are frequently fearful that they will lose a special relationship by violating the confidentiality of a teenager, and sincerely believe (sometimes correctly) that they would be more effective working on their own. However, there is no clear and consistent evidence for this belief; adolescents usually understand quite rapidly why abuse must be reported, especially if a safety plan has been made. Much of the time, the fear of losing the special relationship is more a problem of countertransference on the part of the counselor—it feels good to be the only one who can apparently help and to be confided in. Dawn knew that her counselor had put in a lot of caring hours. After a brief display of anger and disappointment when she learned about the call to child protection services, Dawn resumed her regular weekly visits to "check in" with the counselor.

3. *Adolescents Say Not To.* Adolescents can be very persuasive in arguing why it is in their best interest not to report the abuse even when they acknowledge that they are being victimized. Bright and highly verbal adolescents can lead adults to believe that they are relatively adept at managing their own cases. Dawn had convinced

her counselor for more than a year that the situation was under control.

4. Adolescents Present with Different Serious Problems. Adolescents respond to abuse in ways that may divert attention from the central cause and distinguish them from younger children. The dearth of research on adolescent victims could be in large part the result of reactive behavior that shifts attention away from the abusive incidents to the victims' conduct. For example, until the counselor began to take special interest in Dawn's victimization, all of their previous school meetings had focused on Dawn's attendance and deteriorating performance. Her parents had been supported in the frustrations they felt with her disobedience and challenges to their authority at home. Significantly, delinquency, running away, truancy, drug and alcohol use, schizophrenia, prostitution, teen pregnancy, juvenile homicide, parricide, and suicide have *all* been associated with the abuse of adolescents. While abuse itself does not cause all of the social problems of adolescence, it is turning up with notable regularity in studies of teenagers that do not begin as research into abuse, and it appears to be clearly associated with many social ills.

5. Adolescents Don't Always Look Like Victims. Abuse of teenagers does not typically involve broken bones, spiral fractures, bleeding in the head, or other extreme injuries generally associated with physical child abuse. Although Dawn had sustained serious injuries, they were not as appalling as those typically inflicted upon infants. As with other adolescents, Dawn did not usually act like a "victim." She had a verbal and behavioral repertoire that often included outrageously provocative gestures, such as swearing at her parents for mistrusting her and then shinning down the fire escape after being sent to her room. Additionally, while she may not always have used restraint, she did have better impulse control than young children and so was more responsible for her relationships with others. Further, she was mobile and could participate independently in school and extracurricular activities, so she had access to external social supports if she felt she really needed them. Although Dawn was considerably smaller than her father, she was full-grown, and worked hard, as many teens do, to appear more mature than her

years. In sum, the discrepancies between power and resources that
are so critical to the definitions of abuse employed by professionals
(Finkelhor, 1983) are not usually apparent on first glance in adolescent cases and may thus be overlooked altogether.

6. *We Worry Less About Adolescents.* It is also probable that
adolescent abuse is taken less seriously because the role of adolescents in their families is viewed differently and tends to generate
less concern—particularly if there is no history of child abuse. Dawn
did not receive more than a spanking until she turned 13. Since
then, adults who had seen her struggling ascribed her difficulties to
"the teenage years." It is true that conflict is generally heightened
in families with teenagers, and the developmental tasks of this period often create new problems for family members. Indeed, an
adolescent's rebellious "identity crisis" is typically timed to collide
with the insecure "midlife crisis" of her parents, precipitating painful family changes that members may resist. Although adolescence
is disruptive for many families, the abusive parent views an adolescent's move toward greater independence with particularly intense
frustration and anger. Dawn's father proved to be terrified about
his daughter's increasing self-sufficiency. Paradoxically, he became
violent in part from fear that she would not be safe outside of the
home, beyond his protection.

7. *Abused Adolescents Are Seen by Overwhelmed Systems.* Despite the number of situations in which disclosure is possible, abuse
of adolescents often goes undetected and untreated. Many groups
of professionals come into frequent contact with abused adolescents: child protection workers, runaway/crisis shelter staff, juvenile court and probation officers, police, family court attorneys and
judges, predelinquent diversion counselors, residential treatment
staff, community mental health and child guidance therapists, teachers and school administrators, and primary-care physicians. Professionals in these settings tend to be extremely busy, with in-
numerable daily struggles, since disturbed adolescents often exert
dervishlike energy acting out and otherwise causing attention to be
paid to their problems. However, it is not just impending burn-out
that causes such professionals to focus on the task at hand (e.g.,
teach the teen, adjudicate the shoplifter, do the school physical,

listen to complaints about curfew). Rather, the necessity of these tasks is evident and the abuse may not be.

Furthermore, once abuse is identified, case management can be even more time-consuming. For example, Dawn's counselor was responsible for 250 other students, but had to spend three full days on Dawn's case, making sure she had set up the appropriate interventions and writing all of the reports requested by the school and child protection services.

8. Interventions Are Limited. Even when adolescent-abuse cases are identified, therapeutic resources are scarce and expert opinion is divided and incomplete about what treatments are most effective. Although Dawn and her family cooperated and agreed to individual and family therapy, such a course is not always the most advisable one for adolescents who would not be safe at home. Some adolescents will speak in group therapy but give an individual and family therapist the cold shoulder. Yet, the foster-care system is overburdened, particularly for troubled, hard-to-handle teens. Residential care, meanwhile, is costly and time-limited; without appropriate aftercare planning, teens will return home to find little changed. And, in the interim, abused adolescents stir up other problems— commit crimes, get expelled from school, get caught drinking— which brings in more experts and systems in typical patchwork fashion.

Since abused adolescents are often masters of crisis, I should not have been surprised when the counselor called me the next day to say she had spoken to Dawn and then Dawn swore at her before bolting from school. While I was concerned about this, as I always am when a teenage girl gambles using her safety, I also noted that Dawn may have helped out the counselor by upping the ante. Adolescents frequently escalate their troubling behaviors to communicate the seriousness of a problem when more moderate routes appear unlikely to help. It is impressive, indeed, to examine the magnificent gestures that abused adolescents make (often unconsciously) to get help for their families. In fact, the full spectrum of violent behavior problems, from suicide attempts at one end of the acting-out continuum to homicidal delinquency at the other, can be closely associated with abuse of adolescents.

Indeed, the crisis that Dawn's absence precipitated proved to be just the catalyst that the Dematos needed to agree to family treatment. When she spoke to Ms. Demato, the counselor raised her concerns about Dawn's attendance and performance in school, and went over a dated list of the injuries she had recorded. In an effort to keep Dawn from being blamed for speaking out against her parents, the counselor emphasized that Dawn had denied that any of her injuries had been deliberately inflicted. However, she informed Ms. Demato that she still believed that someone was hurting Dawn and that she had a legal obligation to report Dawn's bruise to child protection. She encouraged Ms. Demato to call me. I later learned that, although Mr. Demato was initially enraged, he gradually grew responsive to his wife's persuasive logic. He agreed, reluctantly, that their participation in family therapy could help them to manage Dawn better and make things run more smoothly at home. (She also suggested that my involvement might get the nosy social workers out of his hair more quickly.) Ms. Demato called me to set up an appointment for the family. I agreed, but requested to see Dawn alone first. If Dawn had been abused, I did not want to place her at further risk by asking her to answer tough questions that might provoke her parents, or get myself in the middle of a shouting match right away.

The Physically Abused Adolescent

Dawn came to her first appointment dramatically dressed. A slender, wiry 15-year-old, she had enormous brown eyes and short dark hair, which was spiked, punk-style, around her small face. Her make-up job was proficient if a little much (perhaps borne of some necessity to disguise both the bruises and herself); her lipstick and nails were both a dark red. At the defiant outer edge of fashion for the suburban neighborhood in which she lived, Dawn wore leopard spandex pants, big loop earrings and stiletto-heeled red shoes. Before she sat down, she sauntered over to my toy shelf and removed a little stuffed monkey. For the duration of that hour, and many that followed it over the next year, she sat with that monkey in her lap, cuddling and stroking it. The mix of pseudo-maturity and childlike innocence she revealed in that instant came to define for me the whole problem of abused teenagers—stuck in time, unable to move ahead with confidence.

After I explained to Dawn that I was a psychologist specializing in working with adolescents and their families (and mentioned the limits of confidentiality), I told her that I could help her if she let me know the truth about what was going on. To assist her in getting past the initial disclosure. I made some educated assumptions about what had happened, based upon my conversations with both the school counselor and her mother. She did not contradict these. Following some more general conversation about her family, friends and school, I asked if she could tell me about the most recent incident. At first, she had many questions about the consequences of telling me; I answered her as honestly as I could. While it is not up to someone outside of child protection to dictate a social-service plan, I knew that the social worker would consider my suggestions seriously. However, I couldn't guarantee anything. I emphasized that everyone would work together to keep her safe, and because of her age, we would consider her thoughts on the subject, too. She expressed hope that she wouldn't have to repeat her tale to lots of other strangers, and real concern that she would be put in a foster home or that someone would go to jail.

Then she did not speak for several minutes. She studied the monkey for a moment, looked up at me and around my room at my dinosaur collection, my dollhouse, and my walls covered with the artwork of younger patients. (Later, she would tell me that all of my "play therapy junk" made her feel that it would be helpful to talk to me—anyone who spent her days "on the floor with little kids couldn't be too bad.") In this weighty silence, so typical of first sessions, I have come to know three kinds of kids. Some are determined not to speak; their fear and confusion paralyzes them into an oppositional stance in which opening up means giving in. Some talk but minimize everything and act scornfully if I try to care for them. And, others, like Dawn, begin to pour out all they have been trying to contain, like the tide coming in over a child's sand fort by the ocean. In the initial minutes, I cannot tell the kids apart, and I frequently feel nervous and uncertain about my own competence and what I really have to offer.

After that eternity, in a little voice, Dawn began to tell her story. She had come in late from a party because her ride had gotten too drunk and she had to wait for someone else to drive her home. Tears began to fall as she recounted walking into her house to find her father sitting in a chair by the door waiting up for her. He had jumped up, called her a "little whore" and a "disgusting slut" and slapped her once, hard enough to knock her to the floor. Apparently, this is all he intended to do, because he then headed up to his bed for the night. By the time Dawn had gotten herself together and put a cold cloth on her cheek, she remembered, she could hear him sleeping soundly. Now, she hugged the monkey to her chest and cried softly, half turned away from me.

In a speech I usually omit from my early sessions with abused adolescents, I became quite impassioned, righteously telling Dawn that no one had the right to hurt her and that she bore no blame for the violence against her. Dawn disagreed. She admitted that her father behaved in frightening ways from time to time, but added, "I know that I have disappointed him. Sometimes I don't do anything wrong and he still gets mad, but other times, it *is* my fault." She shook her head sadly, looking down at the monkey, and added, "I don't really know." While I continue to believe that abusive adults must take responsibility for controlling their behavior, I no longer impose my alien view on teens who think that they know much better than I all they have done to "get it."

Like other adolescents, Dawn may have wittingly or unwittingly contributed to her abuse. Her oppositional acts and sarcastic and disrespectful behavior (e.g., skipping school, violating curfew, talking back) could annoy the most tolerant parent. Even abusive parents usually first attempt less extreme limits but the results do not encourage them to keep being moderate. For example, Ms. Demato noted in a subsequent family meeting that Dawn had been grounded for coming in late just the week before. Mr. Demato had promised Dawn a CD player for her next birthday if she could demonstrate that she was responsible (perhaps making both the gift and responsibility aversive to Dawn). They had tried both punishment and rewards to little effect and were at their wits' end. In fact, it is hard not to be sympathetic with many abusive parents when they describe the irritation they have endured. Although there is no justification for abuse—*none*—the parents' testimony suggests how provocative and annoying adolescents can sometimes be.

In addition, other adolescents may also display "abuse eliciting characteristics" (Belsky, 1980) that can place them at risk no matter how obedient they may seem. For example, both hyperactive adolescents who act impulsively and depressed adolescents who mope around can be unintentionally provocative. Similarly, if they are clumsy, and break things or have more accidents than other teens, or believe that things will work out by magic instead of hard work or planning, their parents may feel particularly infuriated. Some adolescents are hypersensitive and respond to the slightest correction as though they are suddenly under seige. Additionally, developmental difficulties ranging from minor learning disabilities to major handicaps can increase the likelihood of abuse. Such characteristics make teenagers more difficult to raise, through no fault of their own, and can drive parents to violence if they already respond poorly to the stress of their children's adolescence.

THE EFFECTS OF ADOLESCENT ABUSE

As Dawn spoke about her life, she revealed many areas in which she was unhappy and confused. The effects of abuse are severe whether the adolescent is provocative or compliant to begin with. Perhaps more than any other group, teenagers can communicate their distress through a wide variety of symptoms. Since they don't seem like victims much of the time, it may seem ironic that they have so many more ways than infants and children of letting people know that they may be enduring abuse. I have noticed that abused adolescents display four kinds of symptoms:

- Acting out—running away, stealing, abusing drugs, acting in provocative ways, or skipping school

- Depression—making self-deprecating comments, isolating themselves from friends and family, gaining or losing weight, having trouble getting out of bed and keeping up with usual activities, expecting too much from others and then feeling disappointed

- Generalized anxiety—acting untrusting of family and friends, rationalizing and manipulating, experiencing difficulty concentrating and doing more poorly than usual in school

- Emotional thought disturbance—acting homicidally, speaking and thinking in bizarre and disconnected ways, and dissociating.

Like many abused adolescents, Dawn had exhibited various combinations of several of these symptoms simultaneously and in succession. It often seems that if one symptom or set of symptoms does not elicit help, then there will be an escalation into greater disturbance, or a significant change in the symptom constellation, or both. For example, Dawn's early reaction to the abuse was depressive withdrawal; she spent most of her time in her room and shifted her peer group to a more marginal set of friends. She gradually stopped studying for school, and skipped classes whenever she felt like it. She also began experimenting with drugs and drinking vodka straight from the bottle. She expressed some suicidal ideas, though she had never gone through with them. Recently, she had become quite disconnected from reality during the abuse and any other stressful circumstances, and reported that she could "just go away, far away in my head," whenever she wanted to. The unplanned escape to a friend's home after being confronted by her counselor was only the latest variation in a two-year pattern of attempting to cope with the violence.

Whether the abused adolescent communicates distress through angry, self-destructive, anxious, or bizarre behaviors, it is clear that the abuse will also have deep and deleterious effects upon normal development. Just at the time when feelings of competence and consistency are most necessary to enable them to move to independence, abused adolescents are faced with overwhelming feelings of inadequacy and confusion. Regardless of the strengths with which these adolescents have entered this period, it is likely that abuse will impede the development of important age-related communication and problem-solving skills, placing them at a great disadvantage with peers.

Therapy for the Physically Abused Adolescent

It has been my experience that treatment of abused adolescents needs to focus on five key concerns.

1. Development of Abstract and Moral Reasoning. Abused adolescents appear to be slower in attaining the abstract reasoning ability that Piaget (1954) described as formal operational thought. Through such formal operations, adolescents learn to consider possible ways a particular problem might be solved—the foundation of logical and flexible thought. They therefore need compelling situations and models for different methods of problem solving. This is as true for conflict resolution as it is for other dilemmas. Some abused adolescents experience the use of force and power against them as the *only* solution to all problems, and their reasoning will reflect this limiting perception. Dawn handled disagreements with friends by breaking off relations entirely. This extreme approach to minor daily conflicts suggests her difficulty seeing the multitude of ways she might resolve such differences.

2. Development of a Sense of Self. Similarly, the ability to see oneself as complete and separate (despite important emotional ties to others)—what Erikson (1968) called "ego identity"—requires development of a sense of self in the world and a feeling of internal consistency, both more difficult for abused adolescents to attain. Autonomy and "wholeness" cannot be experienced in the context of abuse. Since adolescents focus so many of their concerns on the physical aspects of themselves, it follows that they will have further trouble forming this constructive identity while their bodies are being physically (or sexually) violated.

3. Development of the Ability to be Intimate and to Trust. The legacy of abuse is nowhere greater than in its intrusion into social relationships. Abusive patterns set up an expectation of hurt and betrayal that endures long after the violence has ceased. Adolescents who have been abused often operate with the self-fulfilling prophesy that they will be devastated if they care or trust too much. Often, they unconsciously behave in ways that ensure the rejection they fear the most. Difficulty with intimacy is often covered up by pseudo-intimacy through promiscuous sexual relations, selfless involvement with peers who are even more troubled, or the rapid, passionate shift from best friend to best friend or from group to group. The therapeutic relationship can become the model for other kinds of intimacy if the adolescent is able to stay engaged.

4. Development of Skills Necessary to Separate and Leave Home. Adolescent-abusing families fall into two general categories. The parental style can tend to be authoritarian, with rigid rules and overpowering control, or overindulging, where a pattern of permissiveness is coupled with sporadic, violent attempts at control. Neither system fosters the sense of autonomy and competence required for adolescents to find their own ways successfully. Abused adolescents (quite sensibly) often try to leave home at the first chance they get. This attempt at separation seldom works well without additional intervention or change elsewhere in the family.

5. Development of Ability to Connect Freedom to Responsibility. In many nonabusing families, adolescents gain freedoms gradually, and accept that increasing responsibility for themselves, for others, and for property goes along with such freedom. At the most concrete level, for example, they use the car but fill the tank; they stay out later but call to say when they will be home; they have more money to spend but show up for work on time. Abused adolescents seldom understand this important connection between freedom and responsibility. Those in authoritarian families are given few freedoms, so they take them on the sly; those in permissive families have few responsibilities. However, without the connection between freedom and responsibility, abused adolescents are at increased risk of growing into angry, unhappy adults, dangerous to themselves and to others.

There is some controversy among professionals about whether the effects of adolescent abuse differ depending upon the time of onset. Some have theorized that there might be differences among those whose abuse begins in childhood and continues into adolescence; begins as spanking in childhood but becomes more severe and violent in adolescence; or begins in adolescence (e.g., Farber & Joseph, 1985; Galambos & Dixon, 1984; Garbarino, 1993; Lourie, 1979). It has been suggested that, with the exception of sexual abuse, abuse beginning in childhood is more psychologically damaging than abuse beginning in adolescence since it may be marked particularly by the victims' extreme beliefs that luck, chance, fate, and powerful others have more control over events than they do.

Other evidence indicates, however, that all abused adolescents, regardless of severity or time of onset, react similarly to the violence, with ego deficits and emotional and behavioral problems that make groups indistinguishable from one another (Farber & Joseph, 1985). Ultimately, the duration of the abuse may be less important than the fact of the disturbed adolescent-parent relationship in determining psychological adjustment.

At the end of our initial time alone, I told Dawn that I would have to call child protection, but that I wanted to discuss with her what I should recommend to them. I said that we needed to come up with a safety plan. She first attempted to persuade me that we could solve this without the state becoming involved. She then pondered the safety plan idea briefly before suggesting that she go live with a maternal aunt for a while. She reported that her aunt had always told her that she would be welcome there if things at home became too hard to manage. I asked Dawn if her parents would agree to involving her aunt in their affairs at this time. She expressed confidence that they would go along with the plan if she threatened to run away to her friend's home again. Although they are victims in many ways, abused adolescents are frequently powerful in their families (and sometimes they know it). I laughed, and evoked from her a trace of a smile when I suggested that I would support her in coming up with a less dangerous way to stay safe than running away.

The Family of the Physically Abused Adolescent

I then brought Mr. and Ms. Demato into the room. I took as firm control of the meeting as I could; I wanted to maintain a position of authority while minimizing Mr. Demato's opportunities to explode or feel as though he was being put on the spot. During this portion of the session, I took a family history beginning with the courtship of the Dematos up until the present; at subsequent meetings I asked for more detailed histories of each of their lives.

In our introductory interview, I also attempted to ally myself with their frustration in caring for Dawn, and to assure them that I knew they loved her and really wanted to do what was best for her. However, I expressed firmly my belief that no one deserved to be harmed, not even a wild and provocative teenager, and that I would work with them in every way to ensure that this never happened again. I prepared myself for Mr. Demato's reaction, but he had himself firmly in check that day. I later learned that he had a drinking problem and tended to be quite subdued and depressed when sober. (Interestingly, he drank vodka martinis—recently Dawn's drink of choice as well).

During the family history, I learned that the Dematos were college sweethearts, and that Ms. Demato had dropped out during her junior year when she became pregnant with Dawn. The eldest child of immigrant parents, she had disappointed them bitterly when she ended her schooling prematurely. Now, 16 years later, she still cried when she thought about how she had let them down. She worked as an administrative assistant in a mental-health clinic. Mr. Demato, the elder of two sons, got high marks in college, attempting in vain to win the respect of his father who had evidently been more impressed by the younger son. Mr. Demato had been wild as an adolescent in the 1960s, and his parents had called him their "black sheep"; even his academic honors could not earn him an exit from that paddock. He had planned to take over his father's furniture business, but his brother, who did not go to college, had already assumed that position by the time Mr. Demato graduated. After a few years attempting to find a place for himself at the store, he moved away and got into the parcel delivery business, working in various departments since that time. Like many parents in adolescent-abuse cases, both Mr. and Ms. Demato had struggled to overcome legacies of failure originating in their own adolescences.

Dawn, it seemed, had been the answer to their woes. A bright, beautiful baby and the first grandchild on both sides, she had brought people in both families closer. Several years later, the couple had two sons in close sucession. While the boys were loved, Dawn was her father's favorite, a fact known by everyone in the family, including her brothers. I was interested to learn that Mr. Demato had taken Dawn fishing and snowmobiling more frequently than the boys, even when they became old enough to go. From the time she was five, Dawn had helped out around the house, and had taken care of the boys. She had done well in school and was liked by everyone. By the end of junior high, however, this picture had begun to change. As Dawn began taking more care of her appearance and boys began calling her on the phone, both Mr. and Ms. Demato became increasingly unhappy with her looks and behavior and tightened the reins. Ms. Demato tried to restrain her husband when he became overwrought, but found that marital conflict about Dawn was too severe when she did. Moreover, she generally agreed that Dawn was behaving poorly, and often complained to her husband to "do something." However, she was always quite distressed when he resorted to violence.

In a household that had been relatively calm and happy, Dawn and Mr. Demato gradually began to disagree every time they were in the same room. These arguments did not become physically abusive in any predictable manner, but Mr. Demato's emotional abuse and name-calling were usually sufficient to send Dawn weeping to her room. Additionally, he became highly punitive; Dawn recalled with a wry grin, several weeks into family therapy, that he had once attempted to ground her for 30 years. While he didn't follow through on this extreme sanction, it indicated his feelings of lost control over his daughter.

I noted, perplexed, that Dawn seemed to be disappointing them much as they had upset *their* parents—she was on the verge of dropping out of school, as her mother had done, and was being wild, as her father had been. I wondered aloud if they had ever resolved to do things differently when they had children of their own. This spurred a revealing conversation, uncovering for all of us some of the hopes they had harbored for Dawn. They recalled, with sad smiles, some of the unrealistic plans they had made. Beginning with music and skating lessons, through spelling-bee competitions and special camps, they had spent years fantasizing about her extraordinary talents in one area or another. Unlike their own parents, who had been critical, they were uncompromisingly enthusiastic about her every endeavor. However, when her interests took her outside of their adoring supervision, they became panicky.

Like many distressed parents of adolescents, the Dematos were absolutely spilling over with a need to describe their lives to someone interested in hearing about them. It was very hard to end sessions on time. Once they had viewed themselves as competent parents; now they couldn't handle things without a slew of strangers and relatives getting involved. This change was dramatic, painful, and violent. I asked the Dematos to arrange for Dawn to live elsewhere for a few weeks while we worked together, and told them I would explain to child protection that they were motivated to change things in their lives. We set up a series of appointments, a couple times a week for all of the different members of the family, in different groupings. When abuse is first disclosed, the family crisis that ensues is typically a wonderful opportunity for more intensive involvement and rapid change. Family members are unsure of how to react, and they may be more receptive to external guidance. Moreover, the difficulties within the family that led to the crisis stand in bold relief and are much easier to detect than at any other time. If it can be arranged, I like to see members two or three times a week at first, before tapering off to the more typical weekly or bimonthly treatment. The hovering involvement of child protection can also maintain early and seemingly enthusiastic participation.

When I learned later in the week from Dawn and her brothers that their father consumed several martinis every evening when he came home from work, and up to a case of beer on the weekend, I also confronted Mr. Demato about his drinking. He did not feel that he needed Alcoholics Anonymous, but he agreed to attend four times and report back to me about how he was different from the other people there. Although he was certainly not sold on it immediately, and took his time getting to the meetings we had agreed on, over the following year Mr. Demato acknowledged his alcoholism and began attending AA regularly. (While some therapists refuse to treat alcoholics who are actively drinking, I tend to try and form a relationship with a family and then use the trust as leverage to get the alcoholic member to AA. This is not a matter of rules and laws guiding professional conduct, but a judgment call each time. When patients who are also alcoholic stop working in therapy, I tell them that I cannot continue to see them until they get to AA. If Dawn had not been out of the house, and making connections with me in therapy, I might also have been more persistent.)

Like Mr. Demato, all parents who abuse adolescents resort to violence out of a variety of needs and frustrations that are important to understand in order to stop it. Many clinical investigators have noted that these parents have not had the experience of being mothered or fathered as adolescents. The emotional deprivation and anger that result are perhaps responsible for the role-reversal often observed in such families. These parents expect to be cared for by their children, rather than care for them (Garbarino et al., 1986; Green, 1976; Spinetta & Rigler, 1977). When the adolescent is unable to comply with this unrealistic demand, the parent responds with violence. In Dawn's case, she had been favored by her father, and had steadily served the function of making him feel good about himself. When the focus of her energy turned, as developmentally it should have, to her peer group, he responded as though she were betraying him instead of just growing up.

Mr. Demato had also suffered at his own father's hands throughout his teenage years. The intergenerational-transmission hypothesis—which suggests that being abused as a child is a good predictor of becoming an abuser as an adult—appears to be borne out in families with abused adolescents. Parents who abuse their adolescents were frequently abused themselves as teenagers, and in these cases the contemporary dynamics become clearer in the context of the parents' painful (and violent) attempts to individuate from their own families of origin. During my work with Mr. Demato about his childhood, he came to see how he was recreating the same situation for Dawn that he had endured himself.

The fact that Dawn was not abused before the onset of adolescence was, however, significant. A factor that distinguishes recent-onset adolescent abuse from long-term child abuse is often a relatively benign history, provided by parent and adolescent alike, of the years before the child's 12th birthday. The social and economic stresses associated with child abuse are often absent, and a picture of a relatively ideal childhood emerges. Dawn's case provided a view of this in its purest form: She was obedient and performed adequately in school. Her parents may have had some marital problems, but these were kept under control, and each had had a relationship with Dawn that they looked back on with nostalgia. They even reported their own childhoods as fairly happy and noted that their parents got strict only when they were bad as teenagers—

though they never misbehaved the way Dawn did now. They were suddenly stymied and unable to use the old solutions for resolving conflicts. In turn, they disagreed about how to manage the new problems, fueling the conflict that was then diverted onto Dawn, often in the form of abuse.

Research on the structure of families where adolescents are abused has also yielded some interesting theories about differences associated with whether the abuse is short-term or long-term (e.g., Galambos & Dixon, 1984). Parents who begin abusing their offspring at young ages are more often separated, divorced, or single than parents who first abuse their offspring in adolescence. Generally, perpetrators of long-term child abuse earn half of the income that short-term abusers earn. In addition, these researchers indicate that long-term abusers are more likely to move about than short-term abusers. The general picture of long-term abusers is clearly spelled out in the child-abuse literature: relative poverty, marital instability, and transience complicated by the low availability of personal resources to cope with life's stresses. In contrast, short-term abusers appear to be more settled and stable and are more often middle class. There is also some evidence that, while both parents may be abusive, fathers are more often responsible for abuse beginning in adolescence (Lourie, 1979).

One of the hallmarks of short-term abusive families is a highly conflicted marital relationship. At the onset of therapy, the Dematos denied marital problems other than disagreements over how to manage Dawn. As we delved into their histories, and talked more about their marriage, it became clear that, for a long time, they had aired their differences only indirectly. Ms. Demato tended to gloss over problems as they arose, and then revealed that, for example, she purposely ignored her husband's pile of laundry while doing all the rest of the family's. Mr. Demato was jealous of his wife's free time outside of the home, and admitted that he was rude to her friends and cousins to keep them away. He viewed his home as "his castle" and did not like outsiders around.

In this and many other families with abused adolescents, conflict in the parental relationship often involves threats of emotional or physical harm by one spouse or the other. Although he had not hit anyone else in the family, Mr. Demato's violence against Dawn provided a clear message to his wife (and other children) about his access to them should he be roused to action. Indeed, Ms. Demato believed that Dawn had occasionally been abused when her husband was actually angry with *her*. I have also treated many cases of adolescent abuse where the mother is the aggressor against the adolescent. In these families, the mother is frequently being victimized by her partner. Some battered women say that they decide to abuse their adolescents because they fear their partners would do more harm. They abuse preemptively and justify it this way. In cases of adolescent abuse where the single mother is the perpetrator, I have found that the level of conflict with the noncustodial father or with her current partner is high, even when there is no evidence of battering. In general, abuse of adolescents reflects severe problems elsewhere in the family system that may have little or nothing to do with the behavior of the adolescent.

Additionally, the specter of separation is always present in these families, so during an early family session I asked the couple quite directly about whether they had thought about divorce. Since children invariably "know" the truth about their parents' marriage, I asked about separation in front of the entire family. No one expressed surprise when Ms. Demato remembered a fight and discussion about divorce just two weeks before, ostensibly held long after the kids were asleep. Interestingly, the fear of being left by a spouse is mirrored in the disproportionate anxiety aroused by the impending departure of the adolescent from the home.

Mr. Demato's history also revealed annual bouts of depression, usually in the winter, which he attempted to control by self-medicating with alcohol. In addition to the other sources of conflict, his periods of feeling overwhelmed and depressed also provided major sources of stress for the family. It is not unusual for someone in such families to be depressed; more typically it is the woman, particularly if the husband holds the traditional patriarchal authority.

I saw the Dematos for 10 months. Child protection did investigate and became involved very peripherally for a few months. They recommended that Dawn participate in a girls' group, which she chose not to do, and they visited the home a couple of times before they closed the case. The school counselor and I touched base every couple of weeks when we had information for each other. When I stopped seeing the Dematos, during the fall of Dawn's junior year, the counselor continued to meet weekly with Dawn into Dawn's senior year.

During the course of treatment, I worked with Dawn on matters of taking responsibility for herself, and helped her regain some of the pride and dignity she had lost during the past years. Because she no longer felt safe at home, she had distorted ideas about protecting herself, and how to get others to care for her. Over our time together, she began to take pride in her accomplishments and to achieve in school again. While appearances do not mean everything, it was quite noteworthy that she came for our final session together dressed in jeans and sneakers, looking less like a waif and more like a 16-year-old, with only a hint of makeup on her face. I gave her the monkey she had cared for in my office, so she could have a part of us go with her. I told her I wanted to hear from her from time to time, to learn how things were going.

Dawn called me once during her senior year to say that she was moving out of the home, to live with her aunt. She said that the violence had not returned but that her father continued to be unnecessarily strict and demanding. While she reported that her parents were not thrilled with her plans to move out, they did not forbid it. She noted that they seemed to be understanding about her need to be closer to public transportation (her ostensible reason for the move).

I worked with the parents on communicating more directly, and on finding pleasure in one another again. We spoke at great length about their families of origin, raising children in a dangerous world, and specific problems they were having with Dawn and the boys (who, it must be noted, were an active duo). While they chose not to work too deeply on their marriage, they both ended up feeling closer and more in control of their lives than they had in a long time.

With the family together, we spoke mostly about growing up in a family, leaving home, and what it meant to everyone to be a Demato. The parents worked on setting more realistic goals and expectations for their children and on coming up with consequences that were both positive and negative but not violent or belittling.

However, Mr. Demato continued to react in extreme ways to his children, and remained highly reactive to his wife's requests for his involvement. She would call him in to help her out, and he would be furious that the children had upset her, regardless of the reason she had needed assistance. I was encouraged to learn that Mr. Demato eventually, on his own, apologized to Dawn, though she was not prepared to accept his efforts immediately. This apology may have been an important first step toward healing for the whole family.

The pain of violence experienced by abused adolescents is shared intensely by their immediate families. Everyone must be given the chance to heal; sometimes they can. For Dawn, leaving home at the first opportunity to do so may have been the healthiest solution. Sometimes emotional wounds need air and distance to mend. Her parents permitted her to leave—and stay connected to them. This outcome suggested that the crisis in the development of the family had, for the time, been resolved.

7

Self-Help and
Community Approaches

Where violence in adolescence is concerned, mental-health providers must operate within three concurrent and seemingly contradictory belief systems. First, we have to believe that problems of violence are like all others and can thus be addressed during an hour or two a week in our offices. We are successful if the violence in question decreases or disappears, and the individuals and families we treat feel better when we are done. We have done our jobs when, for example, we change the family communication patterns that lead to adolescent abuse or offer an adolescent the skills and supports that compete adequately with delinquency. In the ecological terms defined earlier in this book, we are satisfied intervening on the first two of four levels, working as we do with individuals and families. The way the community responds to problems of violence in adolescence is outside of our baliwick. Social policy, too, is someone else's concern.

However, it is difficult to sustain such a narrow focus without also adhering to a second kind of belief about what we are doing. Here, we must entertain the Pollyannaish notion that individual change is causally connected to change in families, which in turn affects blocks, then neighborhoods, communities, and society as a whole. We hold our work with one sexually abused adolescent or one adolescent sex offender's family in the arms of this frail notion, knowing that millions of others out there are as yet unserved and

148

that we may really be redefining social problems so *we* can address them individually. While the idea of a ripple effect is comforting, it most often operates in subtle ways, beneath the surface, where something like scuba equipment may be required to detect it.

We have been accused, rightfully, of participating in a blaming-the-victim or medical model approach to adolescent violence in that we concern ourselves with fixing people one at a time instead of adopting a broader ecological perspective, that might include community empowerment and change. Indeed, all one has to do is drive through the center of any large city to see that an environment can be responsible for sustaining violence. As a corollary, it has been amply demonstrated that ecologically based community interventions can serve large numbers of adolescents at a time with great success (e.g., Felner, Ginter, & Primavera, 1982; Leone, 1989; Trickett & Birman, 1989).

Perhaps it is not surprising that many adolescents and their families do not want therapy or feel that they need more than what we can offer them. And so we must also believe, third, that our services are limited. We can better succeed when we work alongside our communities and tie our work in with the self-help groups and neighborhood organizations that are also "treating" problems of violence in adolescence. It is a humbling reality to learn that the local YMCA's midnight basketball league is keeping 150 young men out of trouble all at once, while we fret as our delinquent case arrives late and unmotivated for therapy.

Where we may be found wanting in our philosophies and success rates, we will provide a much more powerful intervention when we work cooperatively, alongside the community organizations that are also trying, directly or indirectly, to reduce adolescent violence. These services fall into two broad categories: self-help approaches and community-based programs.

Self-Help Approaches

Self help groups have a long and varied history. Katz and Bender (1976) trace them back to 18th century England's "friendly societies," which functioned similarly to today's unions. During the 19th century, in both England and America, consumer cooperatives, trade unions, immigrant-aid societies, and worker housing, banking, and educational programs all incorporated elements of self-help.

In the 20th century, the focus of self-help has shifted from economic development to personal growth through both religious and secular traditions. Since the 1960s, in particular, there has been a dramatic increase in the number and variety of self-help groups, which now exist for nearly every major disease, age group, problem, and life situation (Gartner & Riessman, 1977). The Alcoholics Anonymous message has been particularly potent in its adoption by all forms of addictions—including, but not limited to, drugs, food, sex, relationships, and work. The message of AA has also spawned other movements for such groups as "adult children" of alcoholics, "codependents," and "women who love too much." Indeed, the popularity of the notion that many, if not all, families are somehow dysfunctional has permeated the popular press of the early 1990s to the point where it has become something of a cliche. At the very least, the idea of family dysfunction has done much for both the mental-health field and for the geometric expansion of self-help groups in this country.

There are two likely explanations for the recent increase in self-help groups: consumerism and professional acknowledgment. As mental health services have become more available, they are no longer shrouded in mystery. Consumers, better educated now about what they want from such services, have become frustrated by the more established programs' inability to provide services for them and their problems. Some groups (e.g., ToughLove) form in response to professional failures; clients who find that psychotherapy is not assisting them may find the less structured and more personal atmosphere offered by a self-help group to be more beneficial.

Ethical practice requires that we strive to empower our clients and inform them of the limits of what we can offer, suggesting, where appropriate, that such alternatives may be useful for them. Indeed, it may be possible to work cooperatively with a self-help group. For example, an abused adolescent with a drinking problem can attend both therapy and AlAteen. Moreover, it does not always indicate failure of therapy when clients shift toward a self-help strategy. (In fact, it can be a sign of treatment success when clients decide that they can better serve themselves.)

There are really four different types of self-help groups that can be distinguished, based upon their purpose and composition. First, there are groups that emphasize conduct reorganization or behavioral control (e.g., Parents Anonymous, AlAteen). Second, there are groups whose members share a predicament which entails a degree of stress; their aim is not to change the situation but to ameliorate the stress (e.g., groups for adolescents of divorce, pregnant adolescents, incest survivors). The third kind of groups are survival-oriented, its members discriminated against or labeled deviant by society. Such groups' aims include mutual support and consciousness-raising to enhance self-esteem, and publicity and political activity that are aimed at societal acceptance and elimination of discrimination (e.g., groups for gay and bisexual teens, AIDS awareness groups). Finally, some groups are designed so members can share goals of personal growth, self-actualization, and enhanced effectiveness in life. No single problem is shared by all, but the members bring their concerns to such a group in the belief that together they can help one another to better lives (e.g., sensitivity groups).

Even though self-help groups may form for different purposes, they have many similarities. For example, Levy (1976) described nine helping activities offered by self-help groups: Empathy, mutual affirmation, explanation, sharing, morale-building, self-disclosure, positive reinforcement, personal goal-setting, and catharsis. Similarly, Borman (1979) concludes that all self-help groups provide members with five curative factors:

- Universality (recognition by group members that they are not alone)

- Acceptance of the problem rather than disapproval

- Hope that the problem can be addressed and resolved

- Altruism or self-esteem through the experience of giving help

- Cognitive restructuring, which may involve a revised belief system or simply new knowledge about the cause and effect of problems

Despite the many obvious strengths of self-help groups and the self-help approach to common problems of adolescence and family life, there are limitations to what they can offer. All volunteer organizations are difficult to establish and to maintain. By their very nature, they are fluid and transient; leaders must donate a great deal of time and energy to them. Consequently, the leadership (and membership) of a group changes frequently as problems are resolved or interest is lost. When leaders assume too much responsibility, they may alienate other members or burn out from the effort. There is no self-sustaining structure to assure continuity. For groups attempting to engage adolescents, maintaining their involvement can be a particular challenge. Many adolescents, especially those dealing with violence, have difficulty organizing their time around a formalized group activity. If it's a sunny day, or if they are having a particularly hard time, they are apt to "forget" the group.

Internal problems of the groups may also result in conflict or exclusiveness. Unresolved problems regarding leadership or focus, for example, may cause their dissolution. Looking inward for support, groups may become closed, dependent on core members, and no longer open to others who need help. Thus, the group's purpose can shift, become clubby, or otherwise function poorly.

Moreover, many self-help groups serve only a partial function in the resolution of problems. For example, while AlAteen may help adolescents maintain sobriety, it will not explore the other, deeper issues in their lives that psychotherapy would address. Exclusive focus on one kind of problem may mean a lack of insight or interrelatedness with other problems. It often happens in adolescent substance abuse that, when sober or straight, adolescents are overwhelmed by other painful emotional experiences they masked by drinking or drugging. It is not typical for self-help groups to make referrals to professionals; in these situations, the initial benefit of helping the adolescent become clean and sober may be diminished by the emergence of underlying issues that are not addressed.

Group norms can also be a problem, particularly if they reflect confused or deviant thinking. For example, I was asked to consult to a self-help group operating in a child protection agency. The group, which was made up of abusive parents of adolescents, had as its mission mutual support and the pursuit of alternatives to violence in managing their difficult adolescents. The parents met one evening a week in the group room and discussed whatever emergent issue arose. They requested consultation when they felt that they were losing their focus. I agreed to sit in on a few meetings.

My first encounter revealed that they had been sharing antisocial attitudes and wild misinformation to support one another. For example, one father explained how, after throwing his phone at his son and breaking it, he had told the phone company that it had broken off the wall when he was moving the refrigerator. Another mother shared her decision to poison her daughter's dog with tainted hamburger meat because her daughter was not taking adequate care of it. I was not impressed by the helpfulness of these decisions, and I was dismayed that no one else found them questionable. Another parent revealed that he had told his daughter he didn't want her playing softball because she was spending too much time in her room when she was home—and she had no energy for the family, which he thought was wrong. I envisioned a fruitful discussion on this point, but no one in the group challenged his position. One mother vaguely commented to the softball player's father that at least his daughter did something with her time. When I followed this up by asking him if he had ever told his daughter he enjoyed having her in the living room with the rest of the family, or invited her to play cards with him, the group stared at me in amazement. Yet the group needed to know that it was usually a bad idea to eliminate a positive outlet for an adolescent; many members may have recognized this at some level but could not articulate it. Thus, the group had been spinning its wheels rather than working toward new solutions.

I was subsequently invited to attend regularly but I couldn't make much of a dent in the form of the group discussions, which often contained outrageously delinquent notions. However, members did support one another, and the abuse of their adolescents decreased significantly because of the group participation.

The literature on self-help groups is, for the most part, positive. Certainly their popularity indicates that they are offering members important assistance and outlets. It behooves mental-health professionals to know about the self-help groups available in their area and to plan on working cooperatively with them. A coordinated effort provides adolescents and their families their best chance to live free from violence.

A wide range of self-help approaches has evolved in the past two decades to assist parents and adolescents. As problems of adolescence have burgeoned, so has an assortment of groups and publications designed to pick up where therapy leaves off or to replace traditional treatment altogether. These include ToughLove, Parents Anonymous, a variety of groups modeled along the twelve-step program of Alcoholics Anonymous that are designed for both adolescent victims and offenders, other kinds of support groups, and books for parents and their adolescents.

TOUGHLOVE

Of all of the types of parent support groups that have developed in recent years, ToughLove, with 500 chapters across the country, has probably received the most national attention. Based in part on the therapeutic community model, ToughLove is a self-help organization that asks parents to begin by admitting that they are facing a problem they can no longer handle on their own—an inability to control their adolescent's behavior. A basic tenet of ToughLove is the view that parents are often rendered ineffective by a permissive, child-centered culture.

Meeting regularly in parent-support groups and maintaining contact with other group members between sessions, ToughLove parents are encouraged to begin taking firmer positions with their adolescents and setting "the bottom line" on acceptable behavior in their households. When this standard is violated, the parents, supported by other group members, are expected to follow through according to a graduated set of predetermined consequences. The ultimate sanction is having an adolescent move to some other living arrangement—often to be housed temporarily in homes of other ToughLove parents called "advocates," who then help the adolescents and their parents negotiate a contract that sets clear conditions for a return home.

ToughLove was founded in 1978 by David and Phyllis York after their daughters were in chronic trouble (one committed armed robbery). After trying traditional therapy, the Yorks—themselves counselors—concluded that their problems and those of the thousands of others in a similar predicament, required a different approach. They decided that, because their family's problems were really culturally based, they demanded a cultural solution; what was needed was a community approach, including efforts to involve school and youth workers. In the Yorks' view, adolescent problems can be overcome only by uniting adults in community support groups; they caution parents not to try and carry out ToughLove strategies alone, since the group approach is central to the philosophy.

ToughLove makes no pretense of sharing the goals of parenting programs that seek to impart knowledge and help create more affectionate, supportive, and trusting family relationships. Rather, its primary goal appears to be to help parents break free from their adolescent's extreme, destructive, and antisocial behaviors. If such behaviors persist, ToughLove maintains that legal emancipation from the adolescent "is the most agreeable option" (York & York, 1980). ToughLove believes that it is often necessary for parents to "withdraw affection" from an adolescent and to "ignore [their] feelings of love." Parents are taught to refuse to go to jails, courthouses, or hospitals to see their adolescents, to hang up on their runaways when they call, and to deny entry when their runaway returns home. Instead, they send other ToughLove parents into the fray for them.

ToughLove also does not aim to increase understanding—not intellectually, in the sense of how or why behavior occurred and can be changed, or emotionally, in the sense of greater compassion or intimacy. The Yorks (1980) maintain that understanding "only keeps [parents] helpless" and "gives parents a sense of 'false power.'" Their central assumption, that the primary task for parents of acting-out adolescents is to rid themselves of guilt and a sense of responsibility for their offspring, seems to be based on the notion that there is nothing left to learn. As a behavior-modification approach, it relies heavily on threat of withdrawal of positive reinforcement while denying the importance of positive incentives. Of even greater concern is the likelihood that parents are quite angry at their acting-out adolescents and are all too willing to act on their own rage. In some instances, ToughLove may simply replace one form of violence (physical) with another (emotional), and often with little new learning along the way.

It is difficult to assess how effective this approach really is. Other than endorsements from satisfied parents, there do not appear to be any empirical data, or even simple percentages describing families who have benefitted from ToughLove. This lack of research of any kind makes it difficult to recommend ToughLove to particular families or even to know whether such a severe response actually helps in the long run.

Reinforcement is strengthened if it is offered in the context of compassion, understanding, and warmth; ToughLove appears to provide this for parents in groups but to deny it to the adolescents in distress. ToughLove may help parents who have a problem with setting limits and who do not allow their adolescents to experience appropriate consequences. But, in my opinion, it simply leans too far away from those family connections that can be healing. While there are clear reasons why ToughLove has received so much attention, its limitations provoke concern. The idea of community support in dealing with drugs, delinquency, and other forms of violence is a marvelous one, but there is also much to be gained by empowering families with information about how people change and grow.

PARENTS ANONYMOUS

Jolly K., a former child abuser, founded Parents Anonymous (PA) in 1970 as a self-help group for abusive mothers. Since that time, the concept has spread rapidly, and now more than 1,200 PA chapters have been formed in virtually every region of the United States.

The PA design differs from other self-help groups in three important ways. First, a professional is usually present at meetings. This professional "sponsor" acts as a support system, works with parent leaders, and intervenes when the leaders are unable to act because of lack of information, skill, or experience. While preserving confidentiality, the sponsor performs few of the other functions expected of group therapists (Moore, 1983). Second, PA, unlike many other self-help groups, provides no rigid structure (Holmes, 1978); there are no steps to climb or predetermined agendas for group meetings. Third, involvement in PA often leads to, or is concurrent with, more formalized use of other community services. Indeed, one of the functions of PA is to help its participants develop a more positive attitude toward more formal therapeutic interventions.

Ample research exists demonstrating that PA provides a helpful model of intervention for many abusive families. In one study, Hunka, O'Toole, and O'Toole (1985) noted a significant positive change for participants in ten variables of concern: social isolation, self-esteem, dependency needs, impulsiveness, passivity, attitude toward the child, knowledge of child development, problem-solving ability, ability to cope with stress, and child-management techniques. Similarly, Lieber and Baker (1977) found that PA led to these important changes *and* was highly rated by its members in terms of perceived benefits. This satisfaction increased significantly with length of time in the program. Additionally, the frequency of verbally abusive and physically abusive behavior decreased significantly as an almost immediate effect of joining PA, and even more so as a function of time spent in the program.

Many PA chapters also offer groups for children and adolescents. These tend to be more structured by the professional on hand and, as such, are not exactly self-help groups in the traditional sense. Hall, Kassees, and Hoffman (1986) reported on the efficacy of separate PA groups for sexually abused adolescents and their parents. The adolescent groups emphasized assertive interaction, self-awareness activities and problem-solving skills. By contrast, the adult groups focused more generally on self-esteem, competency, independence, and the ability to establish healthy relationships.

Parents Anonymous groups should not be viewed as a panacea for all problems faced by abusive parents, any more than therapy should. In fact, adolescent abuse is often compounded by the very real interactional problems that exist between adolescents and their parents and by the emotional and behavioral problems of the adolescents, that demand their own set of interventions. In addition, some parents are so distressed that support alone is not sufficient to interrupt the cycle of violence. In these situations, PA alone is inadequate and a broader range of options for abusive families is required.

OTHER 12-STEP GROUPS

The most recent edition of *The Self-Help Sourcebook* (White & Madara, 1992) describes an astonishing number of self-help groups for problems of violence in adolescence. While the following list is by no means exhaustive, it does provide a sense of the power of the self-help movement in this area.

1. *Incest Survivors Anonymous.* With more than 300 groups internationally, this 12-step program, founded in 1980, is available to adolescents and offers members the opportunity "to share their experience, strength and hope, so that they may recover from their incest experiences and break free to a new peace of mind."

2. *Sexual Abuse Survivors Anonymous (SASA).* Founded in 1991, this 12-step program hosts only 10 groups nationally, but offers support to a broader range of victims, including those of incest, rape, or "any overt or covert abuse."

3. *Families of Sex Offenders Anonymous.* Founded in 1989, this 12-step group is open to "families and friends of persons afflicted with a destructive sexual addiction" to help "each member work through the shock, denial, shame, and grief of a behavior associated with deviance and criminality."

4. *Molesters Anonymous.* Ten of these men's groups have been formed around the country since 1985 to provide support with anonymity and confidentiality for men who molest children. These groups "use 'thought-stoppage' techniques and a buddy system," and although they are initiated by a professional, members run them once they get off the ground.

5. *Convicts Anonymous.* Founded in 1990, there are just three chapters of this 12-step program "for people desiring to stop criminal behavior in a fellowship to talk things out before acting things out."

6. *Repeat Offenders Anonymous.* This 12-step program has 10 affiliated groups and was developed in 1989 for people who share the common problem of "an inability to remain crime-free."

OTHER SUPPORT GROUPS

The Self-Help Sourcebook (White & Madara, 1992) lists other groups treating problems of adolescents and their parents that do not follow the 12-step model.

1. *Believe the Children.* This is a national program with three affiliated groups for parents of children and adolescents who have been victimized by people outside of the family. Together, parents and professionals address the issues of sexual and ritualistic exploitation of small children.

2. *Because I Love You: The Parent Support Group.* Founded in 1982, the 11 groups formed thus far provide support for parents who have children and adolescents with behavioral problems such as truancy, substance abuse and other forms of authority-defiance. The focus of these groups is "on parents' getting back their self-esteem and control of their home."

3. *Parental Stress Services.* This program was founded in 1979 so that children and parents from stressful family environments could meet in separate groups led by trained volunteers to "talk about feelings and gain understanding and acceptance."

4. *Sexual Assault Recovery Anonymous (SARA) Society.* With 35 groups nationally, this program, founded in 1983, provides education and self-help for adults and teens who were sexually abused as children.

5. *Parents United International, Inc.* While sometimes thought of as self-help groups, Parents United actually sponsors more than 100 professionally run therapy groups for parents whose children have been sexually abused. They also offer groups for adolescents and adults molested as children.

6. *National Victim Center.* Founded in 1985, the Center provides crime victims with information and resources and promotes the development of self-help groups. Acting as a

clearinghouse, the Center offers referrals to existing groups and consultation and guidelines for starting new groups, and links victims one-to-one for mutual support.

BOOKS FOR PARENTS AND ADOLESCENTS

For therapists wishing to suggest "homework" to support their efforts through the written word, or for parents trying to make the family function better on their own, the shelves of bookstores are full of manuals and texts aimed at "surviving" the perils of adolescence. Of the books I have seen, I most frequently use and recommend three.*

1. Steinberg, L. and Levine, A. (1990). *You and your adolescent: A parent's guide for ages 10–20*. New York: Harper-Collins.

    This is a well-written and thorough resource for understanding the tasks and pitfalls of adolescence. The sections on communication and the common emotional problems of adolescents that may benefit from professional help are particularly strong. Parents who are bewildered by the changes they find in their teenagers are usually appreciative when I recommend this book to them.

2. Dinkmeyer, D. and McKay, G. D. (1984). *The parent's guide: The STEP approach to parenting your teens*. New York: Random House.

    This is a wonderful workbook for parents trying to improve communication with their adolescents. It is very useful in systematically applying negotiation skills, developing appropriate consequences, and organizing constructive family meetings. I have suggested this book many times and it has clearly been helpful.

3. Bayard, R. and Bayard, J. (1983). *How to deal with your acting-up teenager: Practical help for desperate parents*.

---

*A longer listing of self-help books for parents and adolescents can be found in the Appendix. While it is by no means a complete directory, it should suggest that ample written resources exist for readers so inclined.

New York: Evans.

This book offers some very practical suggestions for parents who are too overwhelmed by their adolescents to be creative in any way. Unlike ToughLove, it emphasizes understanding and compassion in arriving at solutions to impasses. In tone, it is very encouraging, and works well with parents who feel bullied by their teenagers.

The readership of self-help parenting books is likely to be a concerned and motivated group who already have a relatively high level of awareness about the nature of the problems they are having with their adolescents. Certainly, from the number of titles with the word "survival" in them, it seems that these readers are determined to make it through in one piece. It is impossible to guess whether the very worst-off families read or are able to benefit from these books, but many parents are reading them, for their shelf space grows annually. Most parents share a desire to do well by their children, and to care for them as responsibly as they can. These books are being written in response to the pervasive sense that we all can use help because a parent's job is not as simple as it was a couple of generations ago. Like self-help groups, all the books seem to say, "You're not alone," which in itself is a very reassuring message indeed.

Community-Based Programs

Community-based programs share some characteristics with both self-help groups and more traditional mental health services. Community-based interventions are concerned with remediation, prevention, and the promotion of competencies and general health. They tend to recognize the many influences upon the well-being of an adolescent, including economics, education, physical health, and emotional supports. Services are usually provided in groups, and often use nonprofessionals or paraprofessionals as leaders. Such interventions are not mutually exclusive with more traditional mental-health services or even with self-help groups. Rather, they address change at a higher ecological level: the social structures around adolescents and their families. Additionally, these alternative interventions extend the service base to include segments of the youth population often missed by the traditional mental-health and social-service institutions—rural adolescents and those living in neighborhoods of concentrated poverty in the inner city (Youth and America's Future, 1988). Additionally, because community-based approaches occur in the natural settings in which adolescents live (e.g., schools, neighborhood centers), they are more accessible to adolescents than mental-health clinics and hospitals. There are seven basic types of community-based alternative programs: youth organizations, organized sports, youth volunteer service opportunities, peer-helping programs, mentor programs, work training programs, and church-based programs.

YOUTH ORGANIZATIONS

National surveys of adolescents between the ages of 11 and 18 have revealed that at least 20 percent are enrolled in one of the more than 400 community youth organizations that exist nationally (Erickson, 1982). Although most organizations are largely recreational, some are career- or avocation-oriented (e.g., Junior Achievement, 4-H), some are character-building (e.g., Boys and Girls Clubs of America, Boy Scouts, Girl Scouts), some are politically oriented (e.g., Young Democrats, Young Republicans), some instill ethnic pride (e.g., Ukrainian Youth Organization), and some are religious-oriented (e.g., Christian Youth Groups [Davis & Tolan, 1993]). The Boys and Girls Clubs, in particular, provide outreach to minority youth who might not otherwise receive services. Some youth organizations (e.g., Boy Scouts, 4-H) have as many as 4.4 million members.

The benefits of membership in youth organizations for the involved adolescents have been amply documented. First, a relationship between participation and level of educational aspiration and accomplishment among adolescents has been established repeatedly, even when the researchers control for socioeconomic status, intellectual ability, and academic performance (Hanks & Eckland, 1978; Otto, 1975; Otto & Featherman, 1975). Second, longitudinal studies (e.g., Hanks, 1981; Otto, 1976) point to a relationship between adolescent participation in community- and school-based activities and later membership in voluntary organizations and political activity in adulthood (again, even when controlling for the effects of education, occupation, or income). Third, it appears that this effect is relatively specific to the type of community involvement emphasized by the organization. For example, Hanks found that participation in organizations designed to achieve a social objective was more predictive of later political involvement than was participation in organizations in which recreational and other "expressive" activities were emphasized. Finally, although youth organizations attract only a small fraction of youth who might be eligible—mostly those whose parents and backgrounds support the ideology of that particular group—those who participate do obtain skills and competencies that are not taught in school. Additionally, family involvement in teaching and in the transmission of values to participating adolescents is also more likely (Klienfield & Shinkwin, 1982).

Youth organizations are hampered by several factors that can threaten the stability of program design and lead to high staff turnover. These include, for example, frequent loss of funding, staff burnout due to insufficient salary or relevance to career, the loss of an inspiritional leader whose shoes are hard to fill, and attendant failure to generate sufficient adolescent commitment to the program (Stephens, 1983). If staff could be trained and better renumerated, and greater incentives could be developed for adolescents to participate, it is possible that these problems might decrease.

Such difficulties should not overshadow the enthusiasm of participants in youth organizations or the potential they hold for reaching adolescents who might not otherwise receive any other services. These programs fit naturally with the adolescent emphasis on positive peer relationships, on leadership and on the development of social responsibility, and as such may provide an effective means for prevention of violence in adolescence.

ORGANIZED SPORTS

While mental health research has paid little attention to organized athletics for adolescents, there is still a widespread societal belief that participation in sports can be an important positive outlet for adolescents who might otherwise get into trouble. Indeed, among lower income male youth, those involved with sports display significantly less delinquent activity than their nonathletic counterparts (Schafer, 1969; Segrave & Chu, 1978). However, this finding does not hold true for middle-class adolescents, and the debate over the merits of organized sports as a mental health tool persists.

In Reppucci's (1987) literature review, he noted that, on one side of the debate, youth sports proponents, particularly physical education professionals, stress the heavy value our culture places on physical competition, emphasizing that participants are more physically fit, have greater self-confidence and self-discipline, and, through sports, find an appropriate channel for their aggressive tendencies. On the other side, Reppucci summarizes that sports have not been proven to be a unique socializing experience, that they place an unhealthy emphasis on winning (often by overinvolved parents), result in excessive levels of stress and overcompetitiveness, and that the high structure of such competition undercuts creativity and spontaneity which are other traits that are important for adolescents to develop.

The issues of the impact of sports involvement are complex and may differ depending upon the type of sport, the reason for participating, other available outlets, and characteristics of the individual adolescent. However, the sheer numbers of adolescents participating in sports, their potential for impact on a wide range of adolescents, the social value given to participants, and their ready convenience (given their base in youth organizations, schools, and other community settings) indicates that sports may have a vast mental-health potential that merits more systematic exploration.

One unconventional model of sports as an alternative to violence is the Midnight Basketball League (Simons, Finlay, & Yang, 1991). Begun in 1986 as a deterrent to crime and drug activity in Prince George's County, Maryland, the program has been replicated in Chicago and several other big cities. Since most crimes are committed between 10 PM and 2 AM by men in their teens and early twenties, the MBL was designed to offer such individuals a positive diversion during the hours when they were most likely to get in trouble.

In Chicago, the MBL invites young men to try out for 160 positions on 16 teams—eight teams from each of the two big housing projects in that city. The year-round program mirrors the National Basketball Association in its operation and terminology and by providing top-quality basketball shoes, uniforms, championship rings, all-star games, and awards banquets. Practices are scheduled at odd hours like 3 AM or 6 AM, to determine the player's level of commitment to being on the team. Since attitude is more important than ability, most teams have one superstar and nine average players. There are different gang factions on each team.

Basketball, however, is only one part of the MBL. The program offers discipline and responsibility often lacking in the lives of participants. To stay in the league, players must follow rules barring fighting, unsportsmanlike behavior, profanity, drugs, alcohol, radios, and tape players. If they break the rules, they don't play basketball.

Practices are mandatory, as are workshops after every game. During the workshops, players are encouraged to improve themselves physically, mentally, and economically by seeking appropriate substance-abuse counseling, vocational training and counseling, life-skills assistance, adult education and GED services, basic health care, and various social services. Men in the program for two years are required to get their GEDs.

Obviously, the MBL reaches only a few of those who could most benefit from it; out of more than 6,000 young men in the Chicago projects, only 160 can play in the league at a time. But among those participating, the statistics on educational advancement, job placement, and crime avoidance look quite good. Such a model program merits expansion; at $80,000 a season, it costs a fraction of the expense of monitoring and punishing crime. Although the MBL is only one type of organized athletics, it provides a vivid illustration of the promise such sports may hold for the mental health and well-being of the involved adolescents.

YOUTH VOLUNTEER SERVICE OPPORTUNITIES

Mobilizing adolescents to take on service functions in their community and become direct helpers of others—companions for the aged, tutors, counselors, or mentors for other children and youth—has

attracted increased attention from community psychologists in recent years. These youth service activities actually serve two concurrent functions: Through contributing to others, adolescents, in turn,
have the opportunity to feel important and useful (Nightingale &
Wolverton, 1988; Youth and America's Future, 1988). Rather than
viewing adolescents as problems who need something done *to* or
for them, this approach sees them as *assets* to society who can
extend significant effort in serving others.

Some high schools and colleges encourage or even require students to complete unpaid service hours (Youth and America's Future, 1988). Other youth service efforts include youth corps membership; the VISTA program is probably the best known among
these. Both President Clinton and the U. S. Congress have recently
enacted laws based on this concept by establishing the National
Youth Conservation Corps.

While studies supporting the idea of volunteer service opportunities for youth are scanty and anecdotal, and do not control for
motivation and self-selection, they do consistently indicate that voluntary service reduces feelings of isolation and alienation, increases
understanding of and connection to the community, and develops a
sense of competence and self-worth in the participants (Davis &
Tolan, 1993). Further, the importance of meaningful connections in
decreasing all forms of violence in adolescence has been amply
documented.

Uri Bronfenbrenner and Heather Weiss (1983) have proposed a
"curriculum of caring" in the schools from the earliest grades onward. The purpose of this curriculum would not be to learn about
caring, but to engage in it. As Bronfenbrenner and Weiss stated so
eloquently:

> It is now possible for a young person to graduate from an Ameri-
> can high school without ever having had to do a piece of work on
> which someone else depended. It is also possible for a young
> person, female as well as male, to graduate from high school,
> college, or university without ever having held a baby for longer
> than a few seconds; without ever having had to care for someone
> who was old, ill, or lonely; without ever having had to assist
> another human being who needed help. Yet all of us, sooner or

later, will desperately require such comfort and care, and no society can sustain itself unless its members have learned the motivations sensitivities, and skills that such caring demands. (pp. 405–406)

Engaging adolescents in learning to care for others is more than a method for diverting them from participating in violent activities. Such volunteer services may also be an antidote for the conditions that breed such violence in the first place.

PEER-HELPING PROGRAMS

Peer helpers—mentors, Big Brothers or Big Sisters, and tutors— restructure the helping relationship by transforming the helped recipient or consumer into the producer of help (Reissman, 1989). There are four main benefits of peer-helping programs: (1) a vast expansion of helping resources; (2) conversion of peer interactions into informed, positive help; (3) communication in their own vocabulary among peers; and (4) promotion of strengths to enhance mental health rather than the removal of inadequacies.

Among community-based interventions, the youth-helping approach has received significant attention, with a primary focus on the benefits of enlisting older youth to serve as academic tutors (Cohen, Kulik, & Kulik, 1982; Hedin, 1987; Maher, 1982). Overall, the evaluations of tutoring suggest a reciprocal effectiveness for elementary- and secondary-school recipients, as well as for the adolescent providers. All show small but significant gains in academic and personal functioning, even in studies of older youth who have themselves evidenced problems.

In other peer-helping interventions, adolescents have been placed in the roles of community-based advocates for other introuble youth (Rehabilitation Services Administration, 1974), as peer mediators in youth conflicts in schools (LeFlore, 1989), and in the general capacity of mentors (Mason, 1979). Like youth volunteers, peer helpers are aided by being positioned to assist others. However, the additional success in peer-helper programs also argues persuasively for the curative power of being needed and respected by other children and adolescents.

MENTOR PROGRAMS

Adolescents can also be helped to find their way by being paired with an adult "identification" figure, or a mentor in the community. The concept of one-on-one mentoring is increasingly being promoted as a successful intervention with youth, especially those from impoverished, inner-city areas (Valentin, 1984). It generally refers to a successful adult helping a younger person in an individual relationship. Mentors try to help adolescents succeed in school and in other areas (e.g., work, parenting). These initiatives are being organized through public schools and private corporations, and through partnerships between the public and private sectors (Davis & Tolan, 1993). The mentor-volunteers are solicited through universities, youth organizations, schools, congregations, and, most often, businesses that encourage their employees to participate.

Some of the studies attempting to evaluate the benefits of mentoring have arrived at discouraging or mixed conclusions. While the idea of matching high-risk middle school students with successful business leaders (Kazdin, 1990) or pregnant teens with mature women (Polit, Quint, & Riccio, 1988) makes intuitive sense, implementation appears to be problematic. In the first example, insufficient outreach caused students to miss appointments. A lack of focus on building competence in the young adolescents was associated with an actual grade *de*crease. In the second example, the turnover of mentoring women was high and, even when replacements were found, the pregnant adolescents had great difficulty transferring their loyalties. Five years later, however, the young women who had been paired with a mentor were doing better than their peers who had not on a number of measures—including, for example, mean weekly income, length of time employed, fewer subsequent children, higher vocabulary scores of children, and percent enrolled in Head Start (Polit et al.). The research findings on mentoring point to its potential when implemented carefully. Mentoring works better when the mentor shares racial and cultural characteristics with the adolescent, when the relationships with the adolescents and their families are developed with care and follow-through, and when mentors make a lengthy commitment to their mentees. Additionally, the adolescent needs to acquire concrete skills and attendant self-esteem from the relationship for it to be helpful.

WORK TRAINING PROGRAMS

Commissions and panels on the status of adolescents (e.g., W. T. Grant Commission, Carnegie Council on Adolescent Development, Children's Defense Fund) have endorsed the adolescent work experience as an integral and effective means of developing a sense of independence, bringing adolescents into closer contact with adults, and teaching them the skills they will need as adults. These experts conclude that work experiences also ease the often stressful transition into adult roles, making the workplace an important educational environment.

Schools and other institutions have been criticized for segregating work from the rest of the adolescent's life and adolescent work from the adult workplace (Simons et al., 1991; Steinberg, Greenberger, Garduque, Ruggerio, & Vaux, 1982). Thus, many advocates view better work options and training opportunities as important supplements to traditional schooling. Dropouts, noncollege-bound and impoverished adolescents also need work that can function as an educational alternative (Youth and America's Future, 1988).

One increasingly popular youth-employment initiative has developed through formalized partnerships of private employers, schools, and government. The highest profile among these is probably the National Jobs Corps, which is designed to provide intensive, community-based job-training programs. The Commission on Youth Employment Programs (1985) summarized the results of all of the Jobs Corps programs and concluded that graduates earned more, relied on welfare less time, and were much more likely to have a GED or a high-school diploma than nonparticipants. However, the attrition rates were also high. In some programs the average length of stay was 5.1 months and only one in five participants completed the full 12-month program.

Additional concerns about the value of work for adolescents have been raised by Steinberg (1989). Most adolescents are not enrolled in formal job-training programs and instead have low-paying jobs in fast-food restaurants and similar businesses. In these situations, they are segregated from adult workers and do not acquire skills that can be transferred to adult jobs. Moreover, they are more likely to develop cynical attitudes toward work and the ethics of work practices and, surprisingly, more likely to smoke cigarettes and marijuana. Contrary to expectations, adolescent workers do not become more socially responsible or more committed to personal relationships with friends and family because they work; nor do they develop close relationships with adults on the job. Equally concerning, Gottfredson (1985) found that working did not deter delinquency among high-risk inner-city youth. Others have concluded that employment is, in fact, associated with *increased* delinquent behavior, especially when the working hours are long (Bachman, Bare, & Frankie, 1986; Greenberger & Steinberg, 1986).

However, there does seem to be a dramatic difference between the meaningless dead-end pursuit of flipping hamburgers and the development of skills that actually connects adolescents to adults and enables them to contribute to society. For example, The Youth Action Program in New York City's East Harlem is a model that is being replicated in part or whole by 200 organizations in 35 states across the country through an umbrella organization called the YouthBuild Coalition (Simons et al., 1991). Sixteen- to 24-year-olds who need jobs, job skills, and a second chance at an education join up with the Youth Action Program for 6 to 18 months. They spend half their time in closely supervised, paid work (rehabilitating abandoned buildings to house homeless families) and the other half in classrooms working on their academic skills. The point of the training is to improve their community while improving their own chances for a decent future. At the end of their stay, the program helps to place them in full-time jobs, which are often in the high-paying construction field.

From time to time while they are in the program, these young people also meet with state and local legislators, attend budget hearings, speak out at public meetings, or go on vigils advocating support for youth employment and community improvement initiatives. The idea of combining physical neighborhood improvement, youth employment, and advocacy by youths for youths is both logical and appealing. Every time YouthBuild puts an ad in the paper, it receives seven times as many applicants as it has places.

The Youth Action Program is both thoughtful and comprehensive. At the building sites, for example, the goal isn't to get the job done quickly, but to make sure the trainees get real skills. At the same time, the focus extends beyond obtaining construction skills to life skills, leadership skills, academic skills, and the self-esteem that goes along with this kind of learning, belonging, and purpose.

CHURCH-BASED PROGRAMS

Most churches, synagogues, and religious organizations have programs designed to address the social, emotional, and spiritual needs of adolescents and their families. Religious institutions typically offer counseling and sponsor prevention activities in addition to providing religious services. In poor and minority neighborhoods, the church is often the only glue available to hold the community together, offering food, shelter, clothing, and community outreach as well as prayer (Freedman, 1993). Some adolescents participate in the activities of the church youth group as their only extracurricular experience. In these cases, the youth group leaders are often the first adults approached when adolescents are in crisis.

Recent polls indicate that 96 percent of Americans say that they believe in God (Carter, 1993). Religious belief and and the search for spiritual meaning are still strong forces for most adolescents. Such general observations become more significant when the importance of ideology in the lives of adolescents is considered. Adolescents are acutely susceptible to ideology as an influence on development and identity; they are especially able to make use of it as a personal resource and as a source of resilience (Elder, 1987; Garbarino, 1993).

Religious affiliations provide important buffers from participation in violence as well as its ravaging effects on development. Many observers have described the importance of ideological factors in sustaining the ability to function under extreme stress. For example, in his observations of life in Nazi concentration camps, Bettelheim (1943) notes that those who bore up best were those with intense ideological and religious commitments. Contemporary research similarly associates church involvement with more stable adolescent and family functioning. In fact, in a large number of studies, low "religiosity" (measured by infrequent church attendance) is related to delinquency, substance use, teen pregnancy, school failure, and a myriad of other adolescent problems (Dryfoos, 1990).

Neighborhood churches and synagogues are important also because they provide natural connections for families isolated by problems of violence. Most of us have a spiritual identity whether or not we are consciously aware of it. Establishing stronger ties, reestablishing old ties, or creating new ties to local religious institutions can be significant community-based interventions. These can be instrumental in bringing family members together or providing deeper meaning for adolescents so that they might endure the violence in their lives and triumph over it.

There are many good reasons for mental health professionals to know about and support both the self-help groups and the community-based interventions in their areas. The problems faced by adolescents living with violence are vast and complex, and the mental health implications of violence are profound. There is no one level of intervention or one type of approach that works well on its own consistently over all situations. Problems of violence in the lives of adolescents are also social problems that must be addressed by members of the communities who are most directly affected.

Mental Health in the Community

While outpatient psychotherapy in its many guises has had a 40-year reign as the preferred way to treat problems of violence in adolescence, other mental-health systems and agencies have been developed to supplement or replace therapy for a variety of good economic and political reasons. Like other community approaches, these alternative interventions are designed for high-risk adolescents who do not utilize traditional mental health services. However, unlike other community-based programs, these services are designed by the mental-health establishment to help and rehabilitate troubled adolescents. Furthermore, unlike traditional outpatient psychotherapy, these services have evolved partly *because* of problems of violence in adolescence. Mental health services in the community include shelters, drop-in centers, school-based training programs, juvenile justice system interventions, and residential treatment centers.

SHELTERS

About 500 shelters across the country receive federal and state support to provide crisis intervention, individual counseling, drug and alcohol counseling, long-term foster care, transportation, recreation, and work readiness training for more than one million high-risk adolescents annually. The National Network of Runaway and Youth Services, Inc. prepared a study of these programs in 1984 and found that 57 percent of the adolescents were reunited with their families, placed in foster care or a group home, helped to attain an independent living arrangement, or placed in a nonsecure detention program (Bucy, 1985). The success of these shelters in stabilizing the lives of these high-risk adolescents reportedly depends on the extent to which they offer a variety of different on- and off-site services. On the average, an adolescent in such a program receives 13 different types of services.

DROP-IN CENTERS

Most shelters for runaway and homeless youth have a drop-in component. In fact, twice as many adolescents visit shelters as stay in them overnight (Bucy, 1985). Additionally, many cities now have community-based drop-in programs in which homeless, runaway, out-of-school, and otherwise underserved adolescents can be assisted. Dryfoos (1990) describes an agency in Chicago, called the Neon Street Clinic, that was developed as a comprehensive facility for homeless and runaway youth under age 21. In addition to its general services, Neon Street serves as a drop-in center for homeless youth, where they are allowed to "hang out" for 15 visits before they must subscribe to a "service plan." This clinic allows for contact between social workers and street youth for assistance with social, educational, and vocational problems; AIDS education; and other issues. The program reports that 78 percent of its clients have returned to school, found employment, or enrolled in prevocational training; only 7 percent were still living on the streets.

In New York City, another program, called The Door, houses extensive teen health, family planning, prenatal, and well-baby care facilities; a wide range of educational services for both in-school and out-of-school youths, including a degree-granting alternative high school; counseling on matters from job preparation to substance abuse; legal services; English as a Second Language classes; and a variety of physical, creative, performing, and martial arts programs. About 300 economically or educationally disadvantaged adolescents, of various racial and ethnic groups, come to The Door each day (Simons et al., 1991). Since its inception in 1970, The Door has been used as a model for comprehensive youth services. Its design is built around the concept of a "community of concern" and is furthered by a staff deeply committed to a holistic approach to helping young people.

SCHOOL-BASED TRAINING PROGRAMS

Social-skills training and conflict-resolution training are the alternatives to traditional mental health approaches for adolescents that have had the greatest impact on clinical services (Davis & Tolan, 1993). These school-based services are distinguishable from conventional treatment in their broadening of the definition of mental health beyond the presence or absence of symptoms, their emphasis on competence enhancement, and their prominence as preventive methods.

Social-skills training generally involves teaching adolescents about their own risky behavior, giving them the speaking and listening skills to cope with and, if necessary, resist the influences of their peers in social situations, and helping them to make healthy decisions about their futures, Techniques such as role-playing, rehearsal, peer instruction, and media analysis are typically employed (Dryfoos, 1990). Current curricula are designed to prevent a range of behaviors with negative consequences—including violence. Examples include delaying substance use, delaying sexual activity and using contraception, improving school behavior, and increasing assertiveness with peers (e.g., Davis & Tolan, 1993).

Social-skills training is most effective when it is used in conjunction with other approaches; in the delinquency literature, the benefits of social-skills training alone do not appear to be durable over time (e.g., Henggeler, 1989). To be effective, as Goldstein and Glick (1987) have argued, treatment must combine several types of interventions, including moral education, problem-solving training, social-skills training, contingency management, and peer pressure, to enhance motivation. These researchers believe that positive therapeutic outcome results from a coordinated interplay among these interventions. It is also important to note that, as with all problems of violence in adolescence, it is critical to involve the family and social systems of adolescents to ensure the longevity of any individual changes made.

JUVENILE JUSTICE SYSTEM INTERVENTIONS

The juvenile justice system is actually host to all forms of violence in adolescence. While it is designed to treat offenders (including runaways), it is clear that a significant number of adolescents who come through the system have also been abused. In one review of the literature on juvenile offenders, Pate (1986) concluded that between 40 and 90 percent of youths in trouble with the law have been abused—often repeatedly or brutally. In the past decade, several reputable longitudinal studies have concluded that children who witness and experience violence in their homes are at higher risk for delinquency. Given that more than 4 million adolescents come into contact with law enforcement agencies every year (Monahan, 1976), this association is particularly noteworthy. Moreover, abused offenders are more likely to commit crimes involving interpersonal violence than their nonabused delinquent peers. Adolescent victims may be unusually well-trained in using force to obtain a desired end.

Despite the evidence that many offenders are also victims, outcome research on treatment in the juvenile justice system focuses with great singularity of purpose on recidivism rates. While this shortcoming alone does not account for the disappointing results of such interventions, it does point to a need to understand problems of violence in the broadest context possible.

From its inception, the juvenile justice system has intended to rehabilitate and treat youthful offenders rather than to punish them.

While most would agree that it has fallen short of its lofty goals, three approaches have emerged in response to criticisms and burgeoning recidivism rates: institutional treatment, diversion, and sanctions.

Institutional Treatment

According to The U.S. Department of Justice (1987) statistics, about 25,000 juveniles are currently confined in long-term, state-operated juvenile institutions. The available data on the effectiveness of institutional treatment are mixed. Garrett (1985), and Mayer, Gensheimer, Davidson, and Gottschalk (1986) concluded that, overall, institutional treatment was moderately effective in both aiding community adjustment and reducing recidivism. By contrast, Lab and Whitehead (1988) and Quay (1987) concluded that, while studies usually showed positive behavioral changes within the institutions, the maintenance and generalization of change were problematic. At best, institutional treatment for delinquents is only moderately effective in bringing about lasting change.

Diversion

The impetus for the development of large-scale juvenile-diversion projects came from the President's Commission on Law Enforcement and the Administration of Justice as a part of the deinstitutionalization movement of the 1960s. The primary purpose of diversion was to provide individualized services for adolescent offenders while minimizing their penetration into the juvenile justice system (Blomberg, 1983). Based on the assumptions of labeling theory, advocates of diversion hypothesized that the diversion of youths would reduce the stigmatization that might have occurred if they had become more formally involved in the criminal justice system, and that most juveniles could be better helped if they remained in their communities. Diversion occurs at every possible level. Nonreporting of crimes by citizens, nonarrest by police, and intake into probation all serve to divert adolescents from justice processing, even before a judge gets to hear a case. As Vito and Wilson (1985) note, most cases are diverted—out of 500 potential arrests, police make 200 contacts which produce 100 arrests. Of these, only 40 youths reach the intake stage. Hence, of 500 possible arrests, only 8 percent reach intake and the formal process of diversion.

The emphasis on diversion has created a broad array of public and private organizations and facilities to which a juvenile may be diverted. Some examples include individual, family, or group counseling; halfway houses; Outward Bound; drug and alcohol rehabilitation and treatment centers; and psychoeducational programs. Few conclusions can be drawn from the research about the effectiveness of diversion of juvenile offenders. Reviewers (e.g., Blomberg, 1983; Polk, 1984; Rausch, 1983) have cited several studies that supported diversion and several studies that failed to find differential outcomes for diverted groups versus control groups. In these reports, the most common diversion strategies employed were referrals to other agencies for therapy, tutoring, or job training. Wilderness programs have also been found to have positive effects, but the extent and generalizability of these effects are unclear (Kelly & Baer, 1971; Winterdyk & Roesch, 1981).

More important, and in contrast with the goals of diversion, several investigators have concluded that diversion actually *increases* adolescents' involvement with the juvenile justice system and can have harmful effects (e.g., Adler, 1984; Frazier & Cochran, 1986; Polk, 1984). The diversion of youths who would otherwise be released is especially disturbing in light of findings that associate referral to community agencies with higher recidivism rates than outright release (Klein, 1986).

Finally, there is no unified notion of diversion. Rather, it reflects a variety of psychosocial interventions that vary from study to study, and jurisdiction to jurisdiction. Once touted as something of a panacea, diversion programs have not been shown to be consistently effective in reducing further delinquent behavior.

Sanctions

Deterrence theory, which has become increasingly popular among criminologists, suggests that the threat or the imposition of sanctions for criminal acts can decrease rates of delinquent behavior in adolescents. Most sanctions do not appear to be effective in reducing delinquent behaviors. A possible exception is restitution, which requires the offender to pay a sum of money or perform a useful service for the victim (Schneider, 1986). By contrast, arrest (or the threat of arrest), institutionalization, and the Scared Straight model (in which incarcerated offenders speak to juveniles about the horrors of prison life) have all failed to reduce recidivism in a number of studies (e.g., Henggeler, 1989).

Overall, the juvenile justice system has had a long, uphill struggle accomplishing its mission of helping young offenders. The most favorable findings in the treatment of delinquents have been obtained in studies that used behavioral, individualized, broad-based interventions in community settings—interventions that attempted to improve family functioning and modify the juvenile's social networks. Interventions directed by the juvenile justice system have had, at best, mixed results.

RESIDENTIAL TREATMENT CENTERS

Residential treatment services and psychiatric hospital programs for adolescents are important, costly, and widely used therapeutic modalities designed for individuals who, for a variety of reasons, are not succeeding in a less protective setting. Such programs are generally organized around school, recreational activities, limit-setting with token economies of some kind, and individual, group, family, and/or multifamily therapy (Marohn, 1993).

The pathway into residential treatment is complicated. On the one hand, many severely disturbed adolescents who could profit from residential care are not receiving it (Myers, 1986; President's Commission on Mental Health, 1978). On the other hand, some studies suggest that as many as 40 percent of the adolescents in residential placement do not need to be in such a restrictive setting (e.g., Knitzer, 1982; Marohn, 1993). It is evident that the actual need for residential treatment is often less of a consideration than economic and procedural factors. Similarly, since referrals follow so many different paths, they are subject to all kinds of personal and professional biases. For example, girls are often repeatedly "excused" for deviant behavior, so that by the time they come to the attention of authorities, they may be more seriously disturbed (Offer, Ostrov, & Howard, 1984). Ethnic and racial prejudice also plays a role; minority youth, whose behavior is viewed as criminal, are moved swiftly into and through the juvenile justice system while nonminority youth exhibiting the same behavior are seen as having psychological problems and are more likely to be treated through the medical system. It is evident that how and for whom residential care is applied is a precarious and complex formulation.

However, residential treatment is an important option for adolescents of violence. Several studies have concluded that adolescents who end up in residential care are highly likely to have been victims or perpetrators, to have experienced violent death—through homicide, suicide, accidents—and to behave violently themselves (e.g., Marohn, 1974, 1993). Thus, this group as a whole tends to require the full gamut of therapeutic interventions in order to begin to heal and learn to live without violence.

Interventions that Work

There appears to be a fair degree of consensus among the experts about why interventions with adolescence of violence are successful, although research efforts have not kept up with clinical need. The following four broad principles appear to have been operating when outcomes are positive:

1. Adolescents have the opportunity to develop healing relationships with trustworthy adults in a place that is perceived to be safe.

2. Other services are also provided (e.g., family therapy, tutoring, job placement) because the effects of violence are complex and require flexible, individualized multisystemic responses.

3. The peer group is recognized as a powerful source of support and connection, and efforts to develop this resource are made.

4. Social, cognitive, and problem-solving skills that are stunted or destroyed by violence are given as much attention as the history and relationship-building.

Generally, it is insufficient to treat the experience of violence as an individual problem, removing adolescents from the family and social contexts in which they live. Broad-based interventions have the additional benefit of empowering adolescents to make the personal changes necessary to live without violence. However, they can do this only when the systems that create and perpetuate violence are also addressed.

8

Social Policy

All violence, like politics, is local. People become safe home by home, neighborhood by neighborhood. Yet it is social policy that shapes and organizes the efforts to prevent and control violence in the lives of individual adolescents. Policy is the arm in which the other levels of intervention are cradled—or from which the other levels are dropped. Policy affects, for example, the community supports for families, the resources available to these families that help them protect and care for their adolescents, and the length, types, and availability of interventions.

Current social policies have led to an increase in virtually all forms of violence in adolescence. The problems seem even more insurmountable when we consider the intractibility of underlying attitudes that lead to sexism, racism, and classism. Such "isms" can make violence in adolescence seem inevitable. Yet important reforms that can decrease violence are within reach. In this chapter, I focus on a few of the most glaring of these social policy concerns: prevention, lobbying/advocacy, gun control, and the media.

Prevention

Prevention of adolescent problems, including violence, falls into three general categories of interventions: *early childhood and family interventions* (e.g., preschool, Headstart, parent training and sup-

181

port); *school-based interventions* (e.g., specialized curricula, changes
in school organization, special services offered within the school);
and *community-based and/or multicomponent interventions* (e.g.,
youth organizations, mentor programs, combinations of individual,
family, peer, and community services).

Reviewers of successful prevention programs for adolescent
problems are remarkably consistent in their summaries of what
makes these interventions work (e.g., American Psychological Association, 1993; Bronfenbrenner & Weiss, 1983; Dryfoos, 1990; Garbarino, 1993; Price, Cowen, Lorion, & Ramos-McKay, 1989; Schorr,
1989; Simons et al., 1991). Effective intervention programs share
two primary characteristics: They draw on the understanding of
developmental and sociocultural risk factors leading to antisocial
behavior, and they use proven intervention strategies for changing
behavior, tested program designs, and validated, objective measure-
ment techniques to assess outcomes (American Psychological Association). Effective interventions share other important characteristics: They begin as early as possible in the child's life; they address
violence as part of a constellation of problems that the adolescent
and family have; they include multiple components that reinforce
each other across the child's everyday social contexts, such as the
family, school, peer groups, media and community; and they take
advantage of developmental "windows of opportunity," or points at
which they are either especially needed or especially likely to make
a difference (American Psychological Association).

While no single intervention has magical effects, the application
of a coordinated network of programs and services generally
works, especially when it is tailored to a particular adolescent's
needs. Overall, prevention programs need to include a variety of
different components that have proven efffective for stopping violence in the lives of adolescents.

INTENSIVE INDIVIDUALIZED ATTENTION

Since violence can both cause and be a consequence of isolation,
successful programs attach high-risk children and adolescents to a
responsible adult who pays attention to each one's specific needs.
Thus, children and adolescents benefit from the intense caring of a
concerned adult—to prevent violence from occurring in the first

place and to prevent the effects of violence from leading to other problems. As a corollary, social isolation from someone who cares about the individual adolescent, and from the prosocial support systems the adult is associated with, can be extremely dangerous. As Bronfenbrenner and Weiss (1983) so succinctly phrase it, "In order to develop normally, a child needs the enduring, irrational involvement of one or more adults in care and joint activity with that child . . . In short, someone has to be crazy about that kid" (p. 398).

A good support system provides nurturance *and* feedback (Caplan, 1974). It is not sufficient that the involved adult merely cares for the adolescent (although this, too, is critical); adolescents require that someone be actively engaged in their lives. Thus, regular contact with caring adults needs to include a degree of counseling—for example, about career opportunities and life options, as well as about how to make self-protecting decisions. Ideally, parents play this role. However, when families are not equipped, then adolescents must find mentors in teachers, school counselors, youth workers, clergy, church members, or volunteers in a mentoring program. Every adolescent needs at least one adult willing to be a caring guide into maturity.

COMMUNITY-WIDE MULTIAGENCY COLLABORATION

Participation in recreational and social activities brings adolescents into contact with caring adults and supportive peers and provides constructive outlets for adolescent energy. Subsequently, adolescents also need community-based opportunities in order to feel successful and lead nonviolent lives. Any number of different programs and services can provide this support, including schools, community health and social agencies, businesses, media, church groups, universities, police and courts, and youth groups.

Youth programs can also include opportunities for religious and cultural enhancement, which are especially helpful when family ties are weak or dangerous. Adolescents of violence appear to find important connections, solace, and pride in their cultural and religious roots; in turn, communities are strengthened by providing opportunities for adolescents to celebrate their cultural identities.

Finally, contributing constructively to the community and helping others can give teenagers a stake in the common good and
boost confidence and self-esteem. Community service programs
should give adolescents meaningful tasks and frequent interactions
with other adolescents as well as adults. They should also include
regular opportunities to reflect on and discuss their activities. Community service can include physical labor (e.g., working on a community garden, building a playground) as well as caretaking of other
members of the community. Bronfenbrenner and Weiss (1983) have
proposed that schools add a "curriculum of caring" to the academic
program from the earliest grades onward. The purpose of this curriculum would be not simply to learn about caring, but to *engage* in
it, by caring for those who need help—younger children and elderly, ill, or lonely people. Through community service, adolescents
at risk for being victims or offenders can begin to feel productive
and find caring connections that can benefit them as much as the
community they are helping.

EARLY IDENTIFICATION AND INTERVENTION

Reaching children and their families in the early stages of the development of problem behaviors demonstrates both short- and long-
term benefits for the prevention of violence. At the root of most
serious problems of adolescence lies severe family dysfunction, particularly child abuse and neglect. The link between child abuse and
later difficulties, mentioned in Chapter 6, merits repeating: Child
abuse is associated with delinquency, running away, school problems, parricide, prostitution, sex offenses, and subsequent abuse of
the next generation of children, in excess of 65 percent in some
studies. Therefore, early identification and intervention with children and families at high risk for violence would do much to prevent serious problems later.

Numerous programs have been developed that successfully prevent child abuse or decrease escalation of abuse. These include
home visitation by professionals to support and educate adolescent,
single or low socioeconomic status mothers (Olds, Henderson, Tatelbaum, & Chamberlin, 1986); health, social and educational interventions for handicapped infants and their families following discharge
from the newborn intensive care unit (Soloman, 1979); family sup-

port programs (Weissbourd & Kagan, 1989); and conflict-resolution training for families of adolescents (Alexander & Parsons, 1982). The relationship between child abuse and adolescent problems is clear and merits social policy consideration when programs for troubled families are developed.

SCHOOL-BASED INTERVENTION

As families have increasingly struggled to remain safe and nurturing havens for adolescents, the schools have had to move in and pick up the slack. Even when families are not being effective, a healthy, safe school can help prevent violence. Effective schools buffer adolescents from violence in several ways: They provide sanctuary from dangerous homes and streets; they develop self-esteem and conflict-resolution skills; and they create the link to a safe and productive future.

All adolescents need ambitious education and career goals that promote college or post-high-school training. Inequality in educational opportunity is creating a growing underclass; by the year 2000 more than a third of those entering the labor market will be ill-prepared minorities (Hewlett, 1991). Educational reform can help decrease violence by supplying students with loans, grants, and scholarships sufficient to ensure access to a good education, regardless of ability to pay.

To assist in violence prevention, however, schools must do more than provide an education—which, admittedly, is difficult enough. At the same time, schools must act as referral and delivery sites for coordinated social services for adolescents and their families. To this end, schools require well-trained guidance counselors who will work with families and keep parents involved in their children's education. Schools that serve their adolescents provide effective education *and* effective counseling that in turn provide links to community services (Dryfoos, 1990).

RECOGNITION OF THE IMPORTANCE OF THE PEER GROUP

Program designers, recognizing the importance of peer influence on adolescent behavior, have devised a variety of successful preventive interventions employing peers as mentors, tutors, instructors, and counselors. While peer groups are often seen as the cause of many adolescent problems, this assumption does not fully convey how peer influence evolves. Recent research in particular supports the view that parental abuse and neglect pushes adolescents toward deviant peers more often than peers pull adolescents away from parents (e.g., Condry & Siman, 1974; Kandel & Andrews, 1987). Of course, there are situations where an adolescent gets in with a "bad crowd" and the parents have not been negligent, but this is *not* the most frequent or enduring scenario.

Regardless of the cause of attraction to the bad crowd, structured, educational groups can teach adolescents how to resist the poor judgment of peers and make their own decisions. In particular, social-skills training programs have demonstrated improvements in social competency and decision-making. Outward-Bound-type challenges also appear to be successful in changing poor attitudes and increasing self-esteem. High-risk youth can gain strength from programs that engage them in defined roles, such as tutors for younger students and as classroom instructors for their peers. Trained peer counselors also appear to help divert adolescents from engaging in violence and to connect them with resources in the community.

SUPPORT FOR FAMILIES OF ADOLESCENTS

While prevention programs for adolescents report only limited success in involving parents, a number of models across the various fields have demonstrated that programs directed toward parents can be successful. These programs hold in common an understanding that parental and family involvement is often critical for the reduction and prevention of violence. It does not matter whether the adolescent's problems are simply a continuation of difficulties (like abuse and neglect) begun in childhood, the deterioration of unwise childhood patterns, or the inability of a family that functioned well during childhood to meet new challenges in adolescence. In all instances, the intervention needs to be aimed at helping family members develop new skills and attitudes that will enable them to overcome the obstacles they face raising their adolescents free of violence.

All families raising adolescents need support. For those who are isolated and at risk, communities need to provide access to family resource centers, parent-support groups and various parent-education activities. Furthermore, intensive family-based services for families in crisis should be provided. As much as possible, intervention services and other services designed to prevent the unnecessary placement of youths away from the family should be home-based, aimed at strengthening the family and keeping all members safe. Although some children must be removed from their homes for their own protection or the community's, many more could safely remain at home if their families were assisted in getting the help necessary to better support and nurture them.

LINKS TO THE WORLD OF WORK

Successful prevention programs for adolescents also use innovative approaches to introduce youngsters to career planning and work experiences, and prepare them to enter the labor force. High-risk adolescents need more help to see the value of staying in school if they are to make the transition from school to work. Schools and local businesses must collaborate to motivate students to complete high school and increase employment rates among recent graduates. School-to-work transition programs must include counseling, peer support, and job-training and job-placement skills.

Dropouts also need to be reached through "second chance" education, and job-skill and vocational training. Every state and school district must develop second-chance programs for high-school dropouts and young adults who graduate with poor basic academic skills. The model for such programs (and it merits expansion) is the Jobs Corps, which offers individualized counseling and support services along with remedial education and vocational training.

In addition, high-school graduates not going on to college should have access to a wide range of vocational training options that prepare them for careers in better paying, high-skill occupations. Federal and state governments, as well as local communities, should develop new approaches that combine this training with traditional educational activities. Some examples are youth-apprenticeship programs, collaborative relationships between high schools and community colleges, and other longer term training options that lead to recognized credentials in sizeable or growing occupational areas.

Finally, it should be noted that adolescents raised out of the home—in foster care or some type of residential program—require extra help to make the transition to independent living, and have additional educational and economic needs that require attention.

HEALTH CARE

Adolescents of violence are vulnerable to health problems in some special ways. Physical and sexual abuse can lead to injuries, sexually transmitted diseases, and other kinds of trauma requiring medical attention. Delinquents are increasingly involved in accidents involving weapons. By definition, violence in adolescence is a health problem. Yet few prevention programs address it sufficiently. Instead, adolescent health-related interventions have been targeted at disease prevention (e.g., healthy eating/exercise programs, AIDS awareness); substance-abuse prevention (e.g., drugs, cigarettes, alcohol); sexuality and adolescent pregnancy prevention (e.g., school-based clinics, programs for parenting teens); and the development of health centers that specialize in adolescent medicine (e.g., school-linked clinics, programs designed to address the special health needs of adolescents).

Abused and abusing adolescents may be unlikely to seek and obtain appropriate health care for a variety of reasons. First, they may be poor. Poor 10- to 18-year olds are more than three times as likely as their nonpoor peers to be uninsured, a major barrier to obtaining regular health care (Simons et al., 1991). Second, they may be unable to gain access to medical care if consent—or transportation—is not provided by their parents. If they are victims of abuse or neglect, or if they are out of control, they may not be able to establish an ongoing relationship with a health provider. Third, even if adolescents of violence obtain a check-up, they may be examined by someone unfamiliar to them; they may be too ashamed to disclose what is going on at home—or they may not be asked or believed.

Finally, although well-established, the relationship between abuse and other kinds of symptomatology includes a host of physical and psychological problems. The link is not always apparent to the provider. Migraine headaches, hemorrhoids, depression, and school phobia may be diagnosed, but the violence may not be.

The Children's Defense Fund (1992) has listed four areas of policy reform affecting adolescent health that are particularly critical to the prevention and treatment of adolescents of violence. First, school systems should work with local health agencies, community health centers and community hospitals to develop adolescent-health-care programs accessible to all middle- and high-school students. Programs should be located on or near school campuses or housing projects. It is especially critical for schools serving low-income students to establish clinics, because these students are unlikely to have a regular source of routine health care.

Second, states must make sure that their Medicaid programs cover the services of school-affiliated programs in practice. State programs must eliminate roadblocks like unduly burdensome eligibility processes.

Third, all levels of government should seek opportunities to support comprehensive approaches to teen health care. Services need to be funded at the federal and state levels to allow communities to develop treatment programs to meet the special social, emotional, physical, and educational needs of adolescents. Comprehensive care may include physical exams, general primary health care, pregnancy tests, prenatal care and referrals, immunizations, diagnosis and treatment of sexually transmitted diseases, pediatric care for infants born to adolescents, mental health counseling, and substance-abuse and violence-prevention services.

As this book is being written, President Clinton is working with congress to develop a national health care policy. It is not certain what form the final plans will take, though most versions include important benefits to the poor and currently uninsured. Every child and adolescent should have health insurance coverage. National health care reform, to ensure health insurance for all Americans, is long overdue, but as a first step Congress should act to provide immediate Medicaid coverage to all children and youths with incomes below the poverty level. (Such coverage is currently supposed to be phased in, beginning with infants, and will not benefit adolescents until the year 2002.)

Fourth, while this list is a broad one, the Children's Defense Fund also suggests that adolescents of violence require mental health services designed and funded to meet their needs. Untreated victims and offenders end up costing the health-care, social-service, and legal systems much more later. For an adolescent with post traumatic stress disorder (PTSD), a diagnosis common to survivors of violence, the growing trend in managed health care toward provision of a maximum of 20 psychotherapy sessions can be grossly inadequate. Where the child's ability to trust has been damaged, it can often take many weeks to reassert itself, and the work of therapy for such adolescents cannot begin without basic trust. Cost-containment on the back of an abused or suicidal adolescent makes no sense at all.

ECONOMICS

Although violence in adolescence affects us all, it does discriminate, and its effects are felt most deeply by the poor and minorities. Without a basic standard of living for all teens and their families, the cycle of violence cannot be broken. This standard would include, at a minimum, access to jobs, nutrition, housing, income, and services to meet special needs.

The consequences for teens of growing up poor can be devastating: Young people are more likely to do badly in school, have a range of health problems, and bear children earlier than those from more-comfortably-off families. With their own children, the impact of poverty can be devastating in turn. While jobs and job skills are a key part of the answer, recent economic changes have made it difficult for young workers to support a family even when they work full time. In 1989, for example, nearly half of all hourly workers under 25 were paid wages too low to lift a family of three out of poverty (Simons et al., 1991).

Therefore, along with job skills and job opportunities, the Children's Defense Fund recommends some other key steps to eliminate poverty among children and adolescents. One of these steps is enactment of a child tax credit and child-support insurance. A refundable tax credit to families with children and teenagers would provide a modest amount of assistance through the tax system in recognition of the costs and responsibilities families bear in raising children and preparing them for adulthood. The economic foundation for families provided by this tax credit would be supplemented by a system of child-support insurance that would insure children and teenagers against a parent's desertion or divorce, much in the same way that the federal government now insures many Americans against death and disability. When absent parents are not able to make adequate payments, or when federal or state governments fail to collect such support, the federal government would make up the difference to guarantee that children do not lose basic income support.

Taken together, these nine kinds of interventions offer a multifaceted and comprehensive program for primary and and secondary prevention of violence in adolescence. In a relatively short time, social policy reforms in each of these realms would reduce emotional, physical, and economic costs. Such recomendations provide the basic elements for growing up safely, and making the transition from childhood to adulthood free of violence.

Lobbying/Advocacy

Adolescents need advocates. At the individual level, such advocacy can mean going to school meetings, writing letters of recommendation, or showing up at the band performance even when family members are not interested in going. At the family level, advocacy occurs when parents are given the support and skills necessary to keep their adolescents safe, the adolescent is empowered by the family to make self-protecting decisions, or the adolescent victim is believed and helped with other family members through the criminal justice process. At the community level, advocacy can include sitting on the board of the local YMCA or teen center, publicly speaking on adolescent development and relationships, or helping to develop other community resources and programs.

At the social policy level, advocacy is knowing who the policymakers are, finding out about the issues they are concerned with, and lobbying them through the mail, on the phone, and in person. Anyone interested in the problems of adolescence should know something about lobbying for local changes that could reduce violence in adolescence at home and in our communities. There are many groups responsible for developing policies and getting them funded in Washington. Different groups lobby on behalf of particular issues salient to their work (e.g., the American Academy of Pediatrics lobbies on behalf of disease prevention; the American Psychological Association lobbies on behalf of mental-health services; the Child Welfare League of America lobbies on behalf of child-protection reforms). Among all of the different groups working to reform policies affecting adolescents today, the Children's Defense Fund (CDF) is the most responsive to a broad range of concerns. For the novice lobbyist, a call to the CDF legislative hotline tape (202-662-3678) is a fine place to get started. CDF is the leading advocacy group working on behalf of policy reform for children and adolescents in this country.

Children's Defense Fund
122 C Street, NW
Washington, DC 20001
(202)628-8787

Lobbying can take many forms. Most simply, it can mean writing letters or calling representatives about an issue needing reform. Advocates can lobby on a local, state, or national level.

Contacting a Congressperson
Hon. _____
U. S. House of Representatives
Washington, DC 20515
(202)224-3121

Contacting a Senator
Hon. _____
U. S. Senate
Washington, DC 20510
(202)224-3121

Contacting the President
President Clinton
The White House
Washington, DC 20500
(202)456-1111

Most states have child-advocacy organizations of their own. The National Association of Child Advocates serves as a clearinghouse for different state-based advocacy groups. They assist new advocates in joining forces with existing advocacy groups (or helping to start one) at the state level.

National Association of Child Advocates
1825 K Street, NW
Washington, DC 20006
(202)828-6950

To deal with the the problems of adolescents, the key word is flexibility. Just as parents and programs need to be flexible in providing care to their adolescents, so mental-health professionals need to view their own roles flexibly. This perspective holds the therapy hour valuable, but no more so than any number of advocacy activities done on behalf of the adolescent. Because violence is local, we must know how to lobby for neighborhood policy changes that can keep us all safer. Any and all of the nine areas described above can be singled out for lobbying and advocacy. The adolescents of violence we see in our offices are individuals, but they are also symbols of a system that is failing them. We have an obligation to help them at both levels.

Gun Control

No discussion of violence in adolescence would be complete without reference to guns and the need for gun control in this country. While not the cause of or solution to the whole problem, guns continue to play an increasing role in adolescent violence that merits critical scrutiny.

A comprehensive study of high-school students throughout the United States (Centers for Disease Control, 1991) revealed that 20 percent of all students reported carrying a weapon for protection in the past 30 days; 4 percent of these students carried a gun. By extrapolation, this means that, in any given month, 525,800 U.S. high school students carry a gun to school for self-protection (Clark & Mokros, 1993). Furthermore, a recent national Harris poll concluded that nearly 60 percent of youngsters in grades 6 to 12 could get a gun quickly if they wanted to, and 39 percent said they knew someone who had been killed or wounded by gunfire (Children's Defense Fund, 1994b). While the Harris poll confirmed that 4 percent of adolescents had specifically carried a gun to school in the last month, many more (15 percent) had toted a handgun for some purpose during that time.

The National Center for Health Statistics (1993) has also published some sobering data about homicides. Violence is the leading cause of death among American teens and young adults, especially black males. In 1990, 1 in 4 deaths among all teens aged 15 to 19 was caused by firearms; 60 percent of deaths among black teen males were caused by firearms in that year. The firearm homicide rate among black teen males is more than 10 times the rate among white males of the same age. Black males aged 10 to 24 are about 2 to 4 times more likely (depending upon their age) than their white peers to be victims of handgun crime.

Between 1933 and 1982 the rate of suicide by firearms for all adolescents and young adults between 15 and 24 years old increased by 139 percent, while the corresponding rate for suicide by all other means increased by only 32 percent (Boyd & Moscicki, 1986). The relatively dramatic increase in the suicide-by-firearms rate began in 1970 and is most apparent for males. The same research also showed that the increase coincided with a sharp increase in domestic production of firearms. By 1979, there were 75 guns in civilian hands for every 100 Americans. Estimates of the number of U.S. families owning firearms remained constant at about 50 percent for the period from 1959 to 1977, so these findings suggest that gun-owning households are simply accumulating larger numbers of guns. This research points to a strong association between the increasing availability of firearms with the increasing rates of adolescent suicide (Boyd & Moscicki).

While such a relationship cannot be defined causally, there are other kinds of data to support concern about the increasing suicidal use of firearms. For example, in a review of firearm deaths in one city over a 6-year period, Kellerman and Reay (1986) concluded that people keep guns in their home mostly for self-protection, yet such guns are used for suicide almost 40 times more often than they are used for self-protection.

In a variety of different studies, stricter handgun policies have been shown to reduce both homicide and suicide for adolescents (e.g., Brent et al., 1991; Clark & Mokros, 1993; Sloan, Rivera, Reay, Ferris, & Kellerman, 1990). It is up to Congress and the states to enact tough enough gun-control legislation that may actually help keep deadly weapons out of the hands of children and adolescents and, to some extent, those who prey upon young people through violent drug trafficking. The Brady bill requires just a five-day waiting period before handguns can be purchased; additional legislation to prevent gun-related violence is needed as well. It is one of the sad ironies of policy development in this country that the gun lobby has more funding (and, consequently, a more powerful voice) than all of the children's lobbies combined.

Gun control is urgently needed even though it is not in itself the decisive solution to violence in adolescence. Gun control is not a panacea. Rather, it is one of many different solutions, and an important complement to learning about and applying alternative strategies to violent resolution of problems.

Media

The media play a complicated role in understanding the problems of violence in adolescence. On the one hand, the media present and promote violence in all forms, and our culture is now undeniably saturated with it. From the nightly news to Saturday-morning cartoons, children and adolescents are exposed to large daily doses of violence. Although television is not the sole culprit (other media also serve up hearty portions of violence), the data about television violence are sufficient to make this point: Average American teenagers watch 28 hours of television a week, approximately six times the time they spend on homework; this statistic does not include the time spent watching violent videos or playing violent video games.

By the time children are in sixth grade, they have witnessed about 8,000 murders and 100,000 other acts of television violence in their short lifetimes (Healy, 1990). Again, this does not include movies, magazines, or other media in which they learn of violence, nor does it include the violence in their own lives.

The research on the effects of witnessing television violence is quite consistent, although the degree of effect appears to vary. A large majority of studies conclude that exposure to television and film violence increases the likelihood of subsequent aggressive or antisocial behavior (e.g., Comstock, 1986). In explicit depictions of sexual violence, it is the message about violence more than the sexual nature of the materials that appears to affect attitudes about rape and violence toward women. Male youth who view sexualized violence or depictions of rape on television or in film are more likely to display callousness toward female victims of violence, especially rape (American Psychological Association, 1993).

However, these effects can be reduced by education and training by parents and schools and other organizations (Cofer & Jacobvitz, 1990; Comstock, 1986; Huesmann, Eron, Klein, Brice, & Fischer, 1983). There is little likelihood that the federal government or the entertainment industry will choose to regulate the amount of violence on television. Even the recent move toward "warning" children of impending violent programming does little to reduce the number of hours spent watching this type of programming. Some cynical observers have noted that such warnings may even serve to *increase* viewing of these violent shows.

However, television may be an all-too-easy scapegoat for much that is wrong with our society. One researcher notes that the availability of television is

> an indicator that the family has a fairly sparse repertoire of options—and I'm not just talking about kids in the ghetto. Maybe TV is the only way lots of kids can settle themselves down because no one is there to show them how to work with paint supplies, modeling clay, musical instruments; they have no other nurturance, no one to read them stories, no nature to walk out in, no pets to take care of. We are looking at the absence of all of these things in so many children's lives. TV becomes a side effect. (Coulter, 1989, p. 44)

While lobbying for reforms in the quality of television programming has had modest successes over the years, the effects of television violence will continue to be felt by all who watch, given the importance of First Amendment protection for programmers. At best, more programming designed for children and adolescents will also be provided (Albert, 1978). At the same time, research has demonstrated that TV's effects are amenable to intervention and remedy by parents and schools. One reviewer (Comstock, 1986) summarized the existing studies by concluding that: (1) Effective interventions focus on either increasing the undesirability of the behavior (e.g., parents disapproving of violence and aggressiveness for resolving conflicts) or increasing skepticism and knowledge about the medium; and (2) effective interventions lower the likelihood that young viewers will attribute efficacy, normalcy, or pertinence to a violent act, thus altering the degree to which they are rendered susceptible to acting similarly in their own lives. Lowest-common-denominator competition among the media ensures that, in the future, the level of violence in television, music, and film will probably not be much lower than today and, for the same reason, it may well become increasingly graphic and exhibit greater ferocity. Remedy and intervention do not lie in a greater variety of programming or lobbying efforts against it. The effects of violence in the media can be mitigated only by efforts to the contrary in the home, the school, and the community.

On the other hand, however, the media have an important role to play in raising public consciousness about issues for social policy. It is evident, for example, that policies and laws protecting children from physical abuse in the 1970s and from sexual abuse in the 1980s were in large part brought about by greater public awareness and outrage over these problems. Were television (and newspapers) not to provide dramatic coverage of celebrated cases of abuse, these policies might never have been developed. Cohen (1963) calls this powerful effect *agenda setting*. He notes, "the press may not be successful much of the time in telling people what to think, but it is stunningly successful in telling its readers what to think *about*" (quoted in McLeod, Becker, & Byrnes, 1974, p. 134). Media coverage may not directly alter public attitudes, but it does much to focus public attention on certain events, issues, and people, and to determine how much importance viewers attach to these matters. In this way, media coverage confers status on a subject and, at the same time, burns images in our minds to which we react in countless ways for years afterward (Rubin, 1977). For example, the simple act of coverage on television and in magazines of the VietNam war (body bags, bloody corpses, ravaged villages, etc.) led to the rapid mobilization of antiwar sentiment in this country. By virtue of its presence in the media, a phenomenon may achieve an unprecedented level of status or "worth" in the eyes of the audience (Muenchow & Gilfillan, 1983).

At the same time, simplistic media campaigns are famously ineffective. Among these, the "Just say 'no'" campaigns to reduce participation in sexual activity and drug use had no noticable benefits (Dryfoos, 1990). By contrast, posters and TV commercials can encourage certain behaviors (e.g., using condoms to prevent AIDS) if the ads also include information about where to get the services being promoted (e.g., local family-planning clinic phone numbers).

Violence makes for great drama, news, and entertainment. No other topic is so universally exploited for viewer or listener interest—not even sex. As a result of the disproportionate amount of violence on television, heavy viewers tend to "overestimate the amount of violence in the world, overestimate the chances that they will be victims of violence" and be less trusting of their neighbors (Gandy, 1980, p. 108). At the same time, viewing violence increases desensitization to violence, resulting in calloused public attitudes toward violence directed at others and a decreased likelihood that an individual will take action on behalf of the victim when violence occurs. This leads to a kind of paradox: The more fearful we become of how dangerous our world is, the more inured we become to the commonplace occurence of violent acts. In addition, there is evidence that viewing violence actually increases viewer's appetites for becoming involved with violence or exposing themselves to it (American Psychological Association, 1993). So, the more dramatic the coverage, the more fearful we become, the more indifferently we react, *and* the more interest we show in seeing more violence. This is a cycle of tremendous danger for us all—and one that can be broken only by the systematic application of alternatives.

Agenda-setting can also operate particularly when it involves (or doesn't involve) the problems faced by adolescents of violence. The most powerful media influence on adolescent policy may therefore be the omission of certain news stories that should be of popular concern and the absence of certain characters in television drama. Despite the overemphasis on violence in general, the media have tended to ignore the daily, grinding violence experienced by whole classes of citizens, especially the poor and minorities (Rubin, 1977). Similarly, Gerbner (1980) points out that both television news and drama tend to devalue children and adolescents by grossly underestimating their sheer numerical presence in American society. When depicted, they seldom look or act like youngsters navigating the rising tides of violence; indeed, children and adolescents may be the largest of the invisible minorities.

Newspapers and magazines also tend to relegate coverage of children and adolescents to the "family" pages at the back of the paper (Muenchow & Gilfillan, 1983). While violence may be news, children and adolescents are not. When issues involving adolescents are discussed, they are frequently presented as soft news, something women might want to read about. Coverage of unemployment, inflation, and economic issues make it to the front of the paper as hard news; the impact of these issues on adolescents may not be covered at all.

The chief obstacle to fair, thorough, and persistent coverage of social issues is the conflict between the goals of education and entertainment. (This applies primarily to television but is true of all commerical media ventures.) When the primary goal is to attract the largest audience in order to maintain ratings and thus advertiser revenues, education is bound to take a back seat to entertainment. At the same time, it is also difficult to make social problems sound interesting. The occasional dramatic suicide epidemic or particularly gruesome cult abuse case might supply some temporary fascination, but more in-depth coverage of the policy implications of such news is wearying for most viewers accustomed to the 30-second sound bite. The media want to cover action and events, not the grinding costs of social isolation, mediocre education, and lack of opportunity.

Even when the media do present a social problem in greater depth, the overwhelming demands of news-as-entertainment often lead broadcast and print media to focus on simplistic, even spurious, solutions to these problems. For example, coverage of premature birth complications focuses on neonatal intensive-care units and not on routine prenatal care, preferring the dramatic shots of two pound babies in incubators to those of pregnant women having their urine checked.

There are several ways that advocates who are close to the subject can increase and improve media coverage of violence in adolescence (Muenchow & Gilfillan, 1983). First, decide how an issue can best be covered. For example, the local paper might be able to run a series of in-depth articles, or a favorite radio host might be willing to take on an issue to reach a broader audience. Second, frame the advocacy in such a way that the message is consonant with what the audience can comfortably hear (e.g., don't propose income redistribution to an audience of middle-class Americans). Third, cultivate reporters beyond the regular family and education "beat" (e.g., get to know reporters who cover the front page stories in the local paper). Fourth, focus on specific issues of immediate significance to the audience (e.g., the Children's Defense Fund does not address adolescent policies in general but targets specific areas like adolescent pregnancy and youth employment). Finally, create media events (e.g., the New Right is talented in staging massive antiabortion rallies on the anniversary of Roe v. Wade). Commercial television is here to stay so we must develop strategies to use this and other media to place problems of violence on the public agenda. It cannot be emphasized enough that this, too, is part of advocacy for adolescents.

(Not Quite) Happily Ever After

Social policies affecting adolescent violence are lagging behind other kinds of interventions for many reasons. Adolescents can be difficult and are not always the most grateful or pleasant people to work with; they do not, for example, offer the rewards that preschoolers do. Furthermore, interventions aimed at younger children are generally believed to have greater consequence. By such reasoning, adolescence may seem too late. There are so many problems besetting adolescents that no one really knows where to begin.

Band-aids for social problems are costly, and adolescents are un-likely to demonstrate the rapid healing that they need to earn con-tinued funding. What happens to adults as parents and policymak-ers when they are confronted with the fact that they will be passing the leadership torch on to today's adolescents? Everyone who spends even an hour with an energetic adolescent understands that death approaches more quickly for us than it does for them. We shake our heads wearily and mumble adages about youth being wasted on the young. Our collective resentment bears heavily upon how we individually and as a nation treat our youth.

And even if we want to do something helpful, we can be para-lyzed by the confusing myriad of options. Do we view adolescent problems as the result of personal weakness, or of community mal-function? How do we resolve the struggle between knowing that total social reform would work best but that a patchwork of services may be the best we can provide? As Garbarino (1993) wryly notes, "We have to live as ambulatory schizophrenics if we are to wrestle with adolescent problems. That's the way the world comes to us." Do we develop generic interventions that reach a broad base of adolescent problems, or specific ones that are designed for targeted groups? Do we provide services to those most amenable to interven-tion, or try to reach all who need such services? Do we enhance the functioning of already competent adolescents to prevent their slide into violent options, or do we look for those already sliding? How do we evaluate the success of a prevention program? When we are talking about human lives and spirits, how do we assign a dollar value that makes sense? Who pays? When do they pay? As advo-cates, we must not forget our desire to achieve sweeping social reforms that would diminish violence. At the same time, we must be willing to stand by our efforts, however small, and believe that they have an impact on violence in adolescence.

Perhaps it is fitting that adolescence, a latecomer in history, is also tardy in getting its due. Yet we are beginning to understand how hard it is to get through the teenage years intact and how all of us are touched by the struggles of adolescents we know and love. Merely caring may once have been sufficient; now we have to do more. We must act with a passion equal to the passion of rage and aggression that threatens our children.

Appendix

Self-Help Books

The publishing market generated by problems of adolescence is staggering. I perused the listing of books in print for 1993 to see what was available for parents and their adolescents; it appears that there are literally dozens of books to choose from. This appendix contains samplings of available books.

Books for Parents

Anderson, J. (1990). *Teen is a four-letter word: A survival kit for parents.* Crozet, VA: Betterway.

Apter, T. (1990). *Altered loves: Mothers and daughters during adolescence.* New York: St. Martin's.

Barrish, I., & Barrish, H. (1989). *Surviving and enjoying your adolescent.* Kansas City, MO: Westport.

Baucomb, J. (1988). *Bonding and breaking free: What good parents should know.* Grand Rapids, MI: Zondervan.

Bell, R., & Wildflower, L. (1983). *Talking with your teenager: A book for parents.* New York: Random House.

Brondino, J. (1989). *Raising each other: A book for parents and teens.* San Bernardino, CA: Borgo.

Brusko, M. (1987). *Living with your teenager.* New York: Ivy.

Buntman, P., & Saris, E. (1990). *How to live with your teenagers: A survi-*

vor's handbook for parents. Los Alamitos, CA: Center for Family Life Enrichment.

Desisto, M. (1991). *Decoding your teenager: How to understand each other during the turbulent years.* New York: Morrow.

Fontenelle, D. (1992). *Keys to parenting your teenager.* Hauppauge, NY: Barron.

Forgatch, M., & Patterson, G. (1989). *Parents and adolescents living together.* Eugene, OR: Castalia.

Gardner, J. (1993). *The turbulent teens: Understanding, helping, surviving.* Rolling Hills Estates, CA: Jalmar.

Greydanus, D. (1991). *Caring for your adolescent: Ages 12 to 21.* New York: Bantam.

Herbert, M. (1987). *Living with teenagers.* Cambridge, MA: Blackwell.

Huggins, K. (1989). *Parenting adolescents.* Colorado Springs, CO: NavPress.

Leiter, J. (1991). *Successful parenting: A common sense guide to raising your teenagers.* Deerfield Beach, FL: Health Communications.

McCoy, K. (1991). *Crisis-proof your teenager: How to recognize, prevent and deal with risky adolescent behavior.* New York: Bantam.

McIntyre, R., & McIntyre, C. (1990). *Teenagers and parents: Ten steps for a better relationship.* Amherst, MA: Human Resources Development.

Miller, D. (1989). *A parent's guide to adolescents: Understanding your teenager.* Denver, CO: Accent.

Nelson, J., & Lott, L. (1991). *I'm on your side: Resolving conflict with your teenage son or daughter.* Rocklin, CA: Prima.

Novello, J. (1992). *What to do until the grown-up arrives: The art and science of raising teenagers.* Kirkland, WA: Hogrefe & Huber.

Paine, R. (1975). *We never had any trouble before: First aid for parents of teenagers.* Lanham, MD: Madison.

Pappas, M., & Sadler, O. (1987). *How to survive with adolescence.* Lincoln, NE: Media.

Parsons, R. D. (1988). *Adolescence: What's a parent to do?* Mahaugh, NJ: Paulist.

Rickerson, W. (1988). *This is the thanks I get? A guide to raising teenagers.* Cincinnati, OH: Standard.

Schules, J. (1991). *Teenage years: A parent's survival guide.* Tucson, AZ: Fisher.

Shalov, J. (1990). *You can say no to your teenager and other strategies for effective parenting in the 1990's.* Redding, MA: Addison-Wesley.

Smyth, P., & Benner, J. (1988). *Parent survival training: A guide for parents of teenagers.* Santa Barbara, CA: Joelle.

Weinhaus, E., & Friedman, K. (1988). *Stop struggling with your teen.* New York: Viking Penguin.

Wolf, A. (1991). *Get out of my life, but first could you drive me and Cheryl to the mall: A parent's guide to the new teenager.* New York: Farrar Straus Giroux.

Books for Adolescents

Atanasoff, S. (1989). *How to survive as a teen: When no one understands.* Scottdale, PA: Herald.

Bauman, L., & Riche, R. (1987). *The nine most troublesome teenage problems and how to solve them.* New York: Ballantine.

Cohen, D., & Cohen, S. (1983). *Teenage stress: Understanding the tensions you feel at home, at school and among your friends.* Denver, CO: Evans.

Crutsinger, C. (1990). *Teenage connection: A tool for effective teenage communication.* Carrollton, TX: Brainworks.

Elchoness, M. (1989). *Why can't anyone hear me? A guide for surviving adolescence.* Ventura, CA: Monroe.

Engel, J. (1990). *Adolescence: A guide for teenagers and their parents.* New York: Tor.

Gordon, S. (1981). *The teenage survival book.* New York: Random House.

Nource, A. (1990). *Teen guide to survival.* New York: Watts.

References

Abel, G. G., Mittelman, M. S., & Becker, J. B. (1985). Sex offenders: Results of assessment and recommendations for treatment. In H. Ben-Aaron, S. Hucker, & C. Webster (Eds.), *Clinical criminology: Current concepts.* Toronto: M&M Graphics.

Adams, G. R., & Gulotta, T. S. (1983). *Adolescent life experiences.* Monterey, CA: Brooks/Cole.

Adler, C. (1984). Gender bias in juvenile diversion. *Crime and Delinquency, 30,* 400–414.

Albert, J. (1978). Constitutional regulation of televised violence. *Virginia Law Review, 64,* 1299–1345.

Alexander, J., & Parsons, B. (1982). *Functional family therapy.* Monterey, CA: Brooks/Cole.

American Humane Association. (1986). Definitions of national study data items and response categories. In *Technical Report 3.* Denver, CO: Author.

American Psychiatric Association. (1987). *Diagnostic and statistical manual of mental disorders (3rd ed., rev.).* Washington, DC: Author.

American Psychological Association. (1993). *Commission on youth and violence summary report. Volume 1: Violence and youth: Psychology's response.* Washington, DC: Author.

Arbuthnot, J., Gordon, D. A., & Jurkovic, G. J. (1987). Personality. In H. C. Quay (Ed.), *Handbook of juvenile delinquency.* New York: Wiley.

Bachman, J., Bare, D., & Frankie, A. (1986). *Correlates of employment among high school seniors.* Paper available from the Institute for Social Research, University of Michigan, Ann Arbor.

Belsky, J. (1980). Child maltreatment: An ecological integration. *American Psychologist, 35,* 320–335.

Benward, J., & Densen-Gerber, J. (1973). Incest as a causative factor in antisocial behavior: An exploratory study. *Contemporary Drug Problems, 41*, 322–340.

Berlin, R., & Davis, R. B. (1989). Children from alcoholic families: Vulnerability and resilience. In T. F. Dugan, & R. Coles (Eds.), *The child in our times: Studies in the development of resiliency*. New York: Brunner/ Mazel.

Berman, A. L., & Cohen-Sandler, R. (1980, November). *Suicide behavior in childhood and early adolescence*. Paper presented at the annual meeting of the American Association of Suicidology, Nashville, TN.

Berndt, T. (1988). The nature and significance of children's friendships. In R. Vasta (Ed.), *Annals of Child Development: Vol. 5* (pp. 155–186). Greenwich, CT: JAI Press.

Bettelheim, B. (1943). Individual and mass behavior in extreme situations. *Abnormal and Social Psychology, 38*, 417–452.

Blasi, A. (1980). Bridging moral cognition and moral action: A critical review of the literature. *Psychological Bulletin, 88*, 1–45.

Blomberg, T. G. (1983). Diversion's disparate results and unresolved questions: An integrative evaluation perspective. *Journal of Crime and Delinquency, 20*, 24–38.

Blos, P. (1967). The second individuation process of adolescence. *Psychoanalytic Study of the Child, 22*, 162–186.

Borduin, C. M., & Henggeler, S. W. (1987). Post-divorce mother-son relations of delinquent and well-adjusted adolescents. *Journal of Applied Developmental Psychology, 8*, 273–288.

Borman, L. (1979). Action anthropology and the self-help/mutual aid movement. In R. Hinshaw (Ed.), *Currents of Anthropology*. New York: Mouton.

Bowen, M. (1978). *Family therapy in clinical practice*. New York: Jason Aronson.

Boyd, J., & Moscicki, E. (1986). Firearms and youth suicide. In P. Tolan, & B. Cohler (Eds.), *Handbook of clinical research and practice with adolescents*. New York: Wiley.

Brent, D., Perper, J., Allman, C., Moritz, G., Wartella, M., & Zelenak, J. (1991). The presence and accessibility of firearms in the homes of adolescent suicides: A case-control study. *Journal of the American Medical Association, 266*, 2989–2995.

Bronfenbrenner, U., & Weiss, H. B. (1983). Beyond policies without people: An ecological perspective on child and family policy. In E. Zigler, S. Kagan, & E. Klugman (Eds.), *Children, families and government*. New York: Cambridge University Press.

Brown, S. E. (1982). An analysis of the relationship between child abuse and delinquency. *Journal of Crime and Justice, 5*, 51–55.

Brown, S. E. (1984). Social class, child maltreatment and delinquent behavior. *Criminology, 22*, 259–278.

Bucy, J. (1985, July). *To whom do they belong? A profile of America's runaway and homeless youth and the programs that help them*. Testimony presented to Subcommittee on Children, Family, Drugs, and Alcoholism, United States Senate, October 1, 1985. Washington, DC: National Network of Runaway and Youth Services.

Burgess, A. W., & Holmstrom, L. L. (1978). Accessory-to-sex: Pressure, sex and secrecy. In A. W. Burgess, A. N. Groth, L. L. Holmstrom, & S. M. Sgroi (Eds.), *Sexual assault of children and adolescents* (pp. 85–98). Lexington, MA: Lexington.

Campbell, A. (1993). *Men, women, and aggression*. New York: HarperCollins.

Canter, R. J. (1982). Family correlates of male and female delinquency. *Criminology, 20*, 149–167.

Caplan, G. (1974). *Support systems and community mental health*. New York: Behavioral Publications.

Carey, W. B. (1974). Nightwalking and temperament in infancy. *Journal of Pediatrics, 84*, 756–768.

Carlson, G. A. (1983). Depression and suicidal behavior in children and adolescents. In D. P. Cantwell, & G. A. Carlson (Eds.), *Affective disorders in childhood and adolescence: An update* (pp. 335–353). New York: S. P. Medical & Scientific Books.

Carter, B., & McGoldrick, M. (Eds.). (1989). *The changing family life cycle: A framework for family therapy* (2nd ed.). Needham Heights, MA: Allyn & Bacon.

Carter, S. (1993). *The culture of disbelief: How American law and politics trivialize religious devotion*. New York: Basic.

Centers for Disease Control. (1991). *Youth risk behavior survey*. Atlanta, GA: U.S. Department of Health & Human Services.

Cernkovitch, S., & Giordano, P. (1987). Family relationships and delinquency. *Criminology, 25*, 295–321.

Children's Defense Fund. (1989). *A Children's Defense Fund Budget*. Washington, DC: Author.

Children's Defense Fund. (1992). *The state of America's children 1992*. Washington, DC: Author.

Children's Defense Fund. (1994a). Living in fear: National poll finds violence tops children's list of worries. *CDF Reports, 15*(2), 1–2.

Children's Defense Fund. (1994b). Cease fire: Stopping the war on U.S. children. *CDF Reports, 15*(3), 1–2.

Clark, D., & Mokros, H. (1993). Depression and suicidal behavior. In P. Tolan, & B. Cohler (Eds.), *Handbook of clinical research and practice with adolescents*. New York: Wiley.

Cofer, L., & Jacobvitz, R. (1990). The loss of moral turf: Mass media and family values. In D. Blankenhorn, S. Bayme, & J. Elshtain (Eds.), *Rebuilding the nest: A new commitment to the American family*. Milwaukee: Family Service America.

Cohen, B. C. (1963). *The press, the public and foreign policy*. Princeton, NJ: Princeton University Press.

Cohen, P. A., Kulik, J. A., & Kulik, C. (1982). Educational outcomes of tutoring: A meta-analysis of findings. *American Educational Research Journal*, 237–248.

Cohler, B. J. (1987). Adversity, resilience and the study of lives. In E. J. Anthony, & B. J. Cohler (Eds.), *The invulnerable child*. New York: Guilford.

Coles, R. (1989). Moral energy in the lives of impoverished children. In T. F. Dugan, & R. Coles (Eds.), *The child in our times: Studies in the development of resiliency*. New York: Brunner/Mazel.

Commission on Youth Employment Programs, National Research Council. (1985). *Youth employment and training programs: The YEDPA years*. Washington, DC: National Academy Press.

Comstock, G. (1986). Television and film violence. In S. Apter, & A. Goldstein (Eds.), *Youth violence: Programs and prospects*. New York: Pergamon.

Condry, J., & Siman, M. (1974). Characteristics of peer- and adult-oriented children. *Journal of Marriage and the Family*, *36*, 543–554.

Coulter, D. (1989, February). Personal communication. In Healy, J. (1990). *Endangered minds: Why our children don't think*. New York: Simon & Schuster.

Courtois, C. (1988). *Healing the incest wound: Adult survivors in therapy*. New York: Norton.

Cowen, E., Pederson, A., Babigan, H., Izzo L., & Trost, M. (1973). Long-term follow-up of early detected vulnerable children. *Journal of Consulting and Clinical Psychology*, *41*, 438–446.

Craig, M., & Glueck, S. J. (1963). Ten years' experience with the Glueck social prediction scale. *Crime and Delinquency*, *24*, 231–232.

Curran, J. P. (1979). Social skills: Methodological issures and future directions. In A. S. Bellack, & M. Hersen (Eds.), *Research and practice in social skills training*. New York: Plenum.

Cytryn, L., & McKnew, D. (1980). Affective disorders of childhood. In H. Kaplan, A. Friedman, & R. Sadock (Eds.), *Comprehensive textbook of psychiatry* (3rd ed.). Baltimore: Williams & Wilkins.

Davis, G. E., & Leitenberg, H. (1987). Adolescent sex offenders. *Psychological Bulletin*, *101*, 417–427.

Davis, L., & Tolan, P. (1993). Alternative and preventive interventions. In P. Tolan, & B. Cohler (Eds.), *Handbook of clinical research and practice with adolescents*. New York: Wiley.

Davis, P. A. (1983). *Suicidal adolescents*. Springfield, IL: Charles C. Thomas.

Deisher, R. W., Wenet, G., Paperny, D., Clark, T., & Ferenbach, P. (1982). Adolescent sexual offense behavior: The role of the physician. *Journal of Adolescent Health Care*, *2*, 279–286.

Dentler, R. A., & Monroe, L. J. (1961). Social correlates of early adolescent theft. *American Sociological Review*, *26*, 733–743.

Doane, J. A. (1978). Family interaction and communication deviance in disturbed and normal families: A review of research. *Family Process, 17,* 357–376.

Dolan, Y. M. (1991). *Resolving sexual abuse.* New York: Norton.

Dornbusch, S. M., Carlsmith, J. M., Bushwall, S. J., Ritter, P. L., Leiderman, H., Hastorf, A. H., & Gross, R. T. (1985). Single parents, extended households and the control of adolescents. *Child Development, 56,* 326–341.

Douvan, E., & Adelson, J. (1966). *The adolescent experience.* New York: Wiley.

Dryfoos, J. (1990). *Adolescents at risk.* New York: Oxford University Press.

Earls, F., Beardslee, W., & Garrison, W. (1987). Correlates and predictors of competence in young children. In E. J. Anthony, & B. J. Cohler (Eds.), *The invulnerable child.* New York: Guilford.

Elder, G. (1987). Adolescence in historical perspective. In H. Graff (Ed.), *Growing up in America* (pp. 5–48). Detroit: Wayne State University Press.

Elliot, D. S., Huizinga, D., & Morse, B. J. (1985). *The dynamics of deviant behavior: A national survey progress report.* Boulder, CO: Behavioral Research Institute.

Elmen, J., & Offer, D. (1993). Normality, turmoil, and adolescence. In P. Tolan, & B. Cohler (Eds.), *Handbook of clinical research and practice with adolescents.* New York: Wiley.

Erickson, J. B. (1982). *A profile of community youth organization members, 1980.* Boys Town, NE: Boys Town Center for Youth Development.

Erikson, E. (1956). Late adolescence. In D. H. Funkenstein (Ed.), *The student and mental health* (p. 76). Cambridge, MA: Riverside Press.

Erikson, E. (1963). *Childhood and society.* New York: Norton.

Erikson, E. (1968). *Identity: Youth and crisis.* New York: Norton.

Fanshel, D. (1978). *Children in foster care: A longitudinal investigation.* New York: Columbia University Press.

Farber, E. D., & Joseph, J. A. (1985). The maltreated adolescent: Patterns of physical abuse. *Child Abuse and Neglect, 9,* 201–206.

Farber, E. D., McCoard, W. D., Kinast, C., & Baum-Faulkner, D. (1984). Violence in families of adolescent runaways. *Child Abuse and Neglect, 8,* 295–299.

Farrington, D. P. (1987). Epidemiology. In H. C. Quay (Ed.), *Handbook of juvenile delinquency.* New York: Wiley.

Federal Bureau of Investigation, U.S. Department of Justice. (1987). *Uniform crime reports.* Washington, DC: Author.

Fehrenbach, P. A., Smith, W., Monastersky, C., & Deisher, R. W. (1986). Adolescent sexual offenders: Offender and offense characteristics. *American Journal of Orthopsychiatry, 56,* 225–233.

Felner, R. D., Ginter, M., & Primavera, J. (1982). Primary prevention during school transitions: Social support and environmental structure. *American Journal of Community Psychology, 10,* 277–290.

Felsman, J. K. (1989). Risk and resiliency in childhood: The lives of street children. In T. F. Dugan, & R. Coles (Eds.), *The child in our times: Studies in the development of resiliency.* New York: Brunner/Mazel.

Feshbach, N. D. (1983). Learning to care: A positive approach to child training and discipline. *Journal of Clinical Child Psychology, 12*, 266–271.

Finkelhor, D. (1979). *Sexually victimized children*. New York: Free Press.

Finkelhor, D. (1983). Common features of family abuse. In D. Finkelhor, & R. Gelles (Eds.), *The dark side of families*. Beverly Hills, CA: Sage.

Finkelhor, D. (1984). *Child sexual abuse: New theory and research*. Beverly Hills, CA: Sage.

Finkelhor, D. (1986). *Sourcebook on child sexual abuse*. Beverly Hills, CA: Sage.

Fischer, D. G. (1983). Parental supervision and delinquency. *Perceptual and Motor Skills, 56*, 635–640.

Fishman, H. C. (1988). *Treating troubled adolescents: A family therapy approach*. New York: Basic.

Fish-Murray, C., Koby, E., & van der Kolk, B. (1987). Evolving ideas: The effect of abuse on children's thought. In B. A. van der Kolk (Ed.), *Psychological trauma*. Washington, DC: American Psychiatric Press.

Flanegan, T., & Jamieson, K. (Eds.). (1987). *Sourcebook of Criminal Justice Statistics-1987*. Washington, DC: U.S. Government Printing Office, U.S. Department of Justice, Bureau of Justice Statistics.

Frazier, C., & Cochran, J. (1986). Official intervention, diversion from the juvenile justice system, and dynamics of human services work: Effects of a reform goal based on labeling theory. *Crime and Delinquency, 32*, 157–176.

Freedman, B. J., Rosenthal, L., Donahow, C. P., Schlundt, D. G., & McFall, R. M. (1978). A social-behavioral analysis of skill deficits in delinquent and non-delinquent adolescent boys. *Journal of Consulting and Clinical Psychology, 46*, 1448–1462.

Freedman, S. G. (1993). *Upon this rock: The miracles of a black church*. New York: HarperCollins.

Freeman-Longo, R. E. (1983). Juvenile sexual offenses in the history of adult rapists and child molesters. *International Journal of Offender Therapy and Comparative Criminology, 27*, 150–155.

Freidrich, W. N., Urquiza, A., & Beilke, R. L. (1986). Behavior problems in sexually abused young children. *Journal of Pediatric Psychology, 11*, 47–57.

Freud, A. (1946). *The ego and the mechanism of defense*. New York: International Universities Press.

Galambos, N. L., & Dixon, R. A. (1984). Adolescent abuse and the development of personal sense of control. *Child Abuse and Neglect, 8*, 285–293.

Gandy, O. H. (1980). Information in health: Subsidized news. *Media, Culture and Society, 2*, 103–115.

Garbarino, J. (1993). Enhancing adolescent development through social policy. In P. Tolan, & B. Cohler (Eds.), *Handbook of clinical research and practice with adolescents*. New York: Wiley.

Garbarino, J., Dubrow, N., Kostelny, K., & Pardo, C. (1992). *Children in danger: Coping with the consequences of community violence*. San Francisco: Jossey-Bass.

Garbarino, J., Schellenbach, C., Sebes, J., & Associates. (1986). *Troubled youth, troubled families*. New York: Aldine.

Garbarino, J., & Gilliam, G. (1980). *Understanding abusive families*. Lexington, MA: Lexington.

Garmezy, N. (1981). The current status of research with children at risk for schizophrenia and other forms of psychopathology. In D. A. Regier, & G. Allen (Eds.), *Risk factor research in the major mental disorders* (DHHS Publication No. ADM 81-1068). Washington, DC: U.S. Government Printing Office.

Garmezy, N. (1983). Stressors of childhood. In N. Garmezy, & M. Rutter (Eds.), *Stress, coping and development in children* (pp. 43–84). New York: McGraw-Hill.

Garrett, C. J. (1985). Effects of residential treatment on adjudicated delinquents: A meta-analysis. *Journal of Research in Crime and Delinquency, 22*, 287–308.

Gartner, A., & Riessman, F. (1977). *Self-help in the human services*. San Francisco: Jossey-Bass.

Geller, M., & Ford-Soma, L. (1984). *Violent homes—violent children*. New Jersey: Department of Corrections.

Gerbner, G. (1980). Children and power on television: The other side of the picture. In G. Gerbner, C. Ross, & E. Zigler (Eds.), *Child abuse: An agenda for action*. Oxford: Oxford University Press.

Gibbs, J. C. (1987). Social processes in delinquency: The need to facilitate empathy as well as sociomoral reasoning. In W. M. Kurtines, & J. L. Gewirtz (Eds.), *Moral development through social interaction*. New York: Wiley.

Glueck, S., & Glueck, E. (1962). *Family environment and delinquency*. London: Routledge & Kegan Paul.

Gold, M. (1963). *Status forces in delinquent boys*. Ann Arbor: University of Michigan Press.

Gold, M. (1978). Scholastic experiences, self-esteem and delinquent behavior: A theory for alternative schools. *Crime and Delinquency, 24*, 290–308.

Goldenberg, I., & Goldenberg, H. (1985). *Family therapy: An overview*. Monterey, CA: Brooks/Cole.

Goldsmith, H. R. (1987). Self-esteem of juvenile delinquents: Findings and implications. *Journal of Offender Counseling, Services and Rehabilitation, 11*, 79–85.

Goldstein, A. P., & Glick, B. (1987). *Aggression replacement training: A comprehensive intervention for aggressive youth*. Champaign, IL: Research Press.

Gottfredson, D. (1985). Youth employment, crime, and schooling: A longitudinal study of a national sample. *Developmental Psychology, 21,* 419–432.

Gove, W. R., & Crutchfield, R. D. (1982). The family and juvenile delinquency. *Sociological Quarterly, 23,* 301–319.

Green, A. (1976). Self destructive behavior in battered children. *American Journal of Psychiatry, 135,* 579–582.

Greenberger, E., & Steinberg, L. (1986). *When teenagers work: The psychological and social costs of adolescent employment.* New York: Basic.

Greene, N. B., & Esselstyn, T. C. (1972). The beyond control girl. *Juvenile Justice, 23,* 13–19.

Grogan, H. J., & Grogan, R. C. (1968). The criminogenic family: Does chronic tension cause delinquency? *Crime and Delinquency, 14,* 220–225.

Groth, A. N. (1977). The adolescent sexual offender and his prey. *International Journal of Offender Therapy and Comparative Criminology, 21,* 249–255.

Hains, A. A., & Ryan, E. B. (1983). The development of social cognitive processes among juvenile delinquents and nondelinquent peers. *Child Development, 54,* 1536–1544.

Haley, J. (1980). *Leaving home.* New York: McGraw-Hill.

Hall, G. (1904). *Adolescence.* New York: Appleton.

Hall, R. P., Kassees, J. M., & Hoffman, C. (1986). Treatment for survivors of incest. *Journal for Specialists in Group Work, 11,* 85–92.

Hanks, M. (1981). Youth voluntary associations and political socialization. *Social Forces, 1,* 211–223.

Hanks, M., & Eckland, B. (1978). Adult voluntary associations and political socialization. *Social Forces, 1,* 223–231.

Hanson, C. L., Henggeler, S. W., Haefele, W. F., & Rodick, J. D. (1984). Demographic, individual, and family relationship correlates of serious and repeated crime among adolescents and their siblings. *Journal of Consulting and Clinical Psychology, 52,* 528–538.

Havinghurst, R. J. (1972). *Developmental tasks and education.* New York: McKay.

Healy, J. (1990). *Endangered minds: Why our children don't think.* New York: Simon & Schuster.

Hedin, D. (1987, Winter). Students as teachers: A tool for improving school. *Social Policy,* pp. 42–47.

Henderson, M., & Hollin, C. (1983). A critical review of social skills training with young offenders. *Criminal Justice and Behavior, 10,* 316–341.

Henggeler, S. W. (1989). *Delinquency in adolescence.* Newbury Park, CA: Sage.

Herman, J. (1981). *Father-daughter incest.* Cambridge, MA: Harvard University Press.

Herman, J. (1992). *Trauma and recovery.* New York: Basic.

Hewlett, S. (1991). *When the bough breaks.* New York: HarperCollins.

Hirschi, T. (1969). *Causes of delinquency.* Berkeley: University of California Press.

Hirschi, T., & Hindelang, M. J. (1977). Intelligence and delinquency: A revisionist review. *American Sociological Review, 42,* 571–587.

Holland, T. R., Beckett, G. E., & Levi, M. (1981). Intelligence, personality and criminal violence: A multivariate analysis. *Journal of Consulting and Clinical Psychology, 49,* 106–111.

Holmes, S. (1978). Parents Anonymous: A treatment method for child abuse. *Social Work, 23,* 245–247.

Huesmann, L., Eron, L., Klein, R., Brice, P., & Fisher, P. (1983). Mitigating the imitation of aggressive behaviors by changing children's attitudes about media violence. *Journal of Personality and Social Psychology, 44,* 899–910.

Hunka, C. D., O'Toole, A. W., & O'Toole, R. (1985). Self-help therapy in Parents Anonymous. *Journal of Psychosocial Nursing and Mental Health Services, 23,* 24–32.

Hunter, J., & Schaecher, R. (1990). Teenage suicide: Lesbian and gay youth. In M. J. Rotheram-Borus, J. Bradley, & N. Obolensky (Eds.), *Planning to live: Evaluating and treating suicidal teens in community settings.* Tulsa, OK: University of Oklahoma Press.

Hurley, P. (1985, March). Arresting delinquency. *Psychology Today,* pp. 63–68.

Imber-Black, E. (Ed.). (1993). *Secrets in families and family therapy.* New York: Norton.

Jacob, T. (1975). Family interaction in disturbed and normal families: A methodological and substantive review. *Psychological Bulletin, 82,* 33–65.

Jacobs, J. (1971). *Adolescent suicide.* New York: Wiley.

Janus, M., McCormack, A., Burgess, A. W., & Hartman, C. (1987). *Adolescent runaways: Causes and consequences.* Lexington, MA: Lexington.

Jones, R., Gruber, K., & Timbers, C. (1981). Incidence and situational factors surrounding sexual assault against delinquent youths. *Child Abuse and Neglect, 5,* 431–440.

Jurkovic, G. I. (1980). The juvenile delinquent as a moral philosopher: A structural-developmental perspective. *Psychological Bulletin, 88,* 709–727.

Kagan, J. (1984). *The nature of the child.* New York: Basic.

Kandel, D., & Andrews, K. (1987). Processes of adolescent socialization by parents and peers. *International Journal of the Addictions, 22,* 319–342.

Kandel, E., Mednick, S. A., Kirkegaard-Sorensen, L., Hutchings, B., Knop, J., Rosenberg, R., & Schulsinger, F. (1988). IQ as a protective factor for subjects at high risk for antisocial behavior. *Journal of Consulting and Clinical Psychology, 56,* 224–226.

Kaplan, H. B. (1980). *Deviant behavior in defense of self.* New York: Academic Press.

Karpel, M. A. (1980). Family secrets. 1. Conceptual and ethical issues in the relational context. 2. Ethical and practical considerations in therapeutic management. *Family Process, 19,* 295–306.

Katz, A. H., & Bender, E. (1976). Self-help groups in western society: History and prospects. *Journal of Applied Behavioral Science, 12,* 265–282.

Kazdin, A. E. (1985). *Treatment of antisocial behavior in children and adolescents.* Homewood, IL: Dorsey Press.

Kazdin, A. E. (1990, June). *Prevention of conduct disorder.* Paper presented at the National Conference on Prevention Research. National Institute of Mental Health, Washington, DC.

Kazdin, A. E. (1993). Adolescent mental health: Prevention and treatment programs. *American Psychologist, 48,* 127–141.

Kellerman, A., & Reay, D. (1986). Protection or peril? An analysis of firearm-related deaths in the home. *New England Journal of Medicine, 314,* 1557–1660.

Kelly, F., & Baer, D. (1971). Physical challenge as a treatment for delinquency. *Crime and Delinquency, 17,* 437–445.

Kempe, R., & Kempe, C. H. (1978). *Child abuse.* Cambridge, MA: Harvard University Press.

Keniston, K. (1977). *All our children.* New York: Harcourt Brace Jovanovich.

Kinard, E. M. (1980). Emotional development in physically abused children. *American Journal of Orthopsychiatry, 50,* 686–695.

Klein, M. W. (1986). Labeling theory and delinquency policy: An experimental test. *Criminal Justice and Behavior, 13,* 47–79.

Kleinfeld, J., & Shinkwin, A. (1982). *Youth organizations as a third educational environment particularly for minority youth.* Final report to the National Institute of Education, Washington, DC: Educational Resources Information Center. (ERIC Document Reproduction Service No. ED 240 194)

Knitzer, J. (1982). *Unclaimed children.* Washington, DC: Children's Defense Fund.

Kohlberg, L. (1969). Stage and sequence: The cognitive-developmental approach to socialization. In D. Goslin (Ed.), *Handbook of socialization theory and research.* Chicago: Rand McNally.

Krystal, H. (1978). Trauma and affects. *Psychoanalytic Study of the Child, 33,* 81–116.

Lab, S. P., & Whitehead, J. T. (1988). An analysis of juvenile correctional treatment. *Crime and Delinquency, 34,* 60–83.

Landau-Stanton, J., & Stanton, M. (1985). Treating suicidal adolescents and their families. In M. Mirkin, & S. Koman (Eds.), *Handbook of adolescents and family therapy.* New York: Gardner.

Langway, L. (1982, October 18). A nation of runaway kids. *Newsweek,* pp. 97–98.

Lappin, J., & Covelman, C. (1985). Adolescent runaways: A structural family therapy perspective. In M. Mirkin, & S. Koman (Eds.), *Handbook of adolescents and family therapy.* New York: Gardner.

Lee, M., & Prentice, N. M. (1988). Interrelations of empathy, cognition and moral reasoning with dimensions of juvenile delinquency. *Journal of Abnormal Child Psychology, 16,* 127–139.

LeFlore, F. (1989, December 10). Pat on the back: Educators, students join in a positive approach. *Milwaukee Journal,* p. 2.

Leone, P. E. (1989). Beyond fixing bad behavior and bad boys: Multiple perspectives on education and treatment of troubled and troubling youth. *Monograph in Behavioral Disorders, 12,* 1–10.

Levy, L. (1976). Self-help groups: Types and psychological processes. *Journal of Applied Behavioral Science, 12,* 310–322.

Lewis, D. O., & Balla, D. A. (1976). *Delinquency and psychopathology.* New York: Grune & Stratton.

Lewis, D. O., Shankok, S. S., Pincus, J. H., & Glaser, G. H. (1979). Violent juvenile delinquents: Psychiatric, neurological, psychological, and abuse factors. *Journal of the American Academy of Child Psychiatry, 18,* 307–319.

Lieber, L. J., & Baker, J. M. (1977). Parents Anonymous: Self-help treatment for child abusing parents: A review and evaluation. *Child Abuse and Neglect, 1,* 133–148.

Loeber, R., & Dishion, T. (1987). Antisocial and delinquent youths: Methods for their early identification. In J. Burchard, & S. N. Burchard (Eds.), *Prevention of delinquent behavior* (pp. 75–89). Beverly Hills, CA: Sage.

Lourie, I. (1979). Family dynamics and the abuse of children: A case for a developmental phase specific model of child abuse. *Child abuse and neglect, 3,* 967–974.

Lustig, N., Dresser, J., Spellman, J., & Murray, T. (1966). Incest: A family group survival pattern. *Archives of General Psychiatry, 14,* 31–40.

Maher, C. A. (1982). Behavioral effects of using conduct problem adolescents as cross-age tutors. *Psychology in the Schools, 19,* 360–364.

Marohn, R. C. (1974). Trauma and the delinquent. *Adolescent Psychiatry, 3,* 354–361.

Marohn, R. C. (1993). Residential services. In P. H. Tolan, & B. J. Cohler (Eds.), *Handbook of clinical research and practice with adolescents.* New York: Wiley.

Martin, A. D., & Hetrick, E. S. (1988). The stigmatization of the gay and lesbian adolescent. *Journal of Homosexuality, 15,* 163–183.

Martin, H., & Beezley, P. (1977). Behavioral observations of abused children. *Developmental Medicine and Child Neurology, 19,* 373–387.

Mason, B. C. (1979). *An experiment in cross-age peer interaction.* Washington, DC: Educational Resources Information Center. (ERIC Document Reproduction Service No. ED 185 492)

Masterson, J. (1968). The psychiatric significance of adolescent turmoil. *American Journal of Psychiatry, 124,* 1549–1554.

Mayer, J. P., Gensheimer, L. K., Davidson, W. S., & Gottschalk, R. (1986). Social learning treatment within juvenile justice: A meta analysis of impact in the natural environment. In S. J. Alper, & A. P. Goldstein (Eds.), *Youth violence: Programs and prospects.* New York: Pergamon.

McCord, J. (1979). Some child-rearing antecedents of criminal behavior in adult men. *Journal of Personality and Social Psychology, 37,* 1477–1486.

McCord, W., McCord, J., & Zola, I. (1959). *Origins of crime.* New York: Columbia University Press.

McCoy, K. (1982). *Coping with teenage depression: A parent's guide.* New York: New American Library.

McGarvey, B., Gabrielli, W. F., Bentler, P. M., & Mednick, S. A. (1981). Rearing, social class, education, and criminality: A multiple indicator model. *Journal of Abnormal Psychology, 90,* 354–364.

McLeod, J., Becker, L., & Byrnes, J. (1974). Another look at the agenda-setting function of the press. *Communication Research, 1,* 131–166.

Mikel-Brown, L., & Gilligan, C. (1992). *Meeting at the crossroads.* Cambridge, MA: Harvard University Press.

Miller, D., Miller D., Hoffman, F., & Duggan, R. (1980). *Runaways—Illegal aliens in their own land: Implications for service.* New York: Praeger.

Mirkin, M. P., Raskin, P. A., & Antogini, F. C. (1984). Parenting, protecting and preserving: Mission of the female adolescent runaway. *Family Process, 23*(1), 63–74.

Monahan, J. (1976). *Community mental health and the criminal justice system.* New York: Pergamon.

Moore, J. B. (1983). The experience of sponsoring a Parents Anonymous group. *Social Casework, 64,* 585–592.

Muenchow, S., & Gilfillan, S. (1983). Social policy and the media. In E. Zigler, S. Kagan, & E. Klugman (Eds.), *Children, families and government.* Cambridge: Cambridge University Press.

Murphy, L. B., & Hirschberg, J. C. (1982). *Robin: Comprehensive treatment of a vulnerable adolescent.* New York: Basic.

Murphy, W. D., & Stalgaitis, S. J. (1987). Assessment and treatment considerations for sexual offenders against children: Behavioral and social learning approaches. In J. R. McNamara, & M. A. Appel (Eds.), *Critical issues, developments and trends in professional psychology.* New York: Praeger.

Myers, J. (1986). How public policy affects the role of residential psychiatric care for children and youth. In K. Wells (Chairman), *Division 37 task force on residential treatment report.* Symposium conducted at the meeting of the American Psychological Association, Washington, DC.

National Center on Child Abuse and Neglect. (1981). *National incidence study.* Washington, DC: U.S. Government Printing Office.

National Center for Health Statistics. (November 28, 1990). *Monthly vital statistics report, 39,* Supplement, Advance Report of Final Mortality Statistics, 1988. Washington, DC: U.S. Government Printing Office.

National Center for Health Statistics. (1993, March). Firearm mortality among children, youth and young adults 1–34 years of age, trends and current status: United States, 1985–1990. *NCHS Monthly Vital Statistics Report, 41.*

Nightingale, E. O., & Wolverton, L. (1988). *Adolescent rolelessness in modern society.* Report prepared by the Carnegie Foundation Council on Adolescent Development, Carnegie Corporation, NY.

Nye, F. (1958). *Family relationships and delinquent behavior.* New York: Wiley.

Nye, F. (1980). A theoretical perspective on running away. *Journal of Family Issues, 1*(2), 147–151.

O'Brien, M. J., & Bera, W. H. (1986). Adolescent sexual offenders: A descriptive typology. *Preventing Sexual Abuse, 1*, 1–4.

Offer, D., Marohn, R. C., & Ostrov, E. (1979). *The psychological world of the juvenile delinquent.* New York: Basic.

Offer, D., Ostrov, E., & Howard, K. (1981). *The adolescent: A psychological self-portrait.* New York: Basic.

Offer, D., Ostrov, E., & Howard, K. (1984). Epidemiology of mental health and mental illness among adolescents. In J. Call (Ed.), *Significant advances in child psychiatry.* New York: Basic.

Offer, D., Ostrov, E., & Howard, K. (1989). Adolescence: What is normal? *American Journal of Diseases of Children, 143*, 731–736.

Offer, D., & Sabshin, M. (1984). Adolescence: Empirical perspectives. In D. Offer, & M. Sabshin (Eds.), *Normality and the life cycle* (pp. 76–107). New York: Basic.

Oldham, D. (1978). Adolescent turmoil: A myth revisited. In S. Feinstein, & P. Giovacchini (Eds.), *Adolescent psychiatry: Developmental and clinical studies, Volume 6* (pp. 267–279). Chicago: University of Chicago Press.

Olds, D., Henderson, C., Tatelbaum, R., & Chamberlin, R. (1986). A randomized trial of home nurse visitation. *Pediatrics, 78*, 65–78.

Olson, K. (1992). *A narrative study of resilience in physically abused people.* Unpublished doctoral dissertation, Antioch New England Graduate School, Keene, NH.

Otto, L. B. (1975). Extracurricular activities in the educational attainment process. *Rural Sociology, 40*, 162–176.

Otto, L. B. (1976). Social integration and the status-attainment process. *American Journal of Sociology, 81*, 1360–1383.

Otto, L. B., & Featherman, D. L. (1975). Social, structural and psychological antecedents of self-estrangement and powerlessness. *American Sociological Review, 40*, 701–719.

Parker, J. G., & Asher, S. R. (1987). Peer relations and later personal adjustment: Are low-accepted children at-risk? *Psychological Bulletin, 102*, 357–389.

Pate, M. E. (1986). If we don't want violence, let's do something about abuse. *Justice for Children, 1*, 16–17.

Patterson, G. R. (1982). *Coercive family process.* Eugene, OR: Castilia.

Patterson, G. R. (1986). Performance models for antisocial boys. *American Psychologist, 41*, 432–444.

Pelcovitz, D. (1984). Adolescent abuse: Family structure and implications for treatment. *Journal of the American Academy of Child Psychiatry, 23*, 85–90.

Perry, G. P., & Orchard, J. (1992). *Assessment and treatment of adolescent sex offenders.* Sarasota, FL: Professional Resource Press.

Petzel, S. V., & Cline, D. W. (1978). Adolescent suicide: Epidemiological and biological aspects. *Adolescent Psychiatry, 6*, 239–266.

Petzel, S. V., & Riddle, M. (1980). Adolescent suicide: Psychological and cognitive aspects. In S. C. Feinstein, & P. L. Giovacchini (Eds.), *Adolescent psychiatry*, (Vol. 9, pp. 343–397). Chicago: University of Chicago Press.

Pfeffer, C. R. (1981). The family system of suicidal children. *American Journal of Psychotherapy, 35*, 330–341.

Piaget, J. (1954). *The construction of reality in the child.* New York: Basic.

Piaget, J. (1968). *Six psychological studies.* New York: Vintage.

Polit, D., Quint, J. C., & Riccio, J. A. (1988). *The challenge of serving teenage mothers: Lessons from Project Redirection.* New York: Manpower Demonstration Research Corporation.

Polk, K. (1984). Juvenile diversion: A look at the record. *Crime and Delinquency, 30*, 648–659.

Poznanski, E., & Blos, P. (1975). Incest. *Medical Aspects of Human Sexuality, 9*, 46–76.

President's Commission on Mental Health. (1978). *Report to the President: Vol. 1. Commission Report.* Washington, DC: U.S. Government Printing Office.

Price, R., Cowen, E., Lorion, R., & Ramos-McKay, J. (1989). *14 ounces of prevention.* Washington, DC: American Psychological Association.

Pulkkinen, L. (1983). Finland: The search for alternatives to aggression. In A. P. Goldstein, & M. H. Segal (Eds.), *Aggression in global perspective.* New York: Pergamon.

Quay, H. C. (Ed.). (1987). *Handbook of juvenile delinquency.* New York: Wiley.

Rausch, S. (1983). Court processing versus diversion of status offenders: A test of deterrence and labeling theories. *Journal of Research in Crime and Delinquency, 20*, 39–54.

Rehabilitation Services Administration. (1974). *Teens helping other teens get together: An evaluation of the Baltimore Youth Advocate Project Final Report.* Washington, DC: Educational Resources Information Center. (ERIC Document Reproduction Service No. ED 134 658)

Reid, J. B., Taplin, P. S., & Lorber, R. (1981). A social interactional approach to the treatment of abusive families. In R. Stuart (Ed.), *Violent behavior:*

Social learning approaches to prediction, management and treatment. New York: Brunner/Mazel.

Reidy, T. J. (1977). The aggressive characteristics of abused and neglected children. *Journal of Clinical Psychology, 33,* 1140–1145.

Reissman, F. (1989, August 12). *Restructuring help: A paradigm for the 1990's.* Invited address: Award for Distinguished Practice of Community Psychology, American Psychological Association, Washington, DC.

Reppucci, N. D. (1987). Prevention and ecology: Teen-age pregnancy, child sexual abuse and organized youth sports. *American Journal of Community Psychology, 15,* 1–22.

Roberts, A. R. (1982). Adolescent runaways in suburbia: A new typology. *Adolescence, 17,* 387–396.

Roff, M., Sells, S. B., & Golden, M. M. (1972). *Social adjustment and personality development in children.* Minneapolis: University of Minnesota Press.

Rogers, C., & Tremaine, T. (1984). Clinical intervention with boy victims of sexual abuse. In S. Greer, & I. R. Stuart (Eds.), *Victims of sexual aggression: Men, women and children.* New York: Van Nostrand Reinhold.

Rosenbaum, M., & Richman, J. (1970). Suicide: The role of hostility and death wishes from the family and significant others. *American Journal of Psychiatry, 126,* 128–131.

Rubin, B. (1977). *Media, politics and democracy.* Oxford: Oxford University Press.

Rutter, M. (1979). Protective factors in children's responses to stress and disadvantage. In M. W. Kent, & J. E. Rolf (Eds.), *Primary prevention of psychopathology: Social competence in children, Volume 3.* Hanover, NH: University Press of New England.

Rutter, M. (1987). Psychosocial resilience and protective mechanisms. *American Journal of Orthopsychiatry, 57,* 316–333.

Rutter, M., Giller, H. (1984). *Juvenile delinquency: Trends and perspectives.* New York: Guilford.

Rutter, M., Graham, P., Chadwick, O., & Yule, W. (1976). Adolescent turmoil: Fact or fiction? *Journal of Child Psychology and Psychiatry and Allied Disciplines, 17,* 35–56.

Ryan, G. D. (1991). Incidence and prevalence of sexual offenses committed by juveniles. In G. D. Ryan, & S. L. Lane (Eds.), *Juvenile sexual offending: Causes, consequences and correction* (pp. 9–17). Lexington, MA: Lexington.

Ryan, G. D., & Lane, S. L. (1991). Integrating theory and method. In G. D. Ryan, & S. L. Lane (Eds.), *Juvenile sexual offending: Causes, consequences and correction* (pp. 255–298). Lexington, MA: Lexington.

Sabbath, J. C. (1969). The suicidal adolescent: The expendable child. *Journal of the American Academy of Child Psychiatry, 8,* 272–289.

Satchell, M. (1986, July 20). Kids for sale: The exploitation of runaway and throw away children continues to be a national tragedy. *Parade Magazine*, pp. 4–7.

Schafer, W. E. (1969). Participation in interscholastic athletics and delinquency: A preliminary study. *Social Problems, 17*, 40–47.

Schillenbach, C. J., & Guerney, L. F. (1987). Identification of adolescent abuse and future intervention prospects. *Journal of Adolescence, 10*, 1–10.

Schneider, A. L. (1986). Restitution and recidivism rates of juvenile offenders: Results from four experimental studies. *Criminology, 24*, 533–552.

Schorr, L. (1989). *Within our reach: Breaking the cycle of disadvantage.* New York: Doubleday.

Schwartz, I. M. (1989). *(In)justice for juveniles.* Lexington, MA: Lexington.

Segrave, J. U., & Chu, D. B. (1978). Athletics and juvenile delinquency. *Review of Sport and Leisure, 3*, 1–24.

Shaffer, D. (1986). Development of factors in adolescent suicide. In M. Rutter, C. E. Izard, & P. B. Read (Eds.), *Depression in young people: Developmental and clinical perspectives* (pp. 383–398). New York: Guilford.

Shirk, S. (1988). The interpersonal legacy of physical abuse of children. In M. B. Straus (Ed.), *Abuse and victimization across the life span.* Baltimore: Johns Hopkins University Press.

Shneidman, E. S. (1984). Aphorisms of suicide and some implications for psychotherapy. *American Journal of Psychiatry, 38*, 319–328.

Shoor, M., Speed, M. H., & Bartelt, C. (1966). Syndrome of the adolescent child molester. *American Journal of Psychiatry, 122*, 783–789.

Showers, J., Farber, E. D., Joseph, J. A., Oshins, L., & Johnson, C. F. (1983). The sexual victimization of boys: A three-year survey. *Health Values: Achieving High-Level Wellness, 7*, 15–18.

Simons, J. M., Finlay, B., & Yang, A. (1991). *The adolescent and young adult fact book.* Washington, DC: Children's Defense Fund.

Sink, F. (1988). Sexual abuse in the lives of children. In M. B. Straus (Ed.), *Abuse and victimization across the life span.* Baltimore: Johns Hopkins University Press.

Sloan, J., Rivera, F., Reay, D., Ferris, J., & Kellerman, A. (1990). Firearm regulations and rates of suicide: A comparison of two metropolitan areas. *New England Journal of Medicine, 322*, 369–373.

Snyder, J. J., & Huntley, D. (1990). Troubled families and troubled youth. In P. E. Leone (Ed.), *Understanding troubled and troubling youth.* Newbury Park, CA: Sage.

Snyder, J. J., & Patterson, G. R. (1987). Family interaction and delinquent behavior. In H. C. Quay (Ed.), *Handbook of juvenile delinquency.* New York: Wiley.

Soloman, G. (1979). Child abuse and developmental disabilities. *Developmental Medicine and Child Neurology, 21*, 101–106.

Sonkin, D., Martin, D., & Walker, L. (1985). *The male batterer.* New York: Springer.

Spinetta, J., & Rigler, D. (1977). The child abusing parent: A psychological review. *Psychological Bulletin, 77*, 296–304.

Stanley, E. J., & Barter, J. F. (1970). Adolescent suicidal behavior. *American Journal of Orthopsychiatry, 40*, 87–95.

Steele, B. F. (1986). Notes on the lasting effects of early abuse throughout the life cycle. *Child Abuse and Neglect, 10*, 283–291.

Steinberg, L. (1987). Single parents, stepparents, and the susceptibility of adolescents to antisocial peer pressure. *Child Development, 58*, 269–275.

Steinberg, L. (1989). *Adolescence* (2nd ed.). New York: Knopf.

Steinberg, L., Greenberger, E., Garduque, L., Ruggerio, M., & Vaux, A. (1982). Effects of working on adolescent development. *Developmental Psychology, 18*, 385–395.

Stephens, W. (1983). *Explanations for failures of youth organizations.* Washington, DC: Educational Resources Information Center. (ERIC Document Reproduction Service No. ED 228 440)

Stott, D. H. (1982). *Delinquency: The problem and its prevention.* New York: Spectrum.

Straus, M. B. (1984). *"Acting-in" and "acting-out": A comparison of families with suicidal and delinquent young female adolescents.* Unpublished doctoral dissertation, University of Maryland, College Park, MD.

Straus, M. B. (1988). Abused adolescents. In M. B. Straus (Ed.), *Abuse and victimization across the life span.* Baltimore: Johns Hopkins University Press.

Summit, R., & Kryso, J. (1978). Sexual abuse of children: A clinical spectrum. *American Journal of Orthopsychiatry, 48*, 237–350.

Thomas, A., & Chess, S. (1977). *Temperament and development.* New York: Brunner/Mazel.

Thomas, J. (1991). The adolescent sex offender's family in treatment. In G. D. Ryan, & S. L. Lane (Eds.), *Juvenile sexual offending: Causes, consequences and correction* (pp. 333–376). Lexington, MA: Lexington.

Tierney, K. J., & Corwin, D. L. (1983). Exploring intrafamilial sexual abuse. In D. Finkelhor, R. Gelles, G. Hotaling, & M. A. Straus (Eds.), *The dark side of families.* Beverly Hills, CA: Sage.

Toews, J., Prosen, H., & Martin, R. (1981). The life cycle of the family: The adolescent's sense of time. In S. C. Feinstein, J. C. Looney, A. Z. Schwartzberg, & A. D. Sorosky (Eds.), *Adolescent psychiatry: Developmental and clinical studies, Volume 9.* Chicago: University of Chicago Press.

Tolan, P., Cromwell, R., & Brasswell, M. (1986). The application of family therapy to juvenile delinquency: A critical review of the literature. *Family Process, 25*, 619–649.

Tolan, P., Jaffe, C., & Ryan, K. (1990). *The clinical implications of adolescent epidemiological research.* Unpublished manuscript, University of Illinois at Chicago, Department of Psychiatry.

Tolan, P., & Loeber, R. (1993). Antisocial behavior. In P. H. Tolan, & B. J. Cohler (Eds.), *Handbook of clinical research and practice with adolescents.* New York: Wiley.

Tolan, P., & Mitchell, M. (1990). Families and antisocial and delinquent behavior. *Journal of Psychotherapy and the Family, 6,* 29–48.

Tramontana, M. (1980). Critical review of research on psychotherapy outcome with adolescents: 1967–1977. *Psychological Bulletin, 88,* 429–450.

Tramontana, M., & Sherrets, S. (1984). Psychotherapy with adolescents: Conceptual, practical and empirical perspectives. In P. Karoly, & J. Steffen (Eds.), *Adolescent behavior disorders: Foundations and contemporary concerns.* Lexington, MA: Heath.

Trasler, G. (1987). Biogenetic factors. In H. C. Quay (Ed.), *Handbook of juvenile delinquency.* New York: Wiley.

Trickett, E., & Birman, D. (1989). Taking ecology seriously: A community development approach to individually-based interventions. In L. Bond, & B. Compas (Eds.), *Primary prevention in the schools.* Hanover, NH: University Press of New England.

United States Census Bureau. (1987). *Statistical abstract of the United States—1987.* Washington, DC: U.S. Government Printing Office.

United States Department of Justice. (1988, September). *Survey of youth in custody, 1987.* Washington, DC: U.S. Government Printing Office, Bureau of Justice Statistics.

Valentin, C. (1984). The mentor and the dream: Facilitators of psychosocial competence in inner city adolescents. *Dissertation Abstracts International, 45,* 2705B.

Van Ness, S. R. (1984). Rape as instrumental violence: A study of youth offenders. *Journal of Offender Counseling Services and Rehabilitation, 9,* 161–170.

Vito, G., & Wilson, D. G. (1985). *The American juvenile justice system.* Newbury Park, CA: Sage.

Wallerstein, J. (1983). Children of divorce: The psychological tasks of the child. *American Journal of Orthopsychiatry, 53,* 230–243.

Walsh, A., Beyer, J. A., & Petee, T. A. (1987). Violent delinquency: An examination of psychopathic typologies. *Journal of Genetic Psychology, 148,* 385–392.

Walsh, A., Petee, T. A., & Beyer, J. A. (1987). Intellectual imbalance and delinquency: Comparing high verbal and high performance IQ delinquents. *Criminal Justice and Behavior, 14,* 370–379.

Walsh, F., & Scheinkman, M. (1993). The family context of adolescence. In P. H. Tolan, & B. J. Cohler (Eds.), *Handbook of clinical research and practice with adolescents.* New York: Wiley.

Weissbourd, B., & Kagan, S. L. (1989). Family support programs: Catalysts for change. *American Journal of Orthopsychiatry, 59,* 20–31.

Weisz, J., Weiss, B., Alicke, M., & Klotz, M. (1987). Effectiveness of psychotherapy with children and adolescents. *Journal of Consulting and Clinical Psychology, 55,* 542–549.

Wenz, F. V. (1978). Economic stress, family anomie and adolescent suicide potential. *Journal of Psychology, 98,* 45–47.

Wenz, F. V. (1979). Sociological correlates of alienation among adolescent suicidal attempts. *Adolescence, 14,* 19–30.

Werner, E. (1988). Individual differences, universal needs: A 30-year study of resilient high-risk infants. *Birth to Three, 8,* 1–5.

Werner, E. (1989). High risk children in young adulthood: A longitudinal study—birth to 32 years. *American Journal of Orthopsychiatry, 59,* 72–81.

Werner, E., & Smith, R. (1979). An epidemiologic perspective on some antecedents and consequences of childhood mental health problems and learning disabilities. *Journal of the American Academy of Child Psychiatry, 18,* 292–306.

West, D. J., & Farrington, D. P. (1973). *Who becomes delinquent?* London: Heinemann.

West, D. J., & Farrington, D. P. (1977). *The delinquent way of life.* London: Heinemann.

White, B. J., & Madara, E. J. (1992). *The self-help sourcebook.* Denville, NJ: Saint Clares-Riverside Medical Center.

White, J. L. (1989). *The troubled adolescent.* New York: Pergamon.

Wilson, J. Q., & Herrnstein, R. J. (1985). *Crime and human nature.* New York: Simon & Schuster.

Winterdyk, J., & Roesch, R. (1981). A wilderness experimental program as an alternative for probationers: An evaluation. *Canadian Journal of Criminology, 23,* 39–49.

York, P., & York, D. (1980). *ToughLove: A self-help manual for parents troubled by teenage behavior.* Sellersville, PA: Community Service Foundation.

Young, R. L., Godfrey, W., Matthews, B., & Adams, G. R. (1983). Runaways: A review of negative consequences. *Family Relations, 32,* 275–281.

Youth and America's Future. (1988). *The forgotten half: Pathways to success for America's youth and young families.* Washington, DC: William T. Grant Foundation Commission on Work, Family, and Citizenship.

Yusin, A., Sinay, R., & Nihira, K. (1972). Adolescents in crisis: Evaluation of a questionnaire. *American Journal of Psychiatry, 129,* 574–577.

Zimrim, H. (1986). A profile of survival. *Child Abuse and Neglect, 10,* 339–349.

Index